PEOPLE OF SUBSTANCE:
AN ETHNOGRAPHY OF MORA
IN THE COLOMBIAN AMAZON

D0754278
WITHDRAWN
UTSA LIBRARIES

Over the fifteen-year period that Carlos David Londoño Sulkin conducted ethnographic fieldwork among indigenous groups in the Colombian Amazon, known collectively as the People of the Centre, he noticed that they produced innumerable moral evaluations of themselves and of each other – what he calls 'moral portrayals.' The People of the Centre's understandings of themselves featured qualitative distinctions of worth between what they esteemed and what they despised about persons, relationships, and other aspects of their lives – all in the context of a perspectival cosmos, in which every being (human, animal, or plant) is understood to perceive itself as central in the imagined relationships between the categories of 'nature' and 'culture.'

In *People of Substance*, Londoño Sulkin makes the case that to comprehend the lives of individual persons, the social processes they participate in, and the groups they create, it is best to engage with them interpretatively, attempting to grasp what kinds of beings they understand themselves and each other to be, and how they conceive the cosmos within which their lives take place. This ambitious book contributes to the burgeoning anthropological scholarship focused on morality and related matters such as agency and freedom, while at the same time engages with diverse analytical approaches to indigenous Amazonian social life.

(Anthropological Horizons)

CARLOS DAVID LONDOÑO SULKIN is an associate professor and department head in the Department of Anthropology at the University of Regina.

**ANTHROPOLOGICAL HORIZONS**

Editor: Michael Lambek, University of Toronto

This series, begun in 1991, focuses on theoretically informed ethnographic works addressing issues of mind and body, knowledge and power, equality and inequality, the individual and the collective. Interdisciplinary in its perspective, the series makes a unique contribution in several other academic disciplines: women's studies, history, philosophy, psychology, political science, and sociology.

For a list of the books published in this series see page 215.

CARLOS DAVID LONDOÑO SULKIN

# People of Substance

## An Ethnography of Morality in the Colombian Amazon

UNIVERSITY OF TORONTO PRESS
Toronto Buffalo London

© University of Toronto Press 2012
Toronto Buffalo London
www.utppublishing.com
Printed in Canada

ISBN 978-1-4426-4490-8 (cloth)
ISBN 978-1-4426-1373-7 (paper)

Printed on acid-free, 100% post-consumer recycled paper with vegetable-based inks.

**Library and Archives Canada Cataloguing in Publication**

Londoño Sulkin, Carlos David
People of substance : an ethnography of morality in the Colombian Amazon / Carlos David Londoño Sulkin.

(Anthropological horizons)
Includes bibliographical references and index.
ISBN 978-1-4426-4490-8 (bound). ISBN 978-1-4426-1373-7 (pbk.)

1. Muinane Indians – Social life and customs. 2. Muinane Indians – Rites and ceremonies. I. Title. II. Series: Anthropological horizons

F2270.2.M75L65 2012 305.898′9 C2011-907607-1

This book has been published with the help of a grant from the Canadian Federation for the Humanities and Social Sciences, through the Aid to Scholarly Publications Program, using funds provided by the Social Sciences and Humanities Research Council of Canada.

This book has been published with the help of a subvention award from the Humanities Research Institute, University of Regina.

University of Toronto Press acknowledges the financial assistance to its publishing program of the Canada Council for the Arts and the Ontario Arts Council.

Canada Council for the Arts Conseil des Arts du Canada
ONTARIO ARTS COUNCIL
CONSEIL DES ARTS DE L'ONTARIO

University of Toronto Press acknowledges the financial support for its publishing activities of the Government of Canada through the Canada Book Fund.

Library
University of Texas
at San Antonio

# Contents

# Illustrations

**Figures**



**Tables**

# Acknowledgments

Speakers of the Muinane language in the Colombian Amazon highlight the human need for others in all important endeavours in life with the counsel *'Úro' monótatɨhi* (We are never to say 'I alone.') Certainly concerning the process of production of this book this prescription is a fair one; I was most definitely not alone.

I must first thank the Muinane and other People of the Centre with whom I lived in the Medio Caquetá, Colombia, between 1993 and 1998: Eduardo Paki, Adriano Paki, Abelino Paki, Gricélida Paki, Alicia Kumimarima, Aide Barbosa, Ana Rita Andoke, Nubia Cubeo, Aurelia Jifichiu, Henry Nejedeka, Célimo Nejedeka, Chuchito Nejedeka, and Aidé Mendoza, in Villa Azul; the Ortiz brothers, Jorge, Chucho, and my compadre Segundo, and their spouses Leopoldina Kudo, Celina Hernández, and Blanca Perdomo in Chukiki; further upriver, Rafael Mukutuy and his sons, and Mariano Suárez and his wife and sons. Aniceto Nejedeka and Hernán Moreno each spent a month dedicated almost exclusively to answering my questions in prolonged interviews. Andrés Paki, Sebastián Rodríguez, Arturo Rodríguez, Elías Moreno, Jose Moreno, and their many children also provided me with interesting conversation. Oscar Román's family allowed me to hang up a hammock at their home in Araracuara – most recently in 2007 – and don Hipólito Candre's family welcomed me in Cordillera, on the Igaraparaná river, for two convivial weeks in 2008. Several of them insisted that I be very careful with naming them in my writings lest this attract evil beings' attention to them, so beyond this quick acknowledgment and a couple of picture captions, readers will not see their names again here. I have opted to give most of them biblical names.

Tropenbos Colombia and Gaia Foundation Colombia both started me off in the Amazon while I was still an undergraduate student; for this I am indebted to Camilo Robayo, Maria Clara van der Hammen, Juan A. Echeverri, Martin von Hildebrand, Maria Cecilia López, Nicolás Bermúdez, Helga Dvorjak, and Alejandro Jaramillo. From the crowd pertinent to my early years in Araracuara, I am most indebted to my friend and mentor Juan Echeverri, a veritable encyclopedia on matters Amazonian, a deep and fascinatingly liminal scholar, and my most consistent interlocutor concerning People of the Centre. If my references to kinship manage to sound nicely 'techy' and informed, it is doubtless thanks to his help, and to Sandra Turbay's, at the Universidad de Antioquia. Jakob Kronik, Tom Griffiths, and Monica Espinosa were worthy conversation partners in Araracuara, too.

Joanna Overing, at the University of St. Andrews, got me a President's Endowed Scholarship (1996–9) to do my PhD, and furthermore shaped my interest in anthropological approaches to morality. Don Kulick's course on performativity in Oslo in 1999 radically reshaped my thinking on social life and the anthropological endeavour. His writing, teaching, and editing work are paradigmatic of what scholarship should be like: deep and critical, yet constructive and accessible.

I want to underscore how valuable peer review of various kinds has been in the long process of writing this manuscript and to remind my colleagues of what an edifying – indeed, essential – practice peer review is. Others' engagement with my work has shaped it to such an extent that I feel it to be, itself, an example of a product of dialogical processes very much like those that I address in the manuscript. *'Úro' monótatɨhi*, indeed.

Along these lines, I am particularly grateful to the anonymous peer reviewers at the University of Toronto Press, on the basis of whose judicious and incisive commentaries I overhauled the manuscript quite thoroughly and profitably. Anne Meneley, Donna Young, and Anne Brackenbury of Broadview Press all helped me enormously by showing both contagious enthusiasm for my manuscript and tough rigour in criticizing it.

I have had illuminating, sometimes lengthy email or face-to-face conversations on matters Amazonian or generally anthropological with Fernando Santos-Granero, Ellen Basso, Fuambai Ahmadu, Rick Shweder, Jean Jackson, Steven Rubenstein, Elsje Lagrou, Anouska Komlosy, Nigel Rapport, Dan Rosengren, and Mina Oppas; I admire their capacity for engagement, and thank them for engaging with me.

My students in several courses on the ethnography of Amazonia and on the anthropology of personhood at the University of Regina read and commented on early versions of the book and provided valuable feedback. Jessica Boyachek and Lindsay Springer stood out among these as sharp editors indeed. My student, friend, and research assistant Amy McLachlan contributed to my work with ethnographic data, critical comments, and warm moral support. Jason and Michaela Kraft performed the role of lay readers for a portion of the book, and have relentlessly kept me humble concerning my professorial role over the years; to them, many thanks for the first of these favours!

I have gleaned considerable intellectual benefit and delicious companionship from participation in Society for the Anthropology of Lowland South America (SALSA) conferences and list-serve discussions. I must also acknowledge the participants at the International Symposium on the Anthropology of Ordinary Ethics (University of Toronto, October 3–6, 2008) for our riveting conversations, a few insights from which made it into my discussions here. My father-in-law Antonio Vélez and my siblings-in-law Juan Diego and Ana Cristina Vélez have been assiduous, valuable interlocutors for the last two decades.

My father, Carlos M. Londoño de la Espriella, has subsidized my career and this book in myriad ways. My mother, Lolie Sulkin, has also supplied various forms of material support for my endeavours. My brother, Manuel R. Londoño Mejía, turned my poor photography into this book's cover art. I am indebted to the Wenner-Gren Foundation for Anthropological Research, Inc., for a Richard Carley Hunt Fellowship that allowed me to take a year off from teaching to begin to write this book in 2005–6. I benefited from further fieldwork and research help funded by a SSHRC (Social Sciences and Humanities Research Council of Canada) Standard Research Grant. To facilitate my research, Meigen Schmidt and Sarah Savage at the University of Regina Office of Research Services had to move bureaucratic mountains.

My colleagues in the Department of Anthropology of the University of Regina – Marcia Calkowski, Vernon Eicchorn, Peter Gose, Susanne Kuehling, Gedis Lankauskas, Dan Rosenblatt, Frances Slaney, Tobias Sperlich, Jaro Stacul, Kimberly Hart, Diane Riskedahl, Paul Harms, and Charisma Thomson – have managed to create and maintain a coherent little undergraduate program in social and cultural anthropology that we can justifiably be proud of. They and our students have made it a supportive environment for me. I must recognize here as well the stalwart friendship and intellectual counsel Philip Charrier (Department of

History, University of Regina) has loyally tendered to me. Sergio Mejía (Department of History, Universidad de los Andes) has also been a central background presence overseeing my intellectual life over the years.

My greatest debt is to my wife Maria Isabel Vélez, who has provided me with an attentive, supportive ear and a warm emotional home for twenty-something years. I dedicate this book to her and to my sons Joche and Antonio.

# Notes on Muinane Language

## Generalities and Spelling Conventions

There are a few words in Muinane in this book, always italicized. The alphabet I use for these is a rough working tool, based on the Summer Institute of Linguistics' (SIL's) linguistic research (Walton, Walton, and Pakky de Buenaventura 1997), conversations with the linguist Consuelo Vengoechea, and my own limited linguistic work. Pronunciation on the ground is more complex than I describe here, but these tables should provide enough for an approximation.

### *Vowels*

Muinane vowels sound more like those of the Spanish language than like those of English. I would suggest to readers that they imagine the *a* to sound 'ah,' the *e* to sound 'eh,' the *i* to sound 'ee' as in 'keep,' the *o* to sound like the first vowel in 'order, and the *u* to sound like 'oo' as in 'boot.' The closest sound in English to the Muinane *ɨ* is the 'i' in 'it.' There are also long vowels and diphthongs. See table 1.

Muinane has two phonological tones: high and low. Low tones are sometimes descendant. High tones are presented with a tilde: á, é, í, ó, ú, ɨ́, áá, éé, íí. óó, úú, ɨ́ɨ́;

### *Consonants*

Muinane also has a phoneme made up of a very brief postalveolar occlusive followed by sonorous retroflected apical tap, the closest approximation of which is the Spanish 'tr,' as in 'truco.' Vengoechea (1996, 559)

Table 1
Muinane vowels

| IPA* | Conventions (with pronunciation approximations) |
|---|---|
| [a] | a |
| [e] | e |
| [i] | i |
| [ɨ] | ɨ |
| [o] | o |
| [u] | u |
| [a:] | aa |
| [e:] | ee |
| [i:] | ii |
| [ɨ:] | ɨɨ |
| [o:] | oo |
| [u:] | uu |
| Diphthongs | |
| [ai] | ai |
| [ei] | ei |
| [aɨ] | aɨ |

* International Phonetic Alphabet

describes it rather as an instantaneous sonorous predorsal consonant. I represent it with an 'r.' See table 2.

Vengoechea claims that the syllabic structure of Muinane is CV (consonant + vowel). Many syllables that appear to be merely a vowel would have a phonological glottal stop (1996, 557). I mark this on most occasions with an 'h,' but in some cases do not mark it at all.

Table 2
Muinane consonants

| IPA* | Conventions (with pronunciation approximations) |
|---|---|
| [b] | b (as in *b*ull) |
| [β] | v (like a 'b' in which the lips are not quite put together) |
| [š] | sh (as in *sh*ow) |
| [tʃ] or [tch] | ch (as in *ch*ild) |
| [d] | d (as in *d*og) |
| [dj] | dy (palatalized 'd'; no English equivalent) |
| [ɸ] | f (similar to blowing a candle out gently with pursed lips; no English equivalent) |
| [g] | g (as in *g*o) |
| [h] | j (as in *h*appy) |
| [k] | k (as in *c*at) |
| [m] | m (as in *m*ilk) |
| [n] | n (as in *n*ose) |
| [ñ] | ñ (as in Spanish ni*ñ*o) |
| [p] | p (as in A*p*ril) |
| [s] | s (as in *s*ap) |
| [t] | t (as in *t*one, but with less of an explosion of air than 't' at the beginning of a syllable in English) |
| [tj] | ty (palatalized 't,' no English equivalent) |
| [?] (glottal stop) | h (as in the negation 'nuh-uh') |
| [ɟ] | ll (as in ad*j*acent) |
| [j] | y (as in *y*ellow, sometimes tending towards a light [ɟ]) |

* International Phonetic Alphabet

The Medio Caquetá Region, Colombian Amazon

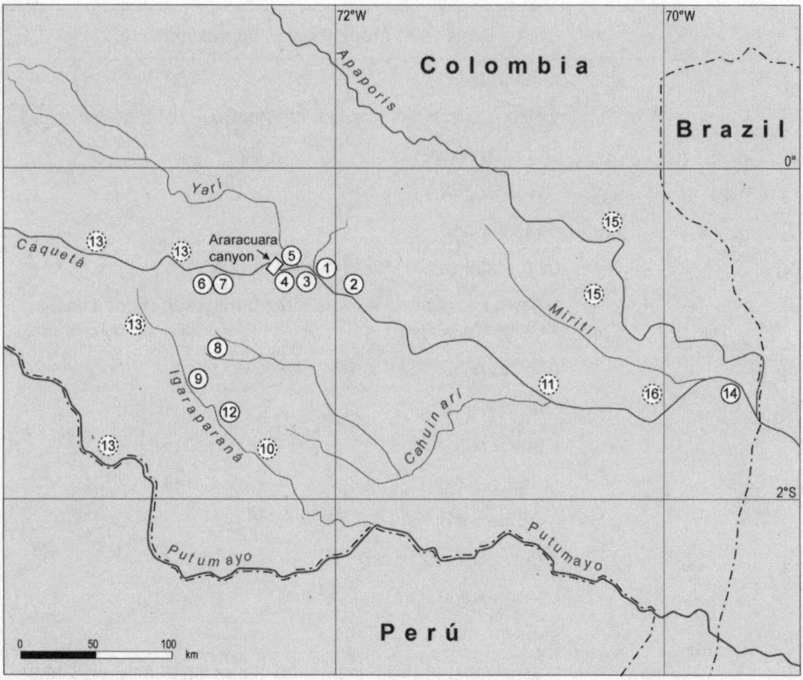


Cartography, Diandra Klinger, 2011

## Key place references

1. Muinane community of Villa Azul
2. Nonuya community of Peña Roja
3. Andoke community of Aduche
4. Puerto Santander
5. Interethnic community of Araracuara

6,7 Interspersed settlements of the Muinane community of Chukiki and Uitoto community of Monochoa

8. La Sabana
9. La Chorrera
10. Bora communities
11. Miraña communities
12. Okaina community
13. Various Uitoto communities
14. La Pedrera
15. Various Tukanoan-speaking communities
16. Various Arawak-speaking communities

PEOPLE OF SUBSTANCE:
AN ETHNOGRAPHY OF MORALITY
IN THE COLOMBIAN AMAZON

# Introduction: People of the Centre

This is a book about the complex indigenous group of people of the Colombian Amazon who call themselves 'People of the Centre,' and specifically about their talk and other practices expressive of their understandings of what it was to be a human being, and the social lives they achieved through such talk and practices. It makes the case that to comprehend the lives of individual persons, the social processes they participate in, and therefore the very groups they create, we do well to engage with them interpretatively, attempting to grasp what kinds of beings these persons understand themselves and each other to be, and how they conceive the cosmos within which their lives take place. A part of this argument is that people's understandings of themselves feature qualitative distinctions of worth between what they esteem and what they despise about persons, relationships, and other aspects of their lives.

My whole account here is rather obsessed with morality. Morality I define at this point, incipiently, as people's evaluative perceptions, reactions, understandings, and claims concerning subjectivities, actions, persons, qualities, and ways of life, in terms of whether these were admirable, despicable, unremarkable, or otherwise distinct in worth. A question that comes to my mind is whether my perception that People of the Centre were particularly prone to call attention to the admirable and the despicable was a function of my biased preferences for this subject matter, or whether it was something any other perceptive ethnographer would have caught on to. In any case, it seems to me that my Amazonian interlocutors produced innumerable moral evaluations of themselves and of each other, in what I came to call in my field diaries 'moral portrayals.' They verbally depicted themselves, others, their groupings, and their interactions, often stressing their own competence and morality or others' lacks thereof. These portrayals came in the form of brief anecdotes, longer narratives, or loose comments in the midst of talk about other matters, and tended to frame individual speakers as exemplifying key virtues or flaws. As such, they purportedly acted out of loving care, manifested great generosity, were pleasant company because of their unvanquishable good temper, or were feared for their dangerous esoteric knowledge. Others appeared in these portrayals as, among other things, angry animals, uncaring misers, or 'itchy' people obsessed with foolishness or incapable of discerning between proper and inhuman behaviour. Such portrayals were so frequent and so explicit during the time I spent in their communities that I soon lost my initial sense of shock at such apparent immodesty and shrewishness. I started to think about them as a matter of puzzlement and curiosity, and then to focus on them as examples of people reiterating socially available narrative frames and symbols.[1]

This book is ambitious. On one hand, it aims to contribute to the burgeoning of anthropological scholarship focused on morality and thus on matters such as structure, agency, and freedom, by borrowing eclectically from the writings of a number of philosophers and anthropologists. On the other hand, it seeks to realize the intellectual benefit of engaging, also eclectically, with what have been called different 'analytical approaches' to indigenous Amazonian social life (Viveiros de Castro 1996a)[2] or 'schools of Americanism' (Taylor 1996). I attend focally to people's practices and understandings of moral, sentient personhood and sociality, along the lines of the 'analytical approach of the moral economy of intimacy' of the 'British school of Americanism.' I also engage eagerly with scholarship of a Franco-Brazilian tenor, with its 'analytical approach of the symbolic economy of alterity' (Viveiros de Castro 1996a), especially concerning the matter of cosmological perspectivism and the various imagined relationships between the imagined categories of nature and culture. My work on morality and selfhood, with its emphasis on performativity, contingency, and temporality, dovetails nicely with these foci and furthermore with other Amazonianist scholars' interests in matters of power and hierarchy, long-term historical processes, and the contextualization of indigenous peoples in modern nation-states.

## People of the Centre: A Brief Ethnographic and Historical Overview

Most of the people with whom I worked between 1993 and 2008 lived in communities constituted by small settlements along the middle basin of the Caquetá river (an area known as Medio Caquetá), roughly at the centre of the Colombian Amazon region (see map, The Medio Caquetá Region, Colombian Amazon). Other important rivers for People of the Centre were the Cahuinarí, the Igaraparaná, and the Putumayo. Much of the region features a very diverse tropical rainforest ecosystem, though there are a variety of non-rainforest ecosystems as well.

The region is a large section of the political divisions known as the Colombian *departamentos* (departments or provinces) of Caquetá, Putumayo, and Amazonas. The most urban sites in the Medio Caquetá are the very small twin towns of Araracuara and Puerto Santander, with the former on the north bank of the river and the latter across from it on the south bank. These have a waxing and waning population of a few hundred people, comprising People of the Centre and smatterings of other groups, settlers and other economic migrants from elsewhere in Colombia, soldiers, the occasional natural or social scientist, and *indigenistas* (people working with NGOs or the Colombian government on matters relating to indigenous peoples as collectives). Araracuara features a landing strip, used by planes hired by fish merchants and traders to transport their goods, and by Satena, the single airline which when I did my fieldwork provided partly reliable flight services once a week to and from Bogotá via any of several small cities or towns, and once a week to and from the Amazonian city of Leticia, stopping in La Chorrera, another small town. For a few years in the early 1990s there was also a small contingent of US Armed Forces at a closely guarded base next to the landing strip, operating a gigantic radar used to track drug-traffickers' flights in the region.

The self-named 'People of the Centre' include clans speaking the Uitoto, Bora, Miraña, Muinane, Andoke, Nonuya, or Ocaina languages. Linguists have classified the Uitoto, Ocaina, and Nonuya languages as constitutive of the Witoto linguistic family; Bora, Miraña and Muinane form the Bora linguistic family, and Andoke is a linguistic isolate. Though some of these languages appear to be unrelated to each other, Julian Steward (1948) classified them as 'the Witotoan tribes' in the *Handbook of South American Indians* (Echeverri 1997, 49). In the 1990s and 2000s, the period during which I did the fieldwork featured in this book, patrilineal clans of different language groups intermarried frequently, held rituals in common, and had similar livelihood practices, together constituting a complex, multilingual aggregate. This multilingualism, I should note, was clearly in decline; older individuals could often speak or understand four or five languages, and some conducted part of their social lives in their vernaculars, but a large proportion of the children and young adults spoke only Spanish.

'People of the Centre' is a translation of the Spanish 'Gente de Centro,' which the Consejo Regional Indigena del Medio Amazonas (CRIMA), a local political organization initially constituted in the 1980s by people of these language groups mainly to represent them in land rights litigations, proposed as an encompassing name for themselves. The common term made sense, for in at least several of these groups' stories of origin, their clans had indeed been created at the very centre of the world. The ready adoption of the term for the purposes of CRIMA's constitution and engagement with the state did feature some ambivalence, however; at times and in the privacy of their own settlements, people expressed an interest in differentiating themselves from some other clans and language groups encompassed by the term, and sometimes insisted that notwithstanding what everybody else said, it had been their own clan or language group that had been created at the very centre of the centre of the world.

In the CRIMA's legal document of constitution, the common defining feature of People of the Centre was that they traditionally consumed tobacco in the form of soft paste or liquid to be licked and swallowed, and coca in the form of a powder to be packed in the cheeks. Some spoke of these same language groups as 'People of Tobacco Paste' (in Spanish, Gente de Ambil) instead of People of the Centre. The key contrast for them was with a variety of Arawakan-speaking (Yukuna, Matapí) and Tukanoan-speaking (Tukano, Cubeo, Desana, Barasana, Makuna, and others) neighbours further up and further down the Caquetá river, and in the Apaporis, Mirití, and Putumayo rivers, people who had different sets of ritual substances, including tobacco in forms other than paste.[3]

The title of this book, *People of Substance*, points on one hand to the importance of key substances like tobacco, coca, and chilies in People of the Centre's practices and understandings of the cosmos, group membership and organization, and moral personhood; indeed, individuals among People of the Centre widely claimed that their very bodies were made of these and other key substances, and that their thoughts/emotions[4] – when tranquil, benevolent, and efficacious – stemmed from them as well. On the other hand, the title plays on the reference in English to wealthy, morally stalwart persons.

People of the Centre associated different areas of the Medio Caquetá and the Predio Putumayo with particular language groups on the basis of either current occupation or of supposed proprietorship of ancestral origin. Clans of various Uitoto dialect-speakers – by far the largest proportion of the local indigenous population – were mostly found to the west of Araracuara and south along the Igaraparaná River, close to settlements of Bora- and Ocaina-speaking clans. The Miraña- and Bora-speaking clans lived mainly near the river mouth of the Cahuinarí into the Caquetá, along the Cahuinarí, and on the Igaraparaná south of La Chorrera. Muinane clans' 'traditional territory' was in La Sabana (the Savannah) of the Cahuinarí River, but only two families, of two patrilines, remained there. The other clans and patrilines had settled up and downriver from Araracuara, on the Caquetá River. The Nonuya, with two surviving patrilines of two clans, had the two-settlement community of Peña Roja, downriver from the Muinane community of Villa Azul. In recent years one of the Nonuya patrilines decided to split itself into two autonomous, named clans, a move their neighbours deemed most unorthodox but which they nonetheless explained quite clearly themselves. In the 1990s there was one large Andoke community with several clans living along a short stretch of the Aduche creek, a tributary of the Caquetá, but in the late 1990s or early 2000s, they split into several communities. Their communities and settlements were rather amoeboid, at times blooming, at times contracting, often splitting up and taking on new names, new members, and new leaders. They also incorporated, without immediately assimilating, individuals or families from a smattering of groups from surrounding regions: mainly Tukano, Desana, Cubeo, Yukuna, and Matapí.

People of the Centre's understandings of kinship – of who was related to whom as 'family' – strongly influenced the constitution of their settlements. They reckoned kinship cognatically or bilaterally, that is, both men and women transmitted 'relatedness,' such that, for instance, an individual's mother's sister's children were deemed to be related to the individual, as were his or her father's brother's children. Their kinship also featured a patrilineal component, however; they established named groups of people – patrilines and patriclans – who were related through male lines exclusively (see appendix on Muinane kinship terminology). The older members of each patriline shared a known common ancestor no further back than three or four generations. Patrilines were part of patriclans (henceforth, 'clans'). These clans were more encompassing, named categories whose individual members were understood to share a common ancestor from First Time (*itíkonɨ bákaje*, in Muinane), the mythical period of the creation of the world. Because their population had been decimated in the early 1900s, however, several of the surviving patrlines and clans were merely single sets of siblings, or the children of such a set.[5]

Patrilineality had corporate implications among these people: in local understandings, the core of each settlement was a group of adult men related to each other as fathers, sons, siblings, and cousins through male lines. When they formed couples, the most common practice was to have the woman – necessarily from another clan and settlement – move in with the man; this is known in the anthropological literature as virilocal post-marital residence. Men, however, were supposed to be on beck and call from their fathers-in-law to help the latter with big tasks such as house building and felling the rainforest to make gardens, a kind of injunction known as brideservice among anthropologists.

During the twenty-odd months I spent in the region between 1993 and 2008 I lived in four settlements of two *comunidades* (communities) widely recognized as belonging to Muinane-speaking clans. I spent six months in Villa Azul, a community of the Cumare Nut clan.[6] The main settlement was a two-hour motorboat ride downriver from Araracuara and Puerto Santander. It centred on one set of four male siblings of the Egret patriline of the Cumare Nut clan, who lived with their aging father and mother, an unmarried sister, and their spouses and children. Between 1993 and 1995 there was also a smaller extended family of the Boobai Nut patriline of the Cumare Nut clan, namely a man in his mid-forties to early fifties, his wife, his married son, and five unmarried sons and daughters. There was also another nuclear family living there at the time, comprising a young Uitoto man who was the son of the sister of the father of the main set of siblings of the settlement. These people lived in wood board houses, many on stilts, roughly one house per nuclear family of man, wife, and unmarried children. The settlement also featured one large maloca, a large, traditional residential and ceremonial house which was in fact used for ceremonies and cooking, but not for residing. Scattered piecemeal further downriver from the main settlement there were lone houses belonging to two Matapí families and to two Muinane-speaking families from Andoke lineages.[7] The composition of this community kept transforming over the years as families or patrilines seceded and others moved in, children married, and so on.

Most of the rest of my fieldwork I carried out in 1997 and 1998 in several settlements of the Muinane community of Chukikɨ, which had seceded in the early 1990s, judicially rather than spatially, from Monochoa, a mixed Uitoto and Muinane community. Uitoto and Muinane patrilines' settlements were interspersed along the river, west of the Araracuara canyon. I lived in the wood board houses of three brothers from the sole surviving patriline of the Pineapple clan; in the maloca of one old man of the Grub clan (of which there was one surviving patriline); and in the maloca of one man of the Wooden Drum clan, of which there were three surviving patrilines dispersed in several communities.

Because I lived in so-called Muinane settlements and developed a modicum of competence in the Muinane language, I used to claim in my writings that the focus of my scholarship was the Muinane people (see Londoño Sulkin 2000, 2004). More recently, however, I decided to have my writings reflect more consistently that the majority of the Muinane men in these settlements were married to women from clans speaking Uitoto, Andoke, or Bora, among others. Except for Uitoto and Bora men, who in the 1990s were somewhat more likely to have spouses from their own language groups, the majority of the marriages of Muinane, Andoke, Nonuya, and Ocaina men and women were with people from other language groups among People of the Centre. This was a necessity given their small size and the prohibition of marriage within the widely encompassing network of people deemed to be each individual's kin. Many claimed that people in the past also married outside their clan, but within their language groups.[8]

People of the Centre's livelihood practices resembled those of many other Amazonian people: their main productive activities were hunting, fishing, gathering, and swidden horticulture. The latter involved making gardens of sizes from half a hectare to two hectares, by means of so-called 'slash-and-burn': felling the rainforest with machetes and axes, allowing the dead vegetation to dry in the sun, and then burning it down to ashes. They then planted manioc,[9] tobacco, coca, chilies, and a wide variety of cultigens. These gardens were kept and harvested for four or five years, after which they were allowed to grow back into forest. People of the Centre also participated in a market economy centred on interactions with a variety of merchants in small towns like Araracuara and Puerto Santander in the Medio Caquetá, and La Chorrera in the Igaraparaná River. Over the years, I witnessed their participation in monetary exchanges with fishing merchants of Andean or mixed local origin who flew several tons of fish into Villavicencio and Bogotá from Araracuara and La Pedrera every month. People of the Centre in the Caquetá occasionally also produced and sold wood planks to inhabitants of Araracuara and Puerto Santander. During the cocaine booms in the 1980s and in the early 2000, some also participated in that paid trade. They were dependent, as they had been for at least a century, on metal axes, guns, matches, salt, sugar, and other trade goods.

My knowledge of People of the Centre before the 1990s is based on word of mouth and secondary sources, rather than of detailed research of primary sources. I will not address the processes that may have occurred prior to the mid-nineteenth century, deeming these to be beyond my interest here. I will only refer to them tangentially, when considering the long-term reproduction of what I will call 'the Amazonian package.' Doubtless there was a large indigenous population in what would later be known as the Predio Putumayo region, and doubtless its social form had already been indirectly affected by diseases, trade, and new forms of slavery brought by European colonization elsewhere in the continent. I will begin this brief review of key historical processes and events with the rubber boom, because it looms large in People of the Centre's own understanding of their own histories, and because discourses and documentation about the period were readily available when I carried out my PhD research.

The territories of clans speaking Uitoto, Muinane, Nonuya, Andoke, Ocaina, Bora, and Miraña were colonized by Colombian and Peruvian quinine harvesters and then rubber tappers in the second half of the nineteenth century, though by that time they had already traded for manufactured goods with people from further downriver, who in turn had received the goods from Brazil. The most egregious period of colonization took place between 1900 and 1930, during the rubber boom, when their region was taken over by the Casa Arana, a Peruvian and British rubber-collecting company (see Casement 1985; Domínguez and Gómez 1994, 123–7; Gómez et al. 1995, 47; Llanos and Pineda 1982, 59; Whiffen 1915). The agents of this company enslaved most of the clans of People of the Centre, murdered thousands, and forced many of the survivors to translocate. They were literally decimated. Muinane elders remembered the names of some twenty Muinane clans, of which only five survived the rubber boom holocaust: the Cumare Nut clan (two patrilines), the Women clan (one patriline), the Grub clan (two patrilines, one of which has become nearly exclusively Uitoto-speaking),

Pineapple clan (one patriline), and Wooden Drum clan (two patrilines). My host at one community often spoke of the Muinane as 'orphans of the Casa Arana.'

In 1932 Colombia and Peru went to war over territorial possessions in the Putumayo and Napo regions, generating further upheaval in the lives of local people. Some were recruited as guides or soldiers, and some as workers to build roads to facilitate the transportation of troops. By then the peak of the rubber boom was well past in the region, given British success in establishing more productive and accessible rubber plantations in Malaysia. The Colombian government started to invest more in establishing its national presence in the region, among other ways by engaging the Catholic church to provide education to indigenous children in missionary boarding schools, and in 1938, by creating a penal colony around Araracuara, in the Caquetá river. The penal colony was closed in 1971 (Useche 1994).

As of the 1930s, some of the indigenous men gathered groups of survivors around them and started to reconstruct their groups, sometimes incorporating the 'orphans' of other clans – young people with few surviving kin – in some cases selectively manipulating myths and rituals concerning their clanic origins in order to make better sense of their novel situations of co-residence (Landaburu 1993 and Echeverri 1997). Some did so in close proximity to their territories of origin, but many moved elsewhere in the Caquetá-Putumayo region – in many cases seeking closeness to missionary boarding schools – before settling.

Many, if not most, of the men and women born in the 1930s or later were forced to attend Catholic missionary schools, at least for a few years. These schools had a mix of clans and language groups. It was forbidden for them to speak any language other than Spanish, and the priests and nuns went far to segregate the boys from the girls. The children learned to speak, pray, sing, read, and write in Spanish. This contributed to the process of language shift.

In the 1960s, the wealthy Summer Institute of Linguistics (SIL), the research arm of the Wycliffe Bible Translators, sent one American family, the Waltons, to live in La Sabana, on the Cahuinarí river, where it quietly competed with the Catholic missionary efforts in La Chorrera. Local families built a landing strip, and for a number of years small SIL planes would land regularly. Some of the Muinane speakers with whom I worked had been trained as informants, and a few had even been taken to the large SIL base in Lomalinda, Meta. The Waltons eventually produced a New Testament in Muinane (Muinane Nuevo Testamento, published by the Wycliffe Bible Translators). By then, however, many families and patrilines had abandoned the area of La Sabana and La Chorrera and moved to the Caquetá river, according to some of them to search increased opportunities to acquire trade goods from the administration and agents of the penal colony. They were soon getting money and trade goods for their produce, and some came to make boats for the penal colony. Some worked as guards, and were even taken to work as such at jails in Bogotá and elsewhere when the penal colony was closed down.

The boom-bust cycle continued throughout the twentieth century. For shorter or longer periods there would be a demand for the products of various gum saps, and later on for the skins of otters, margays, ocelots, jaguars, and pumas, a demand which locals hurriedly responded to. In the eighties the good in demand was cocaine, and many in the Caquetá, Igaraparaná, and Putumayo rivers participated in its production and trade.

Several large-scale processes and events in the 1980s and early 1990s elicited political organizational changes in the Medio Caquetá and Putumayo. With the advice of NGOs and the national organization of indigenous peoples (ONIC), locals organized political groups to seek to defend their territory from its repossession by the Caja Agraria, a Colombian bank that claimed it for itself because it had supposedly paid the Casa Arana for it after the Colombo-Peruvian war. As a result of their strife, the Predio Putumayo was created – the government transferred the inalienable legal ownership of a sizeable chunk of southern Colombia to its indigenous inhabitants (Resolución No. 030 del 23 (888) 6 de abril, INCORA). The coalitions among indigenous groups constituted a new kind of grouping, with new kinds of leaders with unprecedented tasks, challenges, and resources.

In 1988 communities in the Medio Caquetá and in the newly minted Predio Putumayo simultaneously imported and established a new kind of political leadership to complement or replace the now old 'capitanía' (captainship) established during the rubber boom and then developed in the interactions between the indigenous communities and the penal colony (Echeverri, personal communication). Leaders who had spent time in Bogotá, in conversations with indigenous leaders from the Andes and the rest of Colombia, claimed that since they now had a *resguardo* (a reserve) they should have a *cabildo* (something like a small political cabinet), with a governor, a treasurer, a secretary, and perhaps some other minor bureaucratic roles. The process involved some conflict, as some captains who had held considerable sway over several communities resisted the de facto secession of communities that set up cabildos, and thus cut back their authority.

What I witnessed while doing fieldwork in the 1990s was a division of labour among types of leader. The governors and other cabildo members were mostly middle-aged or younger men who could read and write in Spanish, and their signal responsibilities involved legal political negotiations with other cabildos and leaders and with the government. In a few cases young women were part of these cabildos. One key responsibility such leaders had was to pick up the government's monetary transferences to the communities. The other type of leader was constituted by middle-aged or older men with greater knowledge of 'tradition' and entitled to perform large dance rituals. People often spoke of these 'elders' (*mayores*, in Spanish) as the moral source of all authority, including the governors.'[10] *Mambeadores* – basically adult men who consumed ritually a powdered mix of toasted coca leaves and ashes called *mambe* in Spanish – produced much rhetoric about each kind of leader, likening them to each other to the extent that they claimed leaders of both kinds to be 'parents' to the community who felt each member of it to be like a body part that would hurt if the member were somehow in trouble. In a few cases a single strong individual incarnated both forms of leadership. Leaders of both kinds had greater access to money and manufactured goods – forthcoming from NGOs and local government – than most others in the region.[11]

Circulating around the governors and indigenous political organizations there was a great deal of anthropological rhetoric of the 'salvage' type. Certainly by the 1990s *cultura* (culture) had become a buzzword in the region, and people spoke about 'defending' their culture or 'recovering' it, and about protecting indigenous autonomy from the impingements of the Church, the Colombian army, and some aspects of the Colombian government. It was in this context that I was first admitted into a Muinane community – as an advisor for the 'recovery of culture,' specifically in the form of the short stories and formulaic behavioural and dietary counsels collectively known as 'speech of advice.' There were some contrary voices as well, though; I particularly remember a man, who had been a prison guard at the Araracuara penal colony, who told me that he felt indigenous ways should disappear and that the local population should set up factories and live like white people. He informed me that all the stories about the 'recovery of culture' were stratagems to keep Indians from ever becoming powerful or becoming president of Colombia, and that anthropologists were complicit in this.

During the years in which I did most of my fieldwork, between 1993 and 1998, the establishment of small schools in indigenous communities was a matter of much interest, as an alternative to the Catholic missionary boarding schools. The central government's rhetoric subsequent to the national constitution of 1991 privileged the 'respect for diversity,' including among other things, the re-evaluation of policies concerning the education of minorities. This led to greater governmental support for the indigenous peoples' recently acquired legal right to educate their children according to their own 'uses and customs,' and to receive help from the government to do so.[12] It seemed not to cross anybody's mind in the region that the 'education' sought in schools could take place anywhere but in the institutional setting of schools. In any case, in the communities I lived in children attended the communities' small schools every day; in one settlement in Chukikɨ, children from other settlements were boarded and fed at the school. At the time, the schools only had between one and three teachers, who taught the elementary grades. Older children were sent off to the Catholic boarding school in Araracuara.

In the 1980s and 1990s there was also an intensification of research in the natural sciences in the area. Government organizations and NGOs carried out research on the forest canopy, on fish reproduction, on mammal behaviour, and so on. An army of biologists, forest architecture students, fishery experts, and agronomists traipsed through the region, or lived there for up to several years, producing research on the natural environment and in some cases on its potential for eco-friendly exploitation in collaboration with indigenous people (Useche 1994). Many anthropology students also spent time in the region. The local population was beginning to become familiarized with 'white people's' academic interest in the natural environment, and their initially puzzling interest in preserving the forest and its beings. The latter had never seemed to be threatened, as far as my interlocutors were concerned, but they did note that charapa turtles were growing scarce.

In 1999, a few months after I left the Araracuara region to write up my doctoral thesis, the FARC (Revolutionary Armed Forces of Colombia) guerrilla took over the area. They set up their own little police state, demanding that people behave in certain ways. In Araracuara they would have the entire population work every so often on road maintenance, and they would warn and then chastise individuals accused of thievery, wife beatings, disorderly drunken conduct, and so on. Some locals approved of this, but soon they started to threaten some leaders. A member of a Muinane community was murdered, and several other leaders were told to leave the region and stay away. Their occupation of the region lasted until December of 2003, when the Colombian armed forces bombarded some key sites in the area of Araracuara and again took it over (see Tobón 2008).

Quite a few Uitoto, Muinane, Andoke and other People of the Centre had migrated, since the 1930s, to Leticia, and later to towns and cities like Villavicencio, Florencia, Puerto Asís, Puerto Leguízamo, and the Colombian capital, Bogotá. In the time I spent in the Medio Caquetá, there was frequent movement of people, money, and goods between these cities and the communities of People of the Centre, as the occasional youth left to pursue jobs and high school diplomas in these cities, leaders went about bureaucratic and other organizational affairs, and more recent expatriates returned to visit their kin.

**Census Data**

Several anthropologists and other scholars and travellers have carried out censuses in the Medio Caquetá-Putumayo region. Whiffen, who travelled through the region in 1908, around the time when the rubber boom holocaust was really gaining murderous momentum, calculated that Uitoto, Andoke, Muinane, and other local groups numbered around 46,000. Even if this were too generous a calculation, the contrast with the people living in the 1990s reveals the extent of the genocide. Roberto Pineda reported in 1987 that there were some 8,500 (though I believe his data were too optimistic; he suggested there could be as many as 500 Muinane, a good three times as many as I calculated there were myself, ten years later and after a period of population growth). Echeverri reckoned that there were close to 4,400 People of the Centre in the Caquetá-Putumayo region in the mid-1990s: 3,250 Uitoto, 150 Miraña, 400 Bora, 220 Andoke, 150 Ocaina, 140 Muinane, and 60 Nonuya. I performed my own census in 1998, specifically in the two Muinane communities of the Medio Caquetá, and concluded then that there were 110 Muinane in these and in Araracuara and Puerto Santander, with perhaps half again as many married into other communities or gone from the region. There were also significant Bora and Uitoto populations in Peru, in some cases out of touch with those on the Colombian side. In the Medio Caquetá, many clans have become speakers of other languages; several Muinane clans became Uitotoized, and I met several men of Andoke lineages who spoke only Muinane and Spanish. Doubtless episodes of mutual assimilation have been occurring in the region for a long time, suggesting that censuses and interviews concerning ethnic identity in the region need to be taken with a grain of salt.

## Morality, Social Life, and Their Analysis

I am persuaded that social life is best thought of as an ongoing process, and that human social aggregates are achievements the existence and continuity of which depend on the interactions of persons. This is sometimes difficult to grasp in large urban milieus, where an individual's birth or death does not appear to have much effect on our neighbourhoods, cities, or economic patterns: the supermarkets, factories, and roads stay open and all is 'business as usual.' We might thus get the sense that there is such a thing as 'society' of which we are individual 'members'; such a society is like a machine that keeps working, and in which individuals are readily replaceable nuts and bolts, or ephemeral readily replaceable fuel. This image of social life elides the reality that it is individuals acting and interacting with each other in real time that generates not only their own little biographies, but in an aggregate fashion, all of social life.

The individuals in question – who together achieve social groups, invent and maintain institutions, and transform and abandon them – are themselves best understood as ongoing processes rather than as objects with fixed nature and characteristics. Who and what we are is constituted by our activities of understanding (and misunderstanding) ourselves and engaging with others, things we do with language and other more or less shared symbolic forms (to be defined below). The claim is not that we are necessarily what we think we are – we all know people who clearly misunderstand who and what they are – but rather, that what we and others think we are very much shapes us. For instance, there are groups of people who understand themselves to be children of God; independently of the moot point of whether there are gods who beget or otherwise create children, these individuals' everyday lives, the groups they form, the interactions they engage in, and their child-raising practices, weekend rituals, ethical decisions, emotions, and attitudes towards death are all shaped by their sense that that is what they are. We could not account persuasively for their daily lives or the features of the groups they form without bearing in mind who they think they are or what it is they think they are doing when they do what they do. In other words, understanding them involves understanding the way of life they are engaged in.[13]

I particularly like Charles Taylor's manner of articulating these matters and their implications:

> If we are partly constituted by our self-understanding, and this in turn can be very different according to the various languages which articulate for us a background of distinctions of worth, then language does not only serve to *depict* ourselves and the world, it also helps *constitute* our lives. Certain ways of being, of feeling, of relating to each other are only possible given certain linguistic resources. Without a certain articulation of oneself and of the highest, it is neither possible to *be* a Christian ascetic, nor to *feel* that combination of one's own lack of worth and high calling …, nor to be *part* of, say, a monastic order. (1985, 9,10)

The claim here is that the processes constitutive of persons and, *ipso facto*, of their social lives, are symbolic, and this merits further explanation. Symbols are any of a great array of material forms – sounds, images, objects, sensations, perceptions, thoughts, movements – that individuals come to associate with other forms in the very processes of living our lives.[14] Because individuals are immersed in social milieus, we pick up common, shared symbolic forms and associations that others make available for us; for instance, we tend to use the lexicon, grammatical forms, tones of voice, and ways of organizing our sentences that others around us do. We acquire these forms and their associations – linguistic or otherwise – through personal historical engagements in a social milieu, and by redeploying them (or citing them, to use Derrida's and Butler's vocabulary, or borrowing them, to use Mauss's [1979, 102]) make them available for others to pick up as well. Because of the uniqueness of the contingencies of individuals' lives, however, each one will have some symbolic forms and associations peculiar to them.[15]

Our webs of associated symbolic forms are constitutive of our understandings and sensitivities, where reflexivity is key. Charles Taylor points to how we often catch ourselves when we misuse a word and recognize the relevance of challenges from others concerning our use of some term (1985, 229–33). This capacity presupposes that somehow (or at some level) we are constantly reflecting on our own use of language, hearing it and evaluating it. The same is true for other kinds of symbolic deployments, in relation to the ways of life they constitute;

without necessarily focusing reflectively on these matters, we are nonetheless to some extent reflexive about our expressive gestures and our thought processes. We may thus 'correct' our style of walking, our demeanour, our hand movements, or the tone of voice in which we speak to someone, because we find that these are somehow not quite right for our way of life, perhaps not masculine or feminine enough, or too arrogant, or too coarse, or too refined. We also experience reflexive 'second-order' desires the object of which is to have first-order desires, and which similarly incorporate evaluations of the latter (Harry Frankfurt, via Taylor 1985, 16). Thus, we may wish we were more disciplined about reading through dense material, as we experience the desire to abandon the task of plowing through a tough, boring text.

Our understandings of ourselves, of our relationships, and of much else in our lives feature more or less articulate distinctions between things we deem more important or more admirable or of greater worth, and things we deem unimportant, despicable, or of lesser or no worth. In the English-speaking countries where I have lived, for example, people distinguish qualitatively, with terms the understanding of which requires a grasp of contrasts, between persons who are admirably 'objective,' in contrast to those who are contemptibly under the sway of their emotions; at times, though, they deem emotionality to express a goodness, a sensitivity, which 'callous, insensitive' others lack. But qualitative distinctions need not refer to matters concerning some deep issue of the good; people also distinguish bodily shapes, perfumes, gestures, and clothes, among endless other potentially symbolic forms, as manifestations of a certain valued way of life or of being, or as contrary to such. Thus, some people's way of life involves sensitivity to distinctions between what is elegant or classy and what is tacky or cheesy. Distinctions of these and myriad other kinds feature in people's understandings of the kinds of subjects they are or deem it possible and desirable to be. They 'see,' as an obvious, straightforward fact or import of a situation, that a certain action or appearance is admirable, beautiful, cool, cruel, despicably spiteful, and so on.

The constitution of the self is clearly not simply a matter of individuals interpreting themselves autonomously. Among the symbolic deployments that shape us and shape our further deployments of symbols are those that constitute what could be called the footings of relations between persons. The deployments in question include addressing people and being addressed by them in certain terms and not other available ones, positioning our bodies in certain ways when interacting with each other, modulating the tones of our voices, choosing conversational subject matter and expressions, providing or requesting food, services, or gifts or refraining from doing so, and countless other forms. These deployments are objects of our sensitivities; that is, even if we do not have the sense that we are focused on these practices – especially when the deployments are appropriate – we are aware when we or others somehow do not strike the right tone, or overreach ourselves, and so on.[16] These deployments, if felicitous (or effective), make up our relations as intimate lovers, trusting friends, respectfully distant acquaintances, competing siblings, solicitous ritual partners, doting parents and demanding children, curt bosses and meek underlings, and so forth. They also make us, for the duration of the interaction but also in our own and each others' memories, persons of a certain kind: caring lovers, trustworthy and loyal individuals, good parents, awe-inspiring superiors, bullied weaklings, or no-nonsense persons of consequence, and so on. As Lambek (2010, 63) states with slightly different terms, 'speaking and acting entail the predication and appropriation of voice – speaking and acting as oneself (to someone, in the sight or hearing of someone, with reference to someone) – and as such are intrinsically constitutive of ethical subjects and relations.'

I call the sensitivities and judgments in question and the symbolic practices that create them 'morality,' a use of the term which, following Charles Taylor, signals an approach to human life and action that deems it essential to attend to the human personal capacity for reflective, strong, qualitative evaluations of self, while acknowledging the intrinsically social nature of personhood (1985, 15–44). My account here thus engages with the sense that human beings seem to behave in self-aware, purposeful fashion, but yet also at times unreflectively in ways both constrained and enabled by social forms and relations, a sense that has been a central preoccupation of anthropological scholarship on matters of ethics and morality.

For Laidlaw, in a recent example of such scholarship, ethics is any of the ways of answering the Socratic question, 'How ought one to live?' It is an encompassing category, within which Laidlaw distinguishes between a possibly habitus-like, unselfconscious way of acting and a historically produced kind of freedom of thought that involves stepping back from such habitus, objectifying and questioning its meanings and conditions, and choosing between alternatives of action (Laidlaw 2002, 316, 317). He uses the term 'morality' to refer to a limited subset of mainly religious ethical ways of life that centre on self-denial and law-like obligations, rather than as behaviours differentiated on the basis of their place in a continuum from the reflective to the unreflective (ibid., 324). Zigon, though inspired by Laidlaw's Foucaldian concept of freedom, refers to such a habitus, which is not thought out beforehand or noticed when performed, as 'morality'; ethics, in his account, is a reflective and reflexive stepping-away from the embodied moral habitus or moral discourse, brought about by moral breakdown or problematization (2008, 18; 2009). Robbins' categories converge to some extent, if his choice of terms differs as well: for him, there is a Durkheimian, unreflective 'morality of reproduction' on one hand, and a 'morality of choice' dependent on and expressive of (contextualized) freedom (2007) on the other. Keane (2010) treats ethics and morality as synonyms, and sees them as a range of modalities of practice that differ in the extent to which they feature verbal objectification. Some social forms are inarticulate, embodied, and practical, and constitute a background ethical life on which rests an articulate ethical modality involving the self-conscious 'giving of reasons.'[17]

For a number of these scholars, infelicities or crises of various kinds lead from the unreflective reproduction of symbolic forms to the focused awareness of them we call reflexivity. Zigon calls these 'moral breakdowns,' which occur when some event or person intrudes into the everyday life of persons and forces them to reflect consciously upon an appropriate ethical response (2008, 18). For Keane (2010), following Bakhtin, it is contact, and presumably contrast, with other languages, voices, or vocabularies – either from within or from outside competing traditions – that induces consciousness in the first place.

The scholars above seek to avoid the 'mutually repellent extremes' of, on one hand, Sartrean or economistic decisionism, where persons are somehow free from all social structuration, and on the other hand, determinism in its many guises, including accounting for behaviour as fundamentally the product of psychobiological or social mechanical compulsions (Faubion 2001, 18). I do too. I want to insist on the need to attend to human self-awareness if we are to understand social life, but deem the awareness of persons itself to be constituted to an important extent by persons' citations – at the very level of thoughts – of (always) material symbolic forms that social interaction and sensible experience[18] have made available to them. The constitution of persons depends on symbols they cite, symbols whose dense associations with other symbolic forms are never fully and simultaneously available for persons to reflect upon. Similarly, the historical social processes that make these symbolic webs intimately available to persons – and which interpellate them – are never thoroughly available for persons to reflect upon. In short, persons are both conscious of and opaque to themselves.[19]

The symbolic constitution of our personal decisions, our desires, our gestures, and so forth, entails not only that we cannot have a clear-sighted overview or control over their enabling conditions and historical processes, but also that we have very limited control and knowledge of their effects. This is causally related to what seems to me to be an unassailable point of Derrida's about *différance*: that inevitably there will be differences in the meanings the same forms and deployments will have for different subjects. Therefore, the intentions and meanings that we understand our symbolic deployments to convey do not get 'carried across' to others as such; rather, others make their own sense of our expressions with their own webs of associated symbolic forms (Vološinov 2000 [1929], 40, 41). This intrinsically limits our grasp of and control over the effects of what we do and the efficacy of our intentions. Making much the same point, Keane (2003) and Laidlaw (2002, 315) were critical of interpretive anthropologists in the late 1980s and 1990s whose enthusiastic claims about agency conflated the human capacity for self interpretation with the efficacy of their (intentional) actions.[20]

The symbolic deployments that constitute our relationships, our selves, and indeed our moralities, are citations, that is, historical and contingent reproductions, intrinsically susceptible to varied objectifications, transformations, or failures (infelicities). Some discursive and non-discursive forms and their associations are cited more often than others, making them all the more available and perhaps therefore more compelling within a certain set of people at a certain point in time. In such cases they create the kinds of patterns of human social action that we might call 'institutions,' 'styles,' 'languages,' 'rituals,' and 'culture.'[21] We should not lose sight of the fact that the substance of these apparent entities is the temporal reiterations and interpretations of symbolic deployments by and between particular persons – however many of them – in unique historical circumstances. A key virtue of this theoretical approach is that it addresses both the relatively conservative reproduction of symbols and their contexts, and their unavoidable mutability.[22]

The materiality, contingency, and temporality of symbolic deployments, the fact that we individuals are constantly refashioning our webs of associations as we use them in conducting our lives, entails that our moralities, the footings of our relationships, and the kinds of subjects we can be are mutable, and that they differ between social groups that we make up. People of the Centre offer a nice example of such difference: they often judged subjectivities and actions in terms of whether they were truly human as opposed to animalistic; or as anchored in or stemming from moral tobacco and other substances supposedly constitutive of persons, in contrast to 'being empty' or having no substance; or as manifestations of the individual's very body being fabricated out of the substances of this rather than that clan. Individuals among People of the Centre could thus interpret their own and each other's thoughts and actions as potentially stemming from animalistic sources outside themselves, or as manifesting in a laudable way the specifically clanic substances that constituted their bodies. Interpersonal relationships, whether of hierarchy, care, or congenial companionship, were realized in the same symbolic deployments.

Methodologically, my approach calls for attention to individuals, for it is individuals – or historical persons, if you will – who actually iterate symbolic forms. Our actions vis-à-vis one another depend on our (symbolically shaped) motivations and (symbolically constituted) understandings of ourselves in the world. However, I also hasten to add that mine is not a less than sociological approach. Paying attention to individual persons' understandings and actions is pointedly not an alternative to a focus on social relations; rather, persons and relations are mutually constitutive, and cannot, in my understanding, be dealt with apart (see Cohen 1994, 7, for a similar approach). I attended to what people said and did in and about rituals, social organizational practices, and everyday livelihood, but I paid closest attention to talk that seemed to me to centre on evaluations of worth. This included gossip, moral self-portrayals, counsels, scoldings, and harangues, among other more or less recognizable discursive genres.[23]

Symbolic deployments are conditioned, enabled, and limited by histories of the material conditions of people's lives, including previous symbolic deployments and their effects. Such histories could involve, for example, famines or the arrival of conquerors and colonists, and their effects, the establishment of new hierarchies or changes in old ones. Echeverri (1997) describes an instance of such changes in the case of Uitoto, Muinane, Bora, Miraña, Ocaina, and Andoque, whose internal relations, and relations with each other as groups, changed as they engaged with relations with traders and other 'whites.' Early on, the arrival of metal axes may have changed the sizes of their gardens and some of the entailments of the gendered division of labour;

they also led to some clans engaging in the new practice of exchanging their orphans with slavers for manufactured goods. Much later, these people creatively re-imagined their relations with each other in order to make sense within and relate to the nation-state; they created, or started to use in a more encompassing fashion, the category of 'People of the Centre.' This new, larger imagined community's emergence was tied dialogically to that of new kinds of leaders. Echeverri analyses the contradictions between 'public discourses' – narratives that lubricated and helped maintain images of the larger community, and the kinds of leadership it entailed – and 'secret discourses' used in more intimate settings, and which portrayed a picture of leadership, clan origins and interclan relations, and moral hierarchies that contested the public discourses.

Patterns of interaction among people may involve making it more likely that the protests, claims, instructions, and preoccupations of one category of people be hearkened to more than those of others. They may also make it unintelligible, or embarrassing, or punishable for certain people to speak in certain circumstances. When people enact these effects – for instance, when medical doctors in Canada give their patients serious instructions, or when women in some Papua New Guinean societies abstain from speaking in the presence of visiting outsiders (see Kulick 1992, 91) – they contribute to the reproduction of the conditions that shape their own and their consociates' understandings and practices.

Such acts may also lead to what a Marxist analyst might consider the systematic alienation of the labour of some to the benefit of others. Because symbolic deployments are central to the substance of these relations, the latter are subject to slippages, infelicities, and other vicissitudes of symbols. The relations themselves are beyond individuals' clear overview, though new articulations – for example, picking up a Marxist or feminist vocabulary – do enable people to objectify some of their practices and relations in new ways. However, I resist claims to the effect that social change stems from people stepping outside a false, exploitative ideology, on the basis of cognitive access to some fundamental reality about exploitation by dint of some universal, biologically enabled, endowment (for example, Bloch 1977). I would underscore that people's new formulations and understandings are still symbolic, and as such, are always historical and mutable fictions.

I try in this book to be consistent with my theoretical emphasis on the temporality and particularity of symbolic deployments, and so I often describe actual instances of action bearing in mind when these occurred and my own position in time. Hence I use the past tenses throughout, seeking as far as possible to avoid an ethnographic present tense that would veil the temporal and particular nature of what I witnessed People of the Centre doing. The verb conjugations will at times sound clumsy, but I am committed to letting my theoretical emphasis trump, to some extent, the aesthetic standards of academic writing. I must underscore, however, that my verb tense choice does not entail that the groups and practices that I describe are less than alive and well at the time of writing this note (July of 2010).

## The Amazonian Package: Bodies and Alterity in a Perspectival Cosmos

In attending to People of the Centre's understandings of sociality and of personhood, I am in part treading a now well-beaten path in the anthropological literature on the Amazon. This literature seems to me to convey the sense that people in the region share what I will loosely call an 'Amazonian package': interlinked accounts or beliefs to the effect that human bodies are fabricated socially, that this occurs in the context of a perspectival cosmos, and that relations with dangerous outside Others are necessary to the process. Let me briefly explore the three main elements in this package.

A growing number of ethnographers have come to focus on the human body as a primary matrix of social meaning among indigenous peoples of the region.[24] Their ethnographies have shown that the genesis, fabrication, transformation, beautification, and destruction of bodies feature centrally in different people's myths, rituals, and other practices of social organization. Different practices concerning corporeal elements, such as eating, drinking, body painting, dressing, otherwise consuming substances that are extensions or analogues of the body, or talking about these matters, are typically key among the symbolic deployments through which individuals create, maintain, transform, manipulate, and end relationships with each other – in other words, through which they achieve a social life.

It is common in Amazonia to find the notion that human beings – thinking, feeling, interacting persons endowed with specifically human bodies – are the product-in-the-making of their kin and others who surround them. In these accounts, persons are not born as such, but are intentionally manufactured or shaped by kin through rituals, diet, and other practices throughout persons' gestation (or even before their conception), childhood, and adult life. Overing and Passes note synthetically that in much of Amazonia 'social life is about creating good/beautiful people who can live a tranquil, sociable life together" (2000b, 2). The first element in the package – the notion that bodies are fabricated socially – could also be reformulated as the notion that social life is mainly about fabricating bodies.

Following the seminal work of Viveiros de Castro (1998) and his students (for example, Fausto 1999; Lima 1996; Vilaça 2000, 2002), Amazonianist literature on body-making practices also suggests that these depend on the second element of the package, namely, perspectival cosmological premises. Roughly, perspectivism is the belief or claim that every kind of being perceives itself and its co-specifics as human, its lifestyle as a human lifestyle, and its houses and tools as human habitations and tools; other kinds of beings appear to them like animals, plants, or other non-humans. It is their bodies that establish the 'point of view': from a jaguar's embodied point of view, it and other jaguars are human and their claws look like arrows and spears, while we look like wild pigs or large rodents. Some Amazonians would claim that we are jaguars, from the point of view of wild pigs. I will pursue the details of this much further in chapters 2 and 3. For now, however, let me note that perspectivism gives the process of making bodies a certain urgency or edge in a number of Amazonian societies, for the point is to make one's children's and other kin's bodies as much like one's own as possible, lest it become different and Other, and perceive one as less than human.

The third element in the Amazonian package is the related concept that often appears in Amazonian accounts of personhood and sociality to the effect that the creation or formation of proper human bodies and the achievement of a desirable lifestyle also depend on relations of alterity, that is, relations with a panoply of Others who vary in how different and distant they are from the person or group in question. The more encompassing claim is that alterity is the 'given' state of sociality in the cosmos, and that beings attempt to reduce the differences between them to become consanguineal or consubstantial kin – a task never absolutely achieved (Viveiros de Castro 2001). Among the key others that some Amazonian people bring into their accounts are members of the (or an) other sex, affines (in-laws), enemies, and trade partners, and in other cosmological realms, animals, the dead, gods, and forest and river spirits, among others.[25] It is from distant gods, for instance, that

Piaroa shamans in Venezuela must take beautiful, powerful but potentially maddening 'forces of fertility' and place them carefully within youths, to endow them with competences for hunting, fishing, cooking, and having children (Overing 1993, 198, 199). Brazilian Wari' people in the past found it necessary for warriors to kill enemies and ritually incorporate their vitality; this would come to make each killer, and any women he had sex with, vigorous, beautiful, and fertile (Conklin 2001b).[26]

Gow (2001) finds patterns of the kind I call a package here underlying apparent great social changes among the indigenous Piro people in the Peruvian Amazon. His research suggests that certain Piro myths, specifically those concerning twins, differed from certain others in that they were rather stable over centuries, and concluded that the Piro and their ancestors consistently treated distant others – before the European contact, the Inca; afterwards, different kinds of whites – as 'possessors of objects' or traders who had 'twins' beyond the known world. He puts forward that over time the Piro had responded to crises in their lived world by looking for better possessors of objects 'at the edge of the known world,' and that this explained the forms of their successive engagements with slavers, hacienda owners, Catholic missionaries, Evangelical missionaries, and government representatives. Gow's account reveals that many of Piro people's rituals had changed, as did the clothing they wore, but he claims that nonetheless there was an important continuity here: for Piro people, their new rituals and clothes functioned to transform them (partly) into Others, to perceive them and to be perceived by them in turn in such a way as to engage with them effectively and, thereby, to acquire things necessary for their own reproduction and well-being. In their experience, the clothing and the rituals kept performing the transformative function they had always had. In short, the Piro's sense of history was that it was transformational – that they themselves transformed as they interacted with new kinds of Others – and that *that* was continuous. For Piro people, it was the relationship with dangerous white people – who were not themselves part of Piro communities – that had enabled them to create proper communities and live well. For them, relationships with outsiders were prior to, and encompassed, their relations to themselves.[27]

Santos-Granero (2009b) describes, in terms similar to Gow's, the complex transformations in the Peruvian Amazonian Yanesha people's dress over centuries. He calls it a case of 'hybridity,' a native 'cultural praxis,' and, indeed, a 'point of view' operative since pre-contact times.

This praxis – Santos-Granero's description of which situates it very much within the package I described above – is 'an openness to the Other,' manifest in the Yanesha's enduring disposition to transform their bodies in order to incorporate the Other's perspective, whether it be that of Incas, Spanish conquistadores, Catholic or Evangelical missionaries, or hacienda owners, motivated by the desire to establish profitable or at least peaceful relations with them.

A question that Gow and Santos-Granero leave unanswered is how this native sense of history, this willingness to transform into Others, or this 'system in a state of transformation' (Gow 2001, 27) – which I would portray as a version of the Amazonian package – was itself reproduced so conservatively over time. It is beyond my methodological expertise and my more immediate interests here to produce a densely argued account of events of such long duration in Amazonia as scholars like Gow (2001), Santos-Granero (2000, 2009b), Jonathan Hill (1988), Neil Whitehead (2003), and Carlos Fausto and Michael Heckenberger (2007), among others, address. Still, I do insist on the temporal character of symbolic deployments and of the persons, relationships, and groupings these create; furthermore, the likenesses among Amazonian groups that are in some cases geographically very distant from each other and whose ancestors appear not to have had direct contact for perhaps thousands of years, do suggest to me that the elements of the Amazonian package have been cited more or less consistently over time, such that versions of the package are radial transformations of each other.[28]

I will hazard the claim that Amazonian peoples may have cited the elements of the Amazonian package performatively in the symbolic deployments constitutive of their morally evaluative understandings of themselves, and that this might account for its more or less conservative reproduction. I am extrapolating here from my interpretation of People of the Centre's talk and other practices, which reproduced recognizable versions of the Amazonian package. People of the Centre tended to recreate coherent webs of associations that tied together flexibly their accounts of selfhood, their membership in clans and patrilines, their livelihood practices and the substances they produced, their rituals, and their takes on relations among human beings and between human beings and others such as animals and forest spirits. In these accounts, bodies were indeed fabricated by kin in the context of dangerous cosmos densely populated by sometimes inimical, sometimes potentially benevolent beings endowed with their own intentionalities and capacities. In this cosmos, dispensing with alterity would be unimaginable.

Among them, talk of what it was to be a human or an inhuman or a non-human being centred on the morality of their perceptions, points of view, thoughts/emotions, and actions. My sense is that such talk enacted and reproduced the kinds of backgrounds of distinctions of worth that I addressed in the previous section. People constituted themselves and established relationships to an important extent in acts of seeing that these distinctions applied, or in acts and talk motivated by these distinctions. The latter were key means by which people understood what happened in their lives, including what mattered, how it mattered, and how much it mattered. This shaped their actions, which became new citations of the forms that shaped their understandings.

The Amazonian package among People of the Centre, and its versions in much of the Amazon, involved semiotic ideologies – assumptions people made about what things and events in the world could be 'signs' put out there by some being endowed with intentions, and which could not. This included understandings of what kinds of beings were candidates for attributions of agency, in the sense of capacity for intentional action including communication (see Keane 2003, 419). For people in some societies, only members of the human species are candidates for attributions of such agency; among many Amazonians, people, animals, plants, substances, canoes, fishhooks, and a great many more things are understood to be persons, or to share key subjective features with persons. If individuals' sense of self involves their attribution of images, attitudes, and memories of themselves to others, then talk and other symbolic interactions with or referring to various kinds of others – not only human beings but also gods, animals, and the dead – are likely to be among the deployments that shape Amazonian people's morally evaluative understandings of selfhood.[29] These very understandings, and that they shape what matters to people, may have caused people to reproduce them (unwittingly), generating the appearance of a more or less conservative package.

## Structure of the Book

The chapters that follow flesh out my claims. Chapters 2 and 3 address respectively the constitution of moral and immoral selves, with attention to People of the Centre's uses of accounts of body-making for the purposes of making moral claims concerning their own and others' purportedly human or animalistic subjectivities or perspectives. Chapter 4 concerns the gendered human capacities and their manifestations in the livelihood work processes and esoteric knowledge of moral actors, who transform a variety of evil or misanthropic figures of alterity into healthy substances or objects that generate good bodies or enable proper sociality. Chapter 5 describes People of the Centre's discursive and non-discursive practices concerning the substances in question – tobacco, coca, manioc, and other gendering, body-constituting, kinship-making substances – and addresses some of the entailments of their materiality as symbols. Chapter 6 deals with People of the Centre's morally evaluative and prescriptive talk and other practices concerning gender complementarity and hierarchy, their patrilineally inflected kin groups, their dealings with affines, and their need for support from key alters in rituals. The concluding chapter addresses the contingency, temporality, and performativity of the practices that shape personhood among People of the Centre, making the case that I avoid certain common pitfalls of accounts that posit the social structuration of personhood; it recognizes new social practices that shape moral personhood and relationships among People of the Centre, yet also underscores the continuity of the Amazonian package.

# 1 The Constitution of the Moral Self

People of the Centre's talk and non-discursive practices concerning bodies and their fabrication and transformation incorporated key distinctions of worth. They involved complex, coherent notions of the nature of human and non-human bodies and of the ways of life these enabled, of what it was to be a real person or human being as opposed to being something else, and of the relationships between different kinds of beings. I would call this their version of the Amazonian package.

These distinctions of worth were evident in their expressions of admiration or desire for certain thoughts/emotions, attitudes, ways of life, and actions, and of contempt for others. Central among the former were, on one hand, the constructive virtues of loving care, a sense of purpose, coolness or calm equanimity, respect, and good humour and, on the other, the capacity for violent, esoteric predation. My sense with several of these is that they were a matter of 'second-order desires,' that is, desires to have other desires.[1] Second-order desires involve an evaluation of first-order desires that may seem more straightforward and immediate; for instance, we may deem our very real and intimate desire to trip up a rival as something despicable and wish not to have such spiteful feelings. The idea that persons should act out of loving care seems to me often to have been a second-order desire among People of the Centre; people reflected on themselves and their interactions and wanted to act towards others, or at least to portray themselves as persons who acted towards others, as first and foremost motivated by loving care. They asserted that this love was the motivation for acts ranging from nourishing and healing others to co-residing with them, scolding them, and punishing them.

This is not to deny, at all, the intimately felt love that was expressed in what I felt were spontaneous gestures I witnessed, or that people were often purposeful, cool, sincerely respectful, and eager to both enjoy and generate humour. Indeed, all these virtues were the object of aesthetic investment; people to some extent or another valued them, *saw* and *felt* that they were desirable. Underscoring this obviousness allows me to claim that despite my argument that people often intelligently and strategically sought to present themselves in certain ways – akin to Goffman's 'impression management' (1959) – I do not posit a Machiavellian or Hobbesian self-interested, maximizing individual; persons' 'seeing' in this obvious way was a product of their social interactions, but was not itself a product of strategic choice. I shall return to this in greater depth in the following chapter.

Besides being motivated by loving care, real people were supposed to be cool (*sɨɨku-*, in Muinane): tranquil, sociable, content, benevolent, and single-minded in the sense that they did not suffer from confused, obsessive thoughts or manifest careless haste. Coolness was also tied to other key virtues: a stalwart sense of purpose, judicious discernment, and personal rootedness, understood, among other things, as an ability to resist being swayed from properly human courses of action.

The question then is how People of the Centre's understandings of bodies related to ways of life they admired or desired.

**Sociality and the Embodiment of Subject Substances**

In much of the rhetoric of People of the Centre, they were alive, aware, articulate, and capable of competent, moral, and sociable action in part because of 'speeches' and 'breaths' that constituted their bodies and resonated inside them. They spoke of thoughts/emotions as 'speeches' of key substances such as tobacco paste, coca, diverse manioc products, hot chilies, and cool herbs that sounded inside or *through* a body constituted by those substances. Speeches were also the moral talk that people produced as a result of experiencing such thoughts/emotions, and furthermore a number of instrumental discourses. Muinane speakers sometimes used the term 'breath' or 'breaths' as a synonym of 'speech,' but it was particularly appropriate to refer to an animating element, blown into people by the tobacco deity at the moment of birth.[2]

Mambeadores told me speeches of apprising (myths) according to which these substances – tobacco and coca foremost among them – had divine origins. The substances spoke in a 'true' way, virtuously, perspicaciously, and effectively, constituting the normal moral awareness and dispositions of people who lived well, as real people – true human beings – should. The thoughts that people experienced as love and compassion for kin, their judgments when they correctly distinguished between good and evil behaviour, and their strong willingness to assuage conflict, but also the efficacious, predatory anger they experienced in the presence of evil, were examples of the speeches of some of these substances sounding inside the body.

People of the Centre – men more insistently than women – used a variety of metaphors to describe the relationship between substances and speeches as spoken words or as thoughts/emotions; one man, specifically speaking about what I call 'instrumental speeches' – esoteric invocations deployed in the *mambeadero* – stated that just as satellites were far up above, but still the sounds radios made came from them, so too the creator made his speech sound through people from far above, via his substances. Mambeadores deployed this concept to claim their speeches to be the very words of the deity sounding through them, rather than the words of mere mortal men; they thus recognized that there were less powerful, non-divine speeches and thoughts, opening up space for multiple alternatives for the attribution of responsibility for action. In a way, they were also claiming that human subjectivity was a citation of the subjectivity of the divinity, divinities, or other beings. Another comparison I heard elsewhere was that people could only speak if they had tobacco inside them, much as a tape recorder could only sound with a tape inside it. However, the metaphor of the tape was limited; unlike the tape, which was separate from the tape recorder and removable, the tobacco – with its speeches and affects – actually *constituted* the body.[3]

A key aspect of human subjectivity, in contrast to inhuman or animalistic subjectivity, was that real people did not just possess instrumental knowledge – which some non-human (indeed, inhuman) beings did too – but they also discerned between moral action and its spurious counterparts. Muinane people, in particular, spoke of this discernment in terms of 'remembering' properly.[4] In abstract accounts I heard, for example, individuals spoke of antisocial action as a case of miscreants not remembering that another was a kinsman. One term seamlessly brought together discernment and memory: *ésɨkɨnɨhi*. Explaining this term to me, my Muinane friend Pablo – perhaps my most important informant – noted that animals could know (*gájahi*), but unlike real people, they did not remember/discern (*ésɨkɨnɨhi*). As I understand it, such discernment or judiciousness was what led people to treat each other as they should and, thereby, to achieve cool community life. It was mainly tobacco – but at times other substances as well – that 'reminded' people of how to behave.

People of the Centre's reflexive talk on these matters did not seem to be premised on a mind, spirit, or soul that pre-existed the speeches of ritual substances and that constituted the essence – the innate core – of a person's subjectivity. I am thinking here of a contrast between common injunctions in the English-speaking world to be true to one's innermost, true self, where the latter is understood to be a unique, unitary, internal, (often spiritual) essence and centre for volition, and People of the Centre's concept of an extrinsic, ultimately material or literally substantial self. For the most part, People of the Centre treated the moral, thinking and feeling self as constituted in an ongoing fashion by the speeches of the substances embodied in individuals. Sometimes these substances or their speeches (they did not often find it necessary to distinguish between these) did take on a homuncular shape in their descriptions – that is, people attributed to them human body-like features and movements and their own subjectivities. Pablo's explanation of shame posited just such a homuncular speech: he stated that when people felt shame at their own misbehaviour, it was because the speech of tobacco inside them that had become aware of an impropriety and 'lowered its head' (as people did when ashamed). To a limited extent, then, speeches were akin to Hollywood images of the soul as a vaporous, gendered, human sort of body. But neither substances nor speeches compose a unitary, coherent soul; they composed bodies, thoughts/emotions, and inclinations. They were multiple themselves, and they could choose to stay inside a person or not to become fixed to them. They could become sad, rebellious, indignant, or angry, sometimes causing the person they constituted to experience these very thoughts/emotions, but sometimes rather abandoning or attacking the person's body – which is something the soul, as conceived in Western Judeo-Christian societies, would normally never do.

Vilaça claims that in Amerindian understandings, bodies are 'ways of being' actualized in bodily form, rather than substances impregnated with dispositions and affects; the difference is subtle, and it is important to be wary of 'the interference of a Western idea of the body as the starting point that is then reworked' (2005, 450). However, People of the Centre's discursive and non-discursive practices seemed to posit both possibilities: that bodies were basically made of substances that were themselves packages of thoughts/emotions and habits and that bodies were receptacles for such substances. The result in both cases, however, was that the subjectivities of substances expressed themselves in the forms of persons' thoughts/emotions, speeches, and actions.

As an interesting aside, the Muinane term for the body was the morpheme '*–fi*,' which always came with possessives: *tafi, mofi, difi* (respectively, 'my body,' 'our body,' 'your body'). To refer to what we could call character or personality features that people manifested consistently over time, the Muinane language would incorporate a doubled version of the *–fi* morpheme into a verb, turning it into an adjectival verb. Thus, the expression *ákihi*, meaning 'I give,' can be transformed into *ákififihi*, which can be roughly translated as 'I am a giving body,' 'I embody giving,' or 'I am generous.' Similar constructions are *gáijififihi, bañififihi*, and *ímafifihi*, respectively, 'I embody stinginess,' or 'I'm stingy,' 'I embody lying,' or 'I'm a liar,' and 'I embody talking,' or 'I'm a gossip.'

People of the Centre expressed their sense that their subjectivities had concrete, extrinsic, multiple origins in their accounts of men's practice of consuming tobacco paste and mambe, and of women's production of certain drinks and foods. Mambeadores stated that they licked tobacco and consumed mambe because these 'opened [men's] thoughts'; they used this image in claims to the effect that they at times became exceptionally insightful in perceiving troubles in themselves and in others, discerning the proper ways to behave, and in finding the motivation to behave in that manner. The original substances themselves featured these virtues. Men and women also sometimes attributed men's misbehaviours to the lack of coca or tobacco which instilled proper thoughts in them or, in a more abstract fashion, stated that anyone with such a lack was likely to misbehave.

Their talk about substances and thoughts was often simultaneously about family relationships (or kinship), affective bonds, and individuals' sense of who they were in terms of features such as gender, group membership, and a variety of personal qualities. They portrayed kin as *consubstantial*: members of the same clans, lineages, and nuclear families were supposed to be made out of the 'juice' of the same manioc, chilies, cool herbs, coca, and, especially, tobacco. They understood this to be true not only in the sense that they consumed the same stuffs, which was also the case (with minor differences between men and women), but also in the sense that their parents and ancestors had ensured their own reproduction through the ritual use of these substances. Pablo once summarized neatly the constitutive character of substances when he stated that a man's thoughts/emotions of loving care (*Kávajɨ*) and respect for his close kin – those who were made out of the same substances – were the tobacco inside him saying 'This is my own body,' upon recognizing itself in the bodies of others.[5]

Consubstantiality, given that substances generated subjectivity, entailed intersubjectivity, a circumstance that people referred to in their morally evaluative talk. At one large meeting I witnessed, one man stated that Muinane people today were behaving as if they were strangers, contesting and making enemies of each other, and that this was sad and blind, for was it not the case that as People of the Centre they were all made of the same tobacco, and that therefore their thoughts/emotions had to be the same? This kind of hortatory talk urged everyone to recognize their commonalities, and many responded immediately that he was right. However, at other moments, in the privacy of their coca circles, some limited the sameness of the tobaccos and subjectivities to their own smaller subgroups, underscoring what they portrayed as important moral differences between them and other families, lineages, or clans of People of the Centre. Some made affirmations to the effect that their own particular personal virtues and skills stemmed from specific substances unique to their clans.

The implications People of the Centre drew from supposed consubstantiality were not always favourable, for they also explained the immoral behaviour of members of some collectivities in terms of the substantial origin of thoughts/emotions. Many individuals privately pointed out to me that other lineages and clans had intrinsically violent, antisocial, promiscuous, or authoritarian tobaccos and thus similarly undesirable speeches and thoughts/emotions. I also heard much rhetoric about the possibility or purported fact that (perceived) misbehaviours by individuals and entire groups were the product of inhuman beings' usurpation of human subjectivities by means of spurious substances planted in human bodies. The possibility of such usurpations was central to People of the Centre's everyday moral portrayals, and furthermore to accounts of healing and dance rituals, which were meant to address this problem.

The possibility that one's own or one's fellows' thoughts/emotions and actions might cease to be properly human and therefore moral and sociable was a central existential problem for People of the Centre. This problem was causally tied to their accounts of the making and setting of bodies. These accounts were resources that people could use to criticize or inveigh against others' inconsistency or purported immoral ways, thoughts/emotions, or actions but also to posit a somewhat more consistent self, made more steadfast by a properly formed body.[6]

### The Making and Setting of Bodies

In the accounts of several People of the Centre, living pleasantly – and morally – was the product, but also the pre-condition, of the 'multiplication of people.' Pablo and other Muinane, Uitoto and Nonuya elders explicitly treated this multiplication – the growth in numbers of their lineages, clans, or humanity in general – as the ultimate purpose of their rituals and daily work. They seemed to find beauty and the promise of pleasure in the image of a large community in which there was much collaboration and good mutual treatment. Talk of such multiplication often involved references to the making and shaping of the bodies – and thereby the subjectivities – of individual real persons, and to the moral constitution of both shapers and shaped. People presented themselves as concerned, talented, disciplined, and wise performers of people-making practices, or made claims to some desirable aspect of how they themselves had been raised and shaped, and they were often correspondingly critical of others as makers of bodies.

In stark contrast to Westerners' naturalist accounts of new bodies as the product of embryogenesis (the process of formation of a baby in the mother's womb) and a variety of anatomical and physiological processes deemed biological and natural as opposed to social, People of the Centre's talk about bodies was often premised on the notion that these were fabricated intentionally and socially.[7] Among other things, they maintained that a child's gender, bodily shape, virtue, and so forth, were influenced by the actions and interactions of its parents, grandparents, and other kin well before the child was conceived, and continued to be shaped after the child was born. Their understanding of what made kinspeople *kin* – definable for many purposes as 'people whose bodies were alike' – emphasized the social actions and relations involved in the production of persons, rather than the biological linkages.

Muinane, Uitoto, and Nonuya people's talk about conception and pregnancy, which differed from Western scientific accounts, provides a first example of this. To start, some mambeadores described semen as the very purified extract of the properly produced substances which each man consumed: his own tobacco and coca, but also the manioc starch drink and sweet manioc drink his wife and other women made for him. These substances – all of which were produced to some extent or another collectively – were processed by the body's 'fire of life,' which consumed any further impurities and ideally left only nourishing, beneficial elements. The quality of the semen – and thus of the persons made with that semen – could, however, suffer from the consumption of untoward substances such as white men's alcohol, marihuana, or untrustworthy tobaccos; in the following chapter I will provide an example of a man using this possibility to explain his own miscreancy.

Conception and pregnancy depended on the accumulation of semen in a woman's 'cup of life,' an internal receptacle imagined as a hemispheric gourd, where the semen dried up and coalesced into baby form. Several men explained to me that a man generated this process early on in his wife's pregnancy by performing speeches of life in the coca circle; these instrumental speeches likened the process, with magical intentions purportedly empowered by substances, to that of manioc preparation, in which manioc starch initially dissolved in water then sedimented at the bottom and formed a dense cake.

As described in mambeadores' accounts of how it was done, a man continued to use speeches of life in the coca circle throughout his wife's pregnancy, shaping the child properly. For them, these rituals were theoretically at least as important as the insemination in determining the child's constitution and in determining who the child's kin were. For the speeches in question to be strong and effective, the father had to perform them in the form of a ritual dialogue with a 'what-sayer' (Echeverri 1998) or ritual conversation partner, preferably an older kinsman; the speaker would produce statements in a rather verse-like fashion, and the what-sayer would respond by repeating a few key words from what the speaker had said, or with statements and sounds such as 'Yes, that is so,' 'Hmm,' 'What then?' 'You speak the truth,' and so on. Between them, they would ideally achieve a rhythmic dialogue that could go on for anywhere from ten minutes to several hours.

The speeches of life involved the use of certain phrases meant to fashion the bodies of unborn children. For instance, some speeches performatively described how at the moment they themselves were being uttered, the child's bones, or heart, or other body parts were being made *by the speech itself*. Muinane speakers added the double suffix *–nih'* (or *–niji* for the future tense) to transform nouns for body parts into verbs that named and simultaneously created such body parts in a baby being formed in the womb. I recall references to 'making the bones' (*bákinihi)* 'making the foot,' 'making the heart,' 'making the liver,' 'making the eye,' and so forth.

There was a lullaby that made reference to the gendering aspect of this process of 'making the bones' of a child's body:

*Kííllɨ, kííllɨ, kííllɨ, kííllɨme. O, o*
*Jííneje seemene mɨ́ɨ́kɨse táfikaanise? O, o*
*Étɨ gáifi seemene. O, o.*
*Jááseke jíínejeri mábakɨnɨji? O, o*
*Étɨ béremɨkuri. O, o*
*Llííru, llííru, llííruje,*
*besháјeke dihímokɨ́garatɨ ganíkiva! O, o.*
*Állɨ píruje, állɨ míkɨhɨ. O, o*

(Fox, fox, fox,[8] Oh, Oh
*What is this child who always cries? Oh, Oh*
*It is a man child. Oh, oh*
*With what shall we make the bones of this child? Oh, oh*
*With dart palm wood. Oh, oh*
*Snake, snake, snake,*
*come pour your pleasant sleepiness onto my baby boy. Oh, oh*
*Eye closes, eye closes.)*

If the child were a female, the answer to the question as to what child it was who always cried would be: '*Etɨ gáigo seemene*' (It is a woman child). Then the song would ask what this child's bones are to be made of, and would itself respond, '*Eti nɨ́ɨ́feerihori*' (Out of *nɨ́ɨ́feeriho*). The latter was a red-stemmed weed that grew in gardens. We were cutting the ubiquitous *nɨ́ɨ́feeriho* weeds in their garden when my Muinane host Emanuel and his Uitoto wife Eva explained to me that women's bones were made with this so that they would grow quickly, like this plant did, and start bearing children quickly. The dart palm, on the other hand, grew slowly, but its long, thin darts were very hard; similarly, men grew slowly but with hard bones. I commented on how easy *nɨ́ɨ́féeriho* were to cut or break, and Eva said, 'Perhaps it is for this reason that our bones break so easily, whereas men's are so tough.'

People of the Centre averred that other intentional actions, whether ritual or not, also shaped bodies. One of their premises was that the ritual actions, but also the very constitution and past and present moral behaviour of the kinspeople who made a child's body, had an effect upon the latter. Another explicit premise was that youthful bodies were malleable and that the process of maturing or aging involved an increasing setting or hardening of the body and its affects, virtues, dispositions, capabilities, and odours; except for the odours, perhaps, theirs could be understood as a theory of the formation of habitus akin to Mauss's (1979). The similarity between the development of bodies and that of a ceramic dish was overtly underscored, and in certain cases people asserted that once a person's body had set in a certain way, it would not change afterwards. They made claims to virtue by stating that their own or another's body had set in a proper way, but produced harsh critiques, as well, with claims that people misbehaved because their bodies had set in a flawed way.

The similarity between bodies and ceramic extended to the required virtues of their makers. Good potters – women, always – were supposed to follow certain diets so that their pottery would not crack. Along similar lines, individuals praised or blamed themselves and others for behaviours throughout their own youths, during pregnancy, and afterwards during a related child's upbringing, that conferred upon the child's malleable body its beauty, health, fertility, and capacity for work, or else its flaws. The speech of advice featured counsels with the same premise, prescribing that youths follow certain diets because eating certain things would lead to their future children being born too bald or too hairy, undesirably dark-skinned or desirably light-skinned, ugly or beautiful. Children's own ways of interacting with others – that is, angrily or gently, respectfully or disrespectfully – could also affect their future bodily form, both because they induced benevolent or malevolent intentions from others, which would then have an impact upon their bodies, and because such behaviours could become intrinsic to their bodies.[9]

The similarity between body and pottery-making was instituted, as well, in the practice, rare at the time I did fieldwork, of having a kinswoman of a newborn child knead it in order to shape it while it was soft and malleable, so that it would grow up to be beautiful.[10] The Muinane woman Raquel, whom I questioned about this practice, told me that not just anybody could do it; only women who 'dieted' – that is, who steadfastly followed the dietary prescriptions of the speech of advice during their own malleable youth – would shape a child properly. 'Look at my children,' she said. 'My aunt did Arón, Sara, and Rebeca and they are big-bellied and have ugly faces. She did not diet properly. The ones I did myself all have flat bellies and good faces, because I *did* diet.'

I take Raquel to have been pointing to her children as manifest evidence of a double feature of her own moral constitution – her steadfast discipline and obedience to the speech of advice, and her subsequent competence as a person-shaper – and simultaneously as evidence of her aunt's shortcomings. Such statements furthermore reiterated certain criteria of beauty, as well as understandings of the processes of constitution of bodies.

Another ritual that people made reference to in accounts of the making of good or bad bodies and their behaviours was the so-called 'watering' (*nɨɨ́faikunɨhi*). Raquel's husband Pedro, generalizing by using Spanish verbs in the present tense and speaking about an ideal man in an ideal situation, told me that this was done to a child very soon after it was born, and before it received its first breast milk. Pedro himself had done this for his grandchildren when they were older, however, because they had been born in the city. He explained to me that an elder asked to perform a watering would begin by licking tobacco paste and then sitting to think. The tobacco would then speak to him, and tell him what name the child should have according to its *jávarata.*[11] He himself had watered his younger brother Lázaro's daughter, giving her a name that meant 'Striped' (striped in a fashion similar to tabby), because certain specimens of their clan's *jávarata* species were thus striped. Pedro described to me how the watering elder would whistle a long incantation over a small amount of water, rejecting all the evils that could affect the child. To do this he had to be very knowledgeable of speeches of apprising that told of the origins of all manners of disease and of the different origins of each lineage and clan, for individuals of these groupings were particularly vulnerable to tribulations related to their *jávarata.* His whistling followed the tune of the litany (or prayer) he recited mentally, which named and proscribed every possible threat to the child's health that he could remember.

The watering was also a gendering performance. Among the speeches used therein some named the tasks that the child would have to carry out depending on whether it was a boy or a girl. Boys were named as 'coca-pickers,' women as 'manioc-pullers,' among other things.[12] This naming was supposed to ensure that the child would have the proper constitution for these tasks. Only with such properly gendered bodies could women live up to the demands of being proper wives, daughters-in-law, and mothers, and men to the demands of being husbands, sons, sons-in-law, and so on.

After whistling this conjuration into the water, the elder would have the parents give the child a few drops of the water. With this incantation and water, the child was given the name by which it would be called in healing invocations whenever it required them. Thus its future health and strength were ensured.

David, Raquel's brother, questioned his father Francisco's competence as a watering expert. He told me that one of his little sons moved around too much because when Francisco had watered him, Francisco had ritually 'named' (from *nombrar*, in Spanish) his grandson as a certain bird that could walk as soon as it broke out of its eggshell. Though the child did get a forename in watering rituals, this was not the kind of naming in question here. Rather, it was part of a list of words meant to cause the child to become in some way like the regular referents of the terms. In this case, Francisco had blundered, David claimed, because Francisco's naming of that bird during the watering ritual had caused the child to become flitting and overly mobile. He went on to tell me that he had thought carefully about the matter and that a better watering speech would name the child to be like another species of bird, one that laid its eggs and hatched its babies on the forest floor, and yet no other animal would find them, walk over them, or sully them. These hatchlings remained still until they were well grown. Children named thus would be judiciously quiet and still and would suffer no harm. David's father's watering, as David described it to me, seems to me to have been meant to achieve something People of the Centre widely regarded as desirable: quick growth and an early achievement of bodily competence. David himself picked on alternate values on this occasion: fixity and imperceptibility to extrinsic threats.

David's account revealed some of his understandings of the shaping of new individuals' bodies and subjectivities as something done by other individuals, through rituals. It was also, however, part of a series of claims of his to the effect that he himself was a judicious, competent man of knowledge and shaper of new generations, different from his ill-behaved, ignorant father. He sometimes addressed them to his father or produced them in front of him, a habit other mambeadores stated they found deplorable. This matter highlighted, for me, not only that the contributions by individuals to the making of new persons' bodies was a matter of moral concern and evaluation, but also the particularly slippery character of the purported morality or immorality of almost any symbolic deployment among People of the Centre. While this is probably true wherever people interact, perhaps it becomes more frequent where there are more contestations. Certainly among People of the Centre persons' consistency was frequently being put into question, and people may have been motivated to react to this general tendency with frequent pre-emptive presentations of the self.

People of the Centre considered children and young people in general to have malleable bodies that were still in the process of setting into the form, habits, capacities, and demeanour they would always have. They treated certain moments, at least in their rhetoric, as times of more vulnerable and determining malleability. Paradigmatic of these were a girl's menarche and a boy's initiation into mambe At such times, according to the prescriptions, they were supposed to act very judiciously, so that their bodies would take on proper shapes and capacities and become invitingly aromatic, or else desirably odourless, abodes for proper thoughts/emotions, powerful speeches, and desirable 'atmospheres.'[13]

A feature of properly manufactured or set bodies that People of the Centre particularly seemed to find desirable was the capacity to start and finish jobs in one quick, efficient fell swoop. I should rather say 'capacities,' better to translate their rhetoric on this. The first time or times young individuals carried out certain signal tasks – for example, for boys, weaving a basket, toasting coca, or extracting salt, and for girls, grating manioc or harvesting garden products – they were supposed to do so as quickly and with as few mistakes as possible and finish the job. This vigorous efficacy would then become set in their bodies, and they would forever carry out these tasks with admirable efficiency.[14] Boys who interrupted the weaving of their first basket to sleep or rest would, according to the counsels, forever weave that way: slowly and with interruptions. Furthermore, if the quality of that first basket or baskets was good, the young man would forever be able to weave beautiful baskets. The point was that weaving ability became set in the body. Explaining his own success at producing salt quickly and effectively, Lázaro stated that this was so because 'thus I set'[15] (see figure 1.1).

People of the Centre produced myriad counsels, speeches of apprising, and everyday evaluative talk on an endless series of practices – many of which were never actually effected – that had implications for persons' bodily competence, health, aging process, beauty, and judiciousness. Children's and young persons' teeth, skin, singing voice, strength, genital size, and other bodily attributes were susceptible to being affected by a controlled as opposed to a promiscuous diet, by hard

Figure 1.1: Cheo, a young Muinane man of People of the Pineapple, weaves a medium-sized basket in Chukikɨ (1997).

work as opposed to slothfulness, by early morning baths as opposed to late ones, by an erect posture and judicious stillness as opposed to fidgeting, and by abstinence as opposed to untimely or premature sex.

Other talk about the production of people suggested that People of the Centre understood the interactions between people or other beings and children to elicit from the latter desirable thoughts/emotions and virtues, or else inhuman attitudes and dispositions. Children were supposed to be treated in ways that would bring forth proper attitudes from them, and to be taught to act in ways that would cause others to regard and treat them with loving care, respect, and generosity. Many of my interlocutors maintained that in the past, children used to be subjected daily to the formal counsels of the speech of advice, and occasionally given tobacco paste so that the counsels would become fixed to their baskets (explained below); this fixed substance would make them respect their kin and teach them all the other niceties of living together well with other people, in a manner many claimed to be regrettably lost today. In speeches of apprising, evil beings would forever seek to sabotage real people's lives, among other ways, by eliciting antisocial subjectivity and action from children. Schools entered these discussions as well, as people variously considered whether these made youths disrespectful and thieving, or else fostered inside them a desirable esteem for their classmates by sheer force of co-presences.

## Baskets, Hearts, and Shadows

Another element of persons mambeadores spoke of were their 'baskets of knowledge,' their bodies' containers of substances, speeches, and breaths. They described these baskets as something tangible, the material weavework of which was constituted by the ribcage. Several claimed them rather to be intangible and 'spiritual.' These baskets, like the rest of the body, were also fashioned: the moral behaviour of the person in question – and previously, of the person's kin – ideally turned them into sweet, cool, enticing recipients for desirable speeches, and active, winnowing sieves for evil substances and speeches. Baskets of knowledge could be intrinsically 'perfumed' in such a way that particular speeches – for example, the speech of pain (or painful speech)[16] that burned, harmed, or killed evil agents – did not wish to stay in it. David in particular insisted that filth – animal faces, hairs, and feathers – slipped into baskets frequently through food and ritual substances, despite the shamanism and purification these products underwent. This filth could begin to make people experience bad thoughts, speak of gossip, and manifest undue anger or other destructive affects. Though in my experience nobody complied with this, the counsels demanded that people vomit every morning when they bathed, to cleanse their baskets of undesirable filth.

According to the speeches of apprising, and as with many other elements in the cosmos, there were proper baskets and numerous spurious ones. The speeches focused much on the distinction between proper human baskets and animals' improper versions. The former were clean and tightly woven, their weavework such that good speeches stayed in them but the filth sifted through. Animals' baskets, on the other hand, were filthy and fit containers only for spurious foods and substances of the kind that caused the animals to act in immoral ways.

The existential problem of impostorship – of discriminating between real persons, real substances, true speeches, and their spurious counterparts – was presented in very clear, stereotypical form in terms of baskets. Mambeadores often used the image of the mythical Anaconda of Food's basket to highlight how difficult it was to know whether some talk, practice, or person that appeared to be good truly was. The speeches of apprising described the Anaconda's basket as deceptively beautiful, promising, and full of food. Nonetheless, unlike the real basket given to real people, which produced 'true abundance' that brought health and pleasure and enabled the production of yet more abundance, the contents of the Anaconda's basket merely appeared to be true abundance. In reality, however, these contents did not lead to more production and satiety, but to hunger and strife. Jonás and others used this image on several occasions when discussing NGO projects to be set up in their communities and the talk of politicians who visited the Caquetá during departmental elections. The poignant entailment of this image of objects and beings that featured the deceptive appearance of true humanity and its accoutrements, but none of their benign capabilities and effects, was that there was always room for doubt about whether one's own or others' apparently moral thoughts/emotions were actually false.

One of Emanuel's brothers once explained to me in the coca circle that people had two or more baskets: a proper one, inside, for worthy speeches, and then another basket, akin to an animal's, in which to dump all the filth and all the speeches of anger and war that came their way. This seemed typical to me: it reiterated an image of people actively segregating what was admirable, useful, or desirable from what was deleterious and despicable. Saúl produced another account of the multiplicity of baskets that I found interesting, in that it presented in an advantageous moral light an aspect of his social demeanour that he knew others criticized. He was describing himself as an angry-sounding man who, nevertheless, was always cool and peaceful inside. He went on to say that it was always thus among Muinane men of knowledge: their true baskets were always cool and clean, and certainly free of angry or otherwise damaging thoughts. However, any man of knowledge at some point had to scold or counsel angrily the evil of the world. (The term in Muinane for such counselling was *fáfagehinɨhi*, 'to make bitter.') His angry speech at that point, however, did not go downwards into his basket of knowledge to damage his proper substances and speeches, but stayed at a second basket in his throat. This claim that a man could sound angry but, in fact, be cool contrasted with other rhetoric Saúl and others produced concerning how true anger – morally justifiable anger – and the cleansing, ferocious speeches people produced when thus angered, came from true tobacco firmly rooted in the basket of knowledge. Again, this revealed to me how people could cite concepts and images concerning personhood selectively, for their own intelligent purposes.

Basket imagery featured in other ways in accounts of thoughts/emotions and even intersubjectivity. Tobías, for instance, once explained to me that a young man had to weave with particular care the border of the basket which he would take, full of coca, tobacco, game, and manioc starch, as a gift to his prospective father-in-law. A proper border, he pointed out, turned dozens of disparate fibres that pointed in as many directions, into a single, neat structure. Success in this indicated and brought about that the young man's and his future wife's thoughts would all head in the same direction, so that there would be no contestations between them. I sought to pursue deeper research on this marital custom in particular, and found that very few people in the Medio Caquetá practise it any longer.

A key part of the contents of the basket of knowledge was the heart. Pablo claimed once that the heart was a pathway for the speeches spoken by a person. *El espíritu de tabaco* – the 'spirit of tobacco,' as Pedro put it in Spanish – was always on guard, which he explained was the reason the heart never ceased to beat while there was breath in the body. The heart beat slowly when the person slept, for the 'spirit' was at ease and working little. However, when the person was sick or licked tobacco, the heart beat fast; it was the tobacco working intensely, angered at whatever evil could be impinging upon the body. The heart needed frequent mending, sweetening, and cooling through active speeches and the consumption of substances. To that extent at least, it was also produced. Pablo explained to me once that all hearts were made of the same tobacco; killing a person, therefore, meant destroying one's own tobacco, and thus oneself.

People of the Centre spoke of yet another element of persons: their *ɨ́ɨjɨmɨ* (in Muinane) or shadows. The term *ɨ́ɨjɨ* referred to the dark projection of the body when the latter blocked light, to likenesses of the person in the mirror or in a photograph, and to images of a dead person that haunted its living kin. Rhetoric on shadows was rare and not central to everyday accounts of morality. It featured mostly in talk of death. My Muinane hosts showed that they found shadows very dangerous on an occasion when they found me grieving my own dead. On a visit to Araracuara to pick up some supplies, I received a letter from home telling me my cousin Juan Gonzalo had died some weeks before. I expressed my shock and sadness and, furthermore, my frustration at having no way to go home or communicate with my people. Jonás, who had travelled to Araracuara with me, had us carry out a little ritual the following evening. He made some invocations on a cigarette and had me smoke it. He counselled me: should I see my cousin in dreams, I was to tell the shadow that he had already chosen to have another family, a new set of brothers, cousins, and so forth, that he was to go to them and not come back to visit me, for I was no longer his cousin. He explained that people who kept seeing the dead's shadow would grow sad to the point of sickness and could die, too. He stated that should that happen to me, everybody in the region would ask critically which people it was who had let a visitor die of sadness in their midst. Years later, I witnessed a similar death rite when Matusalén died; again, his brother Saúl told the shadow to go away to his new kin. Afterwards, Saúl pointed out that the ease with which he did this showed that his brother had been no sorcerer, for sorcerers' shadows were much more problematic to deal with. This was a moral claim on behalf of his family, whom he knew others sometimes accused of sorcerous tendencies.

This view of shadows of the dear departed as actually dangerous non-kin relates to the view of persons as first and foremost the embodiment of substances that themselves embody affects and ways of life. Shadows as ghosts no longer had a body constituted by true tobacco and other substances of humanity, and so they no longer featured proper human subjectivity. In this, People of the Centre resemble other Amazonian peoples who deem the dead no longer to be properly human, and treat grieving for the dead as a dangerous state (Vilaça 2000; Gow 2001).

# 2 Reflecting on Evil and Responsibility

## The Inhuman Self in a Perspectival Cosmos

In People of the Centre's accounts, real people were intrinsically moral because the substances that constituted their bodies and subjectivities were moral; they were so because they originated in the very bodies of the creator and other cool mythical beings, on those occasions in which these beings succeeded in creating true humans. Ideally, real people acted in such ways as to multiply themselves and achieve a desirable lifestyle in a tranquil community of like-bodied (and therefore like-minded) individuals who were generously supportive of each other. For instance, women's inclination to work hard and nourish their families was generated by the speeches of sweet manioc and cool herbs (*Nɨ́ɨbɨmɨhiijɨ* and others) inside them, and their righteous anger against evil threats, by the speech of chilies (a form of *Áivohiijɨ*, the painful speech which leaders spoke). However, the substance-like and extrinsic character of selves' speeches also enabled the constitution of counterfeit, inhuman selves. According to their rhetoric, if instead of human tobacco, coca, and other desirable substances, the false substances and speeches of animals spoke through persons' bodies, they brought about spurious, immoral subjective states that were not really of the persons in question. Rather, they constituted different, miscreant persons who were nonetheless persuaded of their own authenticity.[1]

In some actual cases of perceived misbehaviour, or in their hypothetical considerations, People of the Centre pointed out to others 'That wasn't your speech! Your own speech does not do thus,' or some other expression to that effect. The notions of selfhood that made such impostors a possibility for them differed from a commonsensical and sometimes academic Western notion of self, in which the thinking self or ego is supposed to be one and the same, consistently guiding or generating almost every action of the individual throughout his or her life.[2] For People of the Centre, true speeches, and thus true selves, were axiomatically good and simply could not speak or do evil.[3] In many situations, they expressed their understandings that other persons' immoral thoughts and actions were forthcoming from a false self constituted by the person's body and a spurious tobacco or other substance.[4] How and why could this happen, for them? The answer requires attention to their cosmological and cosmogonic accounts.

The explicit prescriptions of moral human behaviour and the institutionalized forms of their own lives were one of People of the Centre's yardsticks for judging all beings. In their cosmological rhetoric, different creatures in the world had social lives in some ways like their own, but usually flawed in ways that exemplified the undesirable. For the most part, animals and other forest beings and river beings did not comply with the prescriptions and the recognized institutions of proper social life. Whereas ideally real people married outside their cognatic kin group (people related to them both through male and female lines) and patrilineal clan, lived in properly built malocas, produced an abundance of food and ritual substance through their skilful work and speeches, and interacted with each other coolly and lovingly in everyday life; animals married incestuously, or interacted violently, or lived in filthy mud wallows, tree trunks and nests, or failed properly to produce an abundance of 'true' food stuffs and ritual substances. Animals for the most part thus constituted – each species in its own way – failures in moral sociality.[5]

In Muinane people's speeches of apprising, as in the myths of many Amazonian groups, animals were human in bodily shape at the time of creation. They were among the creator deity's first unsuccessful attempts at creating real people. He gave them his speech of tobacco, which was simultaneously a substance, an animating breath and the capacity for speech; it was to provide them with awareness, motivate them to behave in the cool, moral manner the deity prescribed, and empower them to produce and propagate in a proper fashion. Animals and other non-human beings behaved in different 'hot,' immoral fashions, disobeying the prescriptions of the speech. They did not behave with the love, respect, humility, persistence, discipline, and productivity that the creator had attempted to instil in them. With their disobedience, they ruined the tobacco that motivated and empowered such virtues. Their dialogues,[6] their houses, their ritual dances, their marriages, their cultigens, their food and ritual substance consumption practices, and so on, were inchoate caricatures or outright perversions of the standards of the as yet nonexistent but prefigured versions of human beings. In view of such imperfections and misbehaviours, the infuriated creator transformed them into animals and other non-humans, and banished them to the edges of the world. In the process, he told each one that its original undesirable tobacco and behaviour would belong to it forever, and that it would contaminate people with its evil, causing them disease and other problems.[7]

Since then, as Jonás put it, 'Animals' tobaccos are senseless';[8] in the process of constituting animal selves, they created immoral subjective states, motivated stupid, indiscriminate behaviour – such as incest, for example, for animals 'live with their own sisters' – and empowered destructive intentions. Therefore some animal species had no compassion for their own kin and killed them mercilessly, others were lazy, others foul-tempered, others promiscuous, and so on. Much as real people's cool substances provided them with moral discernment and the capacity for producing desirable goods, animals' hot tobaccos and other substances provided them with perverse capacities and subjectivities. For reasons about which individuals' accounts differed – envy of human beings' way of life, fear and anger at their superior predatory ability, or lack of discernment – animals easily turned to full-blown aggression against humans, and attacked them, among other ways, by replacing humans' proper substances with their own.

Animals' exact means of attack was not a matter of focal attention, though I did hear mambeadores describe a few, such as that the spider webs one tore through in the forest were traps set up by jaguars, and that little filth one found in tobacco paste was feathers and hairs and other paraphernalia of animals and sorcerers. Usually these attacks were diagnosed after the fact, when whoever was doing the diagnosis, or somebody they knew, was already suffering from diseases, accidents, death, or antisocial affects which were deemed to be consequences of such attacks. Diarrhoea, colds, infertility, anger, jealousy, envy, and many other threats to health and to pleasurable, effective community life had their origin in the aggression of these outside agents.

Put in generalizing terms, the claim was that hot speeches or breaths ensuing from animals' tobaccos and other substances altered people's sensibilities so much that they did not perceive or act as real people.[9] This thwarted their uniquely human capacities for moral interpersonal relations and endeavours. Some particular hot thoughts could be attributed to particular animals. For example, when I asked Jonás about the thoughts that stemmed from a jaguar, he answered, '[H]e does not say, "My brother."' I came to understand from this that when a jaguar's speech sounded through a person – and usually it was men who were accused of speaking jaguar's speech – it was experienced by the person as indiscriminately angry thoughts against his own people.[10] It displaced the person's proper thoughts and speech, which would normally make him think 'This is my brother' when acting toward a sibling, or make him address the sibling as 'My brother.' This correct form of address would be evidence that the person 'remembered' – discerned, or was aware of – the relation of kinship and knew that the other was not an enemy or an animal to be attacked. This discerning awareness would normally lead the person to act with love and compassion towards the sibling; the jaguar's speech, on the other hand, made the person (who was not really himself) behave viciously and destructively towards the sibling and other relatives, much as a cannibalistic jaguar would towards *its* kin. In several speeches of apprising, jaguars appeared as merciless murderers who killed and devoured their own kinspeople.[11]

Akin to the speech of a jaguar, the speech of the coati (*Níígomɨhiijɨ*) was the abusive anger of a man against his wife, or else a person's general surliness. I learned about this in a conversation with Pablo about David, a local leader who was rather tyrannical and therefore at risk of losing his following. Pablo attributed the speech of the coati to David, and told me that the owners of this speech, large male coatis, battled any member of their species they met and, for this reason, did not stay with their mates for very long.

Another evil speech, among many others, was that of the mythic figure of the False Woman (in Muinane, *Fáragaigo,* which could also be translated as Woman of Misguided Obsession). This speech made men and women behave purposelessly or experience jealousy, obsessive sexual desire, or vanity. In the First Time, this feminine spirit bore a penis-shaped tobacco container, the contents of which made her desire sex uncontrollably and indiscriminately. She was beautiful and vain, but too lazy, incompetent, and libidinous to produce the food and ritual substances that were her responsibility as a woman. She attempted to seduce her own brothers and, therefore, the creator banished her to the outskirts of the land of moral real people. On diverse occasions I heard her story being used in rituals to heal jealousy, promiscuous tendencies, and some other evils; the rituals involved the angry rejection of that woman back to the edges of the world, with the claim that the victims had their own true tobacco and did not partake of hers. As with many other sources of evil thoughts/emotions, part of the danger of her speech and ways was that they sometimes passed for their proper human counterparts. A claim I heard was that people speaking her speech, indeed, thought they were 'speaking good things.'

Talk about these matters constituted reiterative accounts of persons' subjectivities centred on the materiality and moral quality of thoughts/emotions and actions. I am persuaded that individuals among People of the Centre cited, and were motivated by, ideals of agency that were tied both to the image of the self as materially constituted and to the subsequent possibility of the material usurpation of subjectivity. In other words, these accounts informed People of the Centre of the kinds of beings they were, had to be, and could be. They also informed them of what kind of being it was desirable to be, much as our own talk, our advertisements, our movies, our jokes, also tell us, with qualitative evaluations, what kinds of beings we are or can be; they thereby shape our desires. Part of what made their accounts and ideals particularly plausible to People of the Centre was that they were often articulated in terms of cosmological perspectivism, which People of the Centre used as an account of existence to make sense of their own and other's intimate perceptions and thoughts/emotions.

## Perspectivism and Moral and Ontological Hierarchy

People of the Centre's talk about animalistic impingements upon real people – abstract explanations, speeches of apprising, gossip speculating about others' behaviours, but also screamed accusations – were premised on a perspectival understanding of different kinds of beings' subjectivities. The concept of Amerindian cosmological perspectivism (or cosmological deixis) was systematically developed and disseminated most notably by the Brazilian anthropologist Eduardo Viveiros de Castro (1998), who compared different Amerindian people's cosmological accounts in order to explore the issue of the common 'humanity' of people and animals that many of these accounts posited.[12]

Viveiros de Castro's claim is that in Amerindian cosmologies, different kinds of beings – animals, humans, gods, and others – have souls or some other kind of intentionality or subjectivity exactly like humans.' All such beings perceive themselves as humans and their ways of life as characterized by malocas, gardens, and other accoutrements of a human lifestyle. They also perceive other species as either game or predators. For instance, some Amazonian peoples state that from the points of view of jaguars, snakes, and the moon members of the human species look like white-lipped peccaries appear to humans, and that to peccaries, who perceive themselves as humans, members of the human species look like jaguars. Blood for humans is manioc beer from the point of view of jaguars, and vultures perceive as smoked fish that which humans perceive as maggots in rotting flesh.

Perspectivism could be taken, with a caveat, to be the perceptual aspect of what Descola and Århem would call an animistic understanding of the cosmos. Animistic accounts of the world take sociality to be a fundamental feature of existence; gods, animals, and other beings lead lives in which they interact with their own kind to some extent or another in the ways humans do. They furthermore treat relations between humans and the beings of nature as akin to some relationships among humans. For instance, Descola (1994, 2001) and Århem (1996) argue respectively that the Achuar and the Makuna model the relations between human hunters and game on relations of exchange between men and their affines; hunters 'seduce' prey like men seduce future wives, and they engage with the forest spirits that care for animals in a manner they liken to how they deal with their fathers-in-law. Viveiros de Castro's caveat with the view that Amerindian thought projects the features of the social world onto nature or substantive human qualities onto animals (1998, 474) is that this basically posits that such thinking is merely analogical, and furthermore falls into the eternal regression trap of positing an opposition between a 'really natural' nature and a culturally constructed one.

Viveiros de Castro's alternative interpretation to this substantivist take on animism is that Amerindians feature a 'multinaturalist' system of thought. A clarifying contrast is that where a relativist, multiculturalist thought would posit a single nature or reality represented in as many ways as there are cultures, a multinaturalist system would appear to posit a single culture or way of perceiving natures, of which there are as many as there are kinds of beings. He also calls this system 'cosmological deixis,' noting that the categories of 'human' or 'culture' and its counterpart 'animal' or 'nature' in this cosmos are pronominal rather than substantive. In it the terms 'human' or 'person' are like the pronouns 'I' and 'we' in that their referent depends on who is speaking, unlike nouns with more fixed referential content.

What determines which 'nature' appears as human or animal, or for example, whether a specimen or object observed appears as a peccary, a jaguar, human being, or their accoutrements, is the kind of body from which that specimen or object is observed. The point of view is in the body, where the latter is understood as a bundle of affects and habits rather than as a merely anatomo-physiological entity (ibid., 478). Again, from the point of view of someone with a jaguar body, the reader – who from her own point of view looks human – would look like a wild pig or some other prey animal.

In a radically perspectival account, the only way to perceive the world is a human way; there is no alternative to this phenomenology. Members of our species perceive ourselves as human, and ours as a human world, because we are part of this scheme.

This scheme elegantly accounts for the practices of diverse Amazonian groups for the collective creation and transformation of bodies; these practices are about the making of beings of their own bodily kind – the human *species* – distinct from other kinds of being who nevertheless also perceive themselves as human. Part of the claim is that generic (not specific) humanity is a form of alterity; persons (whatever their species) must engage with it in order to transform still un-specified individuals' bodies, turning them into co-specifics and kin (see Vilaça 2002; Viveiros de Castro 2001).

People of the Centre's cosmological talk and other social practices cohered to a great extent with Viveiros de Castro's general account, and, indeed, reading the latter in 1999 constituted a key moment in my analytical engagement with their social life. His statement to the effect that the Amerindian *Bildung* was more in body than in spirit, because 'there is no "spiritual" change which is not a bodily transformation, a redefinition of its affects and capacities' (Viveiros de Castro 1998, 481), led me to consider People of the Centre's own claims concerning the making and raising of new generations of real people in a new and profitable way (see previous chapter). There was one key aspect of People of the Centre's accounts, however, that differed from Viveiros de Castro's general scheme: while to some extent the phenomenological world of each species resembled others, these worlds also differed in some key respects. This point is of central importance, for it concerns the moral understandings of personhood and social interaction that shaped People of the Centre's social lives.

Two very striking and sociologically relevant characteristics of their animistic and perspectival rhetoric were, first, that it featured prominently in their moral evaluations of individuals' and groups' subjectivities and actions, and second, that in doing so it seemed to be premised on important differences between, and a moral hierarchy among, different creatures' ways of being. In their version of perspectivism, animals' subjectivities and interactions were warped, caricaturesque versions of real people's thoughts/emotions and sociality, to the extent that People of the Centre used them as standards in their evaluations of immoral action. A central aspect of animal predation for People of the Centre was precisely the destruction or sabotage of a true human perspective and the imposition of animals' own immoral or undiscerning views. Their understanding was that people affected by animalistic speeches of anger and other misanthropic thoughts/emotions started to treat other people as some animals treated their own kind, leading to the destruction of pleasurable community life, proper sociality, and eventually, if not dealt with, of the kinship group.

To use an example I previously cited, it was not rare for people to claim that a man who misbehaved had a jaguar inside, or that he spoke the speech of a jaguar. Concerning such evaluations or accounts of uncalled-for anger among kin in everyday life, their point always seemed to me to be perspectival: the person perceived and treated kin as a jaguar perceived and treated *its* kin. And again, an important way in which jaguars differed from proper human beings in the speeches of apprising was that they were violently angry and inclined to cannibalize their own brethren. The man with the jaguar speech inside him gazed upon kin, perceived them as such, but failed to experience the loving, empathetic, and merciful thoughts of a proper human being, and instead felt the desire to burn, maim, hurt, and even kill them in anger. I never heard anyone among People of the Centre claim that angry people perceived kinspeople as peccaries, which in any case I would think would have been phenomenologically untenable as far as their experiences of everyday interpersonal relations among kin were concerned.

For People of the Centre such attributions of forms of animality to others were quite literal. Their everyday talk was full of rich figurative language that people recognized as such, but the accusations in question were not an example of that. I remember an occasion in which Naomi, Pablo's wife, deployed perspectival imagery in an emotional interaction with Pablo. Pablo had angrily berated her for what he deemed was a serious failure on her part. Naomi afterwards tearfully yelled at their little granddaughters – within his earshot – to stay away from their grandfather, because he had 'a big-toothed one' inside and could make them sick. She then cried at him that what he had said to her was not the speech of his father or of his clan, who never spoke that way, but rather the talk of a 'big-toothed' jaguar or puma. 'Kill it! Or let it kill you!' she said again and again. Her harangue did not have the form of a reminder of her humanity to a beast who perceived her as an animal, but rather of an accusation of inhuman thoughts/emotions to somebody who perceived her as human.[13]

Both in speeches of apprising and in People of the Centre's observations of animal behaviour, animals other than jaguars similarly failed to relate in moral ways to their own kind, by being destructively angry, violent, merciless, tyrannical, jealous, incestuous, stingy, disrespectful, lazy, vain, thieving, distractingly playful, and so on, and it was their speeches that were manifest when people behaved in such immoral ways. One speech of apprising described how animals corrupted a child by making it hot and angry, and instructing it to hit and pinch them, clearly an elicitation of antisocial subjectivities. Part of the danger of these inhuman emotions and other false speeches was that when they spoke through another's body they constituted counterfeit selves persuaded of their own authenticity. For this reason, Pablo explained to me, people who manifested evil thoughts/emotions often did not recognize their own faults, but rather denied any wrongdoing. This suggests to what extent self-deluding impostorship – the conviction that one was truly 'oneself' and behaving admirably or at least appropriately, or engaged in a worthy project – was a fundamental existential problem for People of the Centre.

I inquired about attributions of perception so radically altered that people actually perceived other people as animals, because there was literature from the Vaupés about warriors carrying out rituals that would allow them to perceive enemies as large rodents, and because ethnographer Juan Echeverri, conversing with me about perspectivism, mentioned that a Uitoto elder had indeed told him that there were circumstances in which people perceived other people as animals. Barak, a Muinane-speaking Nonuya man, explained to me that this was only so in the case of sorcery.[14] His explanation alluded to the notion, shared in much of Amazonia, that sorcerers were persons who could transform their bodies into those of other species, and in that form either attacked human beings or had fellows of that species do so. Barak stated that sorcerous attacks had nothing to do with anger, however, for the actions of hunting predators weren't angry. He asked, as part of his explanation, 'When have you ever heard of a jaguar scolding its prey? It just seizes it with its claws!' His point was that the sorcerer/jaguar perceived its victims as legitimate prey. Adding another perspectival layer to his explanation, he then added that sorcerers and jaguars also perceived innocent victims as their own fruit – readily available food that could be picked unproblematically from a tree.

According to People of the Centre's cosmological rhetoric, many animals perceived themselves as people, experienced their dens and trees as malocas, and their food, whatever it could be, as manioc bread, chili broth, and legitimate game meat. Intestinal worms, for instance, (mistakenly) saw and treated real people's innards as manioc bread. Their cosmology was not, however, radically perspectival, such that there would be no way of determining a true humanity, since all beings were 'truly human' in their own self-understandings. People of the Centre posited fundamental differences in the moral quality of different species' supposed perspectives. What was most pertinent to them about animals' and other non-human beings' 'humanity' was that it was intrinsically warped and morally and – in crises concerning whose perspective was to dominate – existentially inferior to its counterpart among real people. Thus certain animals perhaps *saw* their kin and co-specifics as people, and could be seen as such in turn; but unlike real people, this visual perception was not accompanied by mutual loving care, respect, and other properly human thoughts/emotions. If the thoughts/emotions of a being regarding its own co-specifics differed from those of real people, then that being could not really be said to have a properly 'human' perspective. This was important, as far as the management of social life – including the always social construction of the self – was concerned. People of the Centre constantly produced depictions of their own and others' thoughts/emotions, actions, and personal histories in terms of the moral contrast between animality and humanity.[15] They may have wanted some of the *capabilities* of great predators and other beasts, but they did not want their affects, habits, or perspectives.

Much of their action seemed to take for granted that human existence was characterized by endless conflict with animals and other kinds of beings who sought to sabotage human bodies, thoughts/emotions, and social relations. Some said animals' animosity was an expression of their angry envy of the proper lives human beings could achieve; they laughed in the forest whenever they successfully generated death, disease, or social tribulations among real people. Other animal attacks were less malignant in intention: they were the unwitting predatory intent of innocent but misguided beasts. In any case, this never-ending war against animals was often the rhetorical justification for hunting and felling the forest. The conflict between kinds of beings and perspectives is a possibility discussed by Lima (in Vilaça 2005, 458, 459) and Viveiros de Castro (1998, 483); the latter argues that in Amazonian thought, when the Other appears to one as human, one's own humanity is in question and one becomes game. In this general scheme, the different perspectives are irreducible to a common underlying reality, and when in conflict, one dominates. In People of the Centre's version, conflicts between morally imbued points of view seem similarly to be resoluble by means of esoterically violent confrontation. However, their rhetoric posits that real people's claims and cases in this regard are the most powerful and, indeed, the true ones.

The stereotypical voice of moral disgust healers assumed at times when healing the intellectual/emotional or bodily tribulations caused by animals' substances suggests that the confrontation with other species involved, at its centre, a moral judgment of their different perspectives, and that animals were found wanting. In their healing rites, mambeadores would use tobacco-empowered speeches to address animals at large, inveighing against them for attacking real people. The tone of such harangues that I witnessed took the form of indignant protests that a filthy beast would dare to touch a real person. As a result of such harangues, mambeadores told me, animals felt shame at attacking real people; presumably, they came to know or had to admit that they themselves were not real people. Another result was that the tobacco would prey upon the animal, killing it or placing it in a hunter's path.

For People of the Centre there was a substantive humanity – both a species and a condition – characterized by propriety, moral acumen, and a certain way of life. The perspective of real people was 'true' because it was moral; it was moral because 'true tobacco' (*míyabaañoho*, in Muinane) and its speech established its morality; and finally, its truth and morality endowed it with a capacity for discernment and effective action greater than that of other perspectives. That is, it had the capacity to disrupt the perceptions that non-humans had of themselves as humans and the predatory capacity to destroy them.[16]

The profound moral inequality between humans and animals featured centrally in People of the Centre's everyday articulate interpretations of what they deemed to be admirable, desirable, acceptable, or despicable in their own and other's actions and thoughts/emotions.

In other words, they articulated part of the background of strong evaluative distinctions between desirable and undesirable actions and thoughts/emotions, partly in terms of the unequal perspectives of humans and animals. Such distinctions thereby motivated people, who behaved in ways that cited these perspectival images anew.

Parenthetically, I should temper this rather dark view of animals. Most animals were immoral in some way or another, but this did not preclude the possibility that in other ways they behaved properly and may, indeed, have been paradigms of some desirable behaviours. Mochileros – large birds known for their hanging nests – were given prominence and importance by one Muinane clan for their violent, usurping authoritarianism, and by a Muinane-speaking Nonuya clan – the People of the Mochilero – for their admirable willingness to remain together as a patrilineal, virilocal group under a single leader.[17] Similarly, many animal species were understood to feature love for their kin comparable to the love that real people felt for theirs. People of the Centre thus slipped back and forth between very frequent claims that made use of the point that each faunal species was guilty in some way or another of villainy or ineptitude, and rarer claims citing rather their desirable traits.

## Interpreting and Portraying Miscreant and Moral Selves

People of the Centre's talk to the effect that persons were manufactured bodily by others in a multiplicity of collective processes, that awareness was substantial in nature and origin, and that anger, authoritarianism, laziness, and so on, could be spurious extrinsic speeches that constituted animalistic selves was clearly not abstract rhetoric they produced with detachment.[18] Individuals used these concepts and images to interpret their own and others' subjectivities, actions, and life processes, or in their interactions, to make a case for others to interpret these matters in certain ways. Their interpretations and portrayals often involved moral evaluations, expressing their sense of what was admirable and good or what was despicable or evil in what someone had done or thought. Some also constituted attributions or negotiations of responsibility, portraying virtuous or miscreant selves as either autonomous agents or helpless dopes.

I witnessed many cases in which individuals implied or explicitly averred that what they or others had experienced at some moment or another had not been their own true thoughts/emotions, but rather the lying, fallacious (but clearly, nonetheless compelling) speech of an animal. Sometimes brought about through dialogues, the realization that their experience was a counterfeit subjectivity profoundly affected their emotions and self-interpretations.

Emanuel, who was middle aged and the leader of his patriline, provided me with an eloquent anecdote about this. He told me that at one time he had suffered from the 'disease' of jealousy and had mistreated his wife because of it. Later, through a ritual, he had realized that the jealousy had been caused by the False Woman, a despicable being rejected to the edges of the world during First Time. He explained: 'She is the one who makes one say, when one's wife laughs, that she is laughing at one; she makes one say when one sees her speaking to herself, that she is speaking about one. It is all lies! I told her I did not wish to lick her tobacco, for I have my own.' I found this story to be very revealing; I understood him to believe that the jealousy he had thought/felt had been his experience, as inner speech, of the False Woman's speeches.[19] Then he became aware, through a ritual, that his jealousy had not been his true 'speeches,' though he had experienced them. In other words, he came to doubt the authenticity and humanity of his thoughts/emotions. The point I want to call attention to is that his new awareness, enabled by his re-description of his problems in terms of immoral, extrinsic substances, changed how he perceived the situation – how he *felt*, I dare say – and, especially, how he behaved. A Goffmanian question comes to mind, concerning the possibility that Emanuel could have been doing some impression management when telling me all this: was he reflectively and strategically presenting himself in a better moral light, namely, as someone who had overcome an immoral personal constitution? Probably; still, it remains that he and other People of the Centre had accounts such as his available as symbolic resources with which to think about their own thoughts/emotions and to make sense of their experiences.

That was one of the most suggestive accounts of experience I witnessed among People of the Centre, and, perhaps, the most illustrative of the importance of narratives that posited a perspectival cosmos and a material, extrinsic origin to the self, in their self-interpretations. I witnessed other similarly enlightening moments in which they used such imagery to interpret others' actions and thoughts/emotions, and to negotiate with them. I remember particularly Pedro and Pablo arguing heatedly, the latter accusing the former of speaking the speech of animals (*ásimɨ hiijɨ*), because he had carelessly allowed his domestic pigs to walk freely and damage the other's manioc garden. According to Pablo, such an unfeeling disregard for the fate of his kin, who ran the risk of going hungry if their manioc was destroyed by the pigs, could only be the thought/emotion of an animal who loved its pig kin more than it loved real people. At some point in the discussion, the brothers lowered their voices and I heard, with surprise, as Pedro recognized that he had not been a real person when he had acted as he had. They then made plans to build a pig pen together.

As I have discussed, the possibility of spuriousness or impostorship in persons' speeches, objects, projects, and so forth, was a matter of preoccupation for People of the Centre, and one causally tied to their understandings of the cosmos and of personhood. Its palliative counterpart was the possibility of personal consistency, suggestive of a personal constitution that had 'set' firmly and well. In some cases this criterion was explicit; this was the case when Pablo, bidding me farewell when I left his home in 1998, congratulated me for 'always being the same' throughout the months I had lived with him. He claimed that I had been cheerful all the time, and had never become surly or sad. From this and other conversations, I gathered that the consistency of my emotional state was almost as important to him as it was that the state was a sociable one to begin with.

This emphasis on consistency cohered with cosmological talk that treated true humanity as unfailingly moral, and inconsistency (rather than consistent immorality) as a signature of animality, of inhuman, spurious selfhood and bad upbringing. Articulations recognizing the possibility of consistent selfhood – specifically of persons who thought/felt and behaved in an unswervingly judicious fashion – were a resource people could cite, making references to the history of the formation of their bodies to make a case about the permanence of their stalwart morality or that a potentially morally reprehensible act they had carried out was, actually, a proper, justified action. They also reiterated in different circumstances that old people were already 'hard,' and, therefore, had little to fear from foods and behaviours that threatened more malleable youths.

There were, thus, frequent tugs of war between portrayals of consistency and accusations of inconsistency that underscored the understanding that thoughts/emotions were speeches produced in an ongoing fashion by substances, and that the proper nature of the latter was not something people could be sure others would recognize. No one was insured against animalistic usurpation – though there were symbolic resources with which to articulate the claim that they were – and certainly no one was absolutely safe from the threat of being accused of having animal substances and speeches inside. There was always leeway for accusations and unfavourable interpretations of behaviour that portrayed the latter as inhuman or otherwise improper, and for claims to the effect that nobody was an absolutely finished product.

But people who made claims suggesting personal malleability among adults did not always do so to portray actions as inconsistent and inhuman, however. An institutionalized aspect of the ongoing shaping of the self was that people could undergo ritual action, even as adults, that continued to shape them: healing rituals to remove sources of anger, jealousy, and so on, or naming rituals. The latter depended on the understanding that personal names were, among other things, powerful titles for a personal constellation of characteristics; when the person in question had 'set' poorly, his elders (I never heard of a woman changing names) could change his name and thereby cause him to behave in virtuous new ways and leave behind certain entrenched misbehaviours. I learned about this from David, in a conversation in which he protested that his brothers still called him by his Muinane childhood name, ignoring a newer one his father had given him a few years previously. 'That is why I sometimes misbehave again … they call me by my old name,' he stated.

David's claim here was also an example of People of the Centre's citation of this general account of persons to stress or deny responsibility for miscreancy. Some of the details I described earlier could be understood to indicate that they accounted for their behaviours and interactions in terms of unoriginal thoughts/emotions of extrinsic and substantial origin that became embodied. Such an interpretation would conclude that People of the Centre thought of themselves as creatures akin to golems, animated clay puppets from medieval Jewish mythology, constrained to behave according to sacred instructions inscribed in their bodies, or for a more current metaphor, that People of the Centre thought of themselves as computer-like beings collectively programmed or hardwired to think and behave in certain way.

Thus interpreted, theirs was a rather 'de-centring' account of selfhood that denied reflexivity, that is, that people could be aware of, and evaluate, their own thoughts and emotions, or at least that this awareness could change them. Particularly in the case of purported evil subjectivities, their accounts could be interpreted as positing an ultimate lack of agency in the philosophical sense of autonomous, clear-sighted self-awareness and control: people's misbehaviours were radically determined by foreign subjectivity-generating substances.

On the other hand, they also produced much rhetoric that emphatically made the case that persons were autonomous and reflexive beings. They made explicit their understanding that people were conscious of their thoughts/emotions and bodies and their sense that such consciousness was an important element in their accounts of action. I recall an occasion in which Jonás and Saúl were speaking about people who misbehaved or were feeling discontent. Jonás, portraying abstractly one such situation, suggested to an imaginary miscreant or discontented man '*Difííko meeki*!' (Look at your body!) This was a prescription very much along the lines of an Anglophone's 'know thyself.' As a prescription, it was premised on the notion that miscreants' and discontented persons' thoughts/emotions at that point in time were not really 'their own,' but rather the perverted subjectivity of a beast or jungle spirit. 'Looking into their bodies' involved licking tobacco and consuming coca, which would enable them to 'see' what it was that was causing them to think/feel and act in a certain inhuman way.

The logical question that this begged, if one presupposes that there must be a subject to every action, concerns who would do the seeing if the self in question was already one created by immoral extrinsic substances. People of the Centre did not ask it. I imagine that an answer one of them could have come up with was that the demand for introspection *elicited* thoughts/emotions from the tobacco and other proper substances that the person had consumed or that in some more permanent fashion constituted them. Such reflexive agents were not, however, radically independent from other people; in cases of usurped subjectivities, another real person had to point out to the person that he or she was not being him or herself.

They also made the case for the uniqueness of individuals, and for the inscrutable privacy of their thoughts. I recall individuals protesting publicly that one could not know what another person was thinking, nor speak for that person. Emanuel furthermore told me that tobacco did not say the same things to everyone. He mentioned that youths should be warned not to assume that because another man had been told by his tobacco in a dream that he had to build a house or hold a ritual, that they should do so too. Rather, they should wait till the tobacco addressed them directly, for it spoke differently to each one. When they spoke of the 'sameness' of thoughts, they were referring to purposes and moral inclinations on the one hand, and to the knowledge of instrumental speeches on the other, rather than to something akin to computer programs that were exact copies of one another.

Eneas's case is pertinent for a discussion of People of the Centre's morally evaluative constructions of personhood and identity, their takes on agency and responsibility, and the contestations and strategic uses to which they subjected symbolic resources. He was much criticized by his community and by others when it was discovered that he had seduced or allowed himself to be seduced by a very young woman, and more so when he threatened to shoot his wife when she repeatedly inveighed against him for his behaviour. At one point in the midst of the scandal he protested publicly that he was not to blame – the blame was his father Saúl's, who as a young man had smoked marihuana and drunken *aguardiente* (cane alcohol) carelessly. These hot substances of white men had become Saúl's semen, and out of that semen he had made Eneas. It was those substances that made Eneas misbehave in the ways he did.

Eneas's rejection of his own guilt seemed to be positing that he had been subject to compulsions over which he had no control, and which shaped his subjectivity and actions. In a sense, Eneas actively redeployed public discourses on selfhood to present himself as being strictly constrained to behave according to an alien but incarnated script or program (my metaphors) – or incapable of wittingly curbing actions generated by thoughts/emotions for which he was not responsible. I do not know how persuaded Eneas was by his own claims, but in any case, they were fully intelligible citations of local narrative frames.

Nonetheless, these narratives did not constitute a single, unchanging story that could only be told one way. In this case, people produced different accounts of what had caused the problem. Eneas's kin were quick to say that their own tobacco did not cause people to behave in Eneas's fashion, and so indeed, that his actions stemmed from some evil, foreign substance, perhaps placed in him through sorcery. For them, he was in need of healing. A few members of other clans and language groups, however, framed the event differently, but also in such a way that they reconstituted the symbolic boundaries of groups. They pointed out to me that Eneas's clan was all like that: 'hot' people, violent and prone to anger. 'That is the coca that they mambe,' one Uitoto told me, questioning the morality of the fundamental substances, and thus the proper humanity of the entire clan. At least one man, however, to some extent agreed with Eneas, telling me that Saúl was indeed to blame but, specifically, for not counselling his son properly rather than for imbuing him with a spurious substance.

Others scoffed at Eneas's demand for sympathetic understanding and contested his denial of culpability. The gist of their critiques was that the least a mambeador could do would be to 'sit firmly,' lick tobacco, and resist evil thoughts/emotions, or 'look into his own body' and request help to get rid of his diseases and evil thoughts/emotions. To me, their evaluations indicated that for them there was a bodily locale of accountability for virtuous or flawed action. They could still deem the origin of some behaviour to be a divine or animalistic substance, but at least temporarily, this material subjectivity and the body it resonated in coalesced into a locatable real person, a self who was deserving of praise or needful of healing if not chastisement. At least some of this rhetoric was enabled by, and reiterated, the recognized possibility of an embodied consistency, a certain 'setting' of virtues, that for the purpose of negotiation of responsibility made the body a centre of volition.

I visited Eneas in 2007, by which time his account of his own past actions was a denser story. He had taken yagé, a powerful, vision-inducing (or entheogenic) drink made out of the *Banisteriopsis caapi* vine, and it had revealed to him that several deaths in his lineage and his own actions had been the product of an old Muinane man's sorcery.[20] The yagé showed him how the old man had promised to kill all the members of the clan, beginning downriver and heading up. The sorcery had killed Eneas's brother and uncle, and it was set up so that Eneas would kill either his own wife, somebody else, or himself. The yagé, however, managed to reveal the plot and disrupt it, and as a consequence of that very substance's vengeful power, the old sorcerer had died. Eneas stressed that no one had cared when this happened; he had fallen off his canoe and drowned, and his body had been found several days later floating close to a community downriver. They could only recognize him from a conspicuous mark on his skin. I found Eneas's description of the purported sorcerer's lonely death to echo claims to the similarity between sorcerers and the more dangerous animals, none of which had proper relations with others.

Finally, I will note one young man's very different take on misbehaviours in general. He did not seem to think of virtuous or flawed behaviour in terms of agential substances, but rather in terms of undesirable personality features, which he called *vicios*, 'vices.' His rhetoric seemed to me to be premised on the point that Eneas (and every other miscreant) was very much his own man, autonomous, and responsible and punishable for his own misbehaviours. For this young man, attempts at explaining misbehaviour in terms of extrinsic agencies seemed to be a travesty and acceptance of them intolerable leniency.

Despite resources that enabled them to defer responsibility, it was not the case that People of the Centre could perpetrate miscreancies with impunity.[21] Among people who consistently treated good behaviour as one prime manifestation of proper bodily formation, a person whose body and subjectivity had proven to be susceptible to usurpation would become the object of criticism, jabs, and even insults. People could mercilessly flag instances of such usurpation, gossip about them, seek to explain them, and most importantly, remember them for a long, long time. As Emanuel used to say, when a person misbehaved, 'he now had a number.' He explained this initially mysterious claim by reference to different soccer players' place in the field and to how their expected behaviour differed according to the number on their shirt; everybody knew what the places and actions of a number one, nine, or ten were. So too, everybody would expect the person who had misbehaved to behave in that fashion again.

## Continuity and Power

The phenomenological plausibility (or psychological persuasiveness) and effectiveness of accusations to the effect that a person's thoughts/emotions and actions were immoral and inhuman were tied to People of the Centre's understandings that subjectivity stemmed from foreign, agential substances inside their bodies, in conjunction with their take on a perspectival cosmos. These accusations, among other performative practices, were dialogically related to motivating ideals of the admirable or desirable in human subjectivity and action, and reproduced these understandings and motivations. Individuals made manifest the sense that they were, or desired to be, a certain kind of agent, or in any case presented themselves as such.

People sometimes produced moral self-portrayals precisely because they were motivated to do so by these ideals and by their awareness of the possibility – indeed, the likelihood – that their actions and subjectivities would be framed as immoral, animalistic, or otherwise incompatible with their ideals of morality and agency. They sought to pre-empt the very real and perceived political threat for individuals and groups, in my experience actualized in cases in which people questioned the humanity of the personal constitution of leaders and of their personal and community projects. Cases in which people admitted to the inhumanity of their own (past) actions and thoughts only buttressed the persuasiveness of the rhetoric about the extrinsic, substantial origins of subjectivity.[22]

Despite the awareness of self and of how the self could be presented strategically or interpreted by others, the selves that were thus aware and strategic need not be thought of as the essentialized individualist subjects of humanism; rather, they were themselves aggregates of affects and understandings, which in turn were the products of cited symbolic deployments. Personal constitution at that level was not a project people could easily be strategic about or that they could undertake freely and with an overarching view of its conditions. It was obvious to people that they were People of the Centre of this or that language group or clan, that their lives centrally involved an engagement with substance production, and that their worth, virtues, and flaws as persons were at least in part tied to that engagement. This was hardly a choice, though within the project there were choices. Yet, with their more or less self-aware actions they mostly unwittingly (re)produced these projects and, thereby, the kinds of persons they and people in new generations could be. It is likely that for generations people had identified with these projects, on one hand, and, on the other, had linked undesirable ways of being with particular animals, and likely, as well, that the stories and motivations this involved had been reproduced.

I must add that their accounts and expressions of recognition of esteemed and despised qualities featured much variety, nuance, and contradiction, a reflection of the inevitability of differences among people but also of a history of change as new kinds of persons, kinds of relationships, and life projects swam into their horizons. One such way of being that individuals among People of the Centre identified and, in some cases, sought to reproduce was that of leaders savvy in dealing competently and trickily with white men in white men's institutions – also not an alternative more than a couple of generations back. Some common details of this project or way of being revealed that individuals were by no means limited to expressing only righteous moral evaluations, or idealizing the corresponding virtues. This project was framed by common, explicit descriptions of naughty indigenous leaders who stole money from the government and from their communities, spent it on prostitutes and booze in Leticia, and generally knew how to come out on top in legal skirmishes, debates, arguments, and fights with their elders or with 'white people.' Among the various admired features of these usually young leaders was that they could not be tricked or lied to, were critical of the bossy, self-serving interests of the older mambeadores, and were frankly incorrigible.

My sense with this kind of mischievous ideal is that though it was doubtless new in many ways, it did have moral precedents. One such was People of the Centre's grudging admiration or appreciation for the Muinane mythical trickster frog *Mɨméhuje*'s sheer cheek, as he brazenly pursued a variety of funny but lustful, murderous, or cannibalistic courses of action. Perhaps, this frog's stories scaffolded, as they were expressions of, an enduring second-order desire to be tough, wily, autonomous, and irreverent.

I dare not be too categorical in my separation of the new and the old, for as Echeverri (1997), Gow (2001), Kulick (1992), Rubenstein (2002), and Sahlins (1985) clearly show for different peoples, the new and the old mix in deceptive ways, due to transformative citationality or structures of conjunctures in which older forms are deployed in perennially changing contexts and in the process transformed. These transformations do cause new kinds of persons to appear and become available as ideals. For instance, becoming a polite man or woman whose demeanour revealed schooling was simply never a project before schools came in, but some People of the Centre were engaged with such a project; likewise, a woman's acceptance of labour pains and rejection of the very prospect of anaesthesia at that point could only be an expression of her engagement with a certain way of relating to God once Christian missionization and the local arrival of Western-style medicine allowed her to frame it that way.

# 3 Agency and Transformation

## Social and Moral Manipulations

People of the Centre's most frequent expressions of concern, claims, and evaluations concerning the admirable and the despicable, the human and the inhuman, and matters of worth in general, cohered well with the picture of the cosmos, of personhood, and of social life that I have already described. Many of them were articulated in terms of persons' bodily composition, and often particularly in terms of the qualities of substances. Their semiotic ideology – basic assumptions about signs and how they function in the world (Keane 2003, 419) – had them treat these substances, but also malocas, animals, trees, the earth, and a variety of climatic phenomena, as beings endowed with subjectivity, a certain kind of moral (or immoral) engagement with the world, and the capacity to act purposefully. 'True' versions of key substances like tobacco paste, mambe, hot chilies, water, herbs, and others, featured dispositions and key capabilities that became features of the persons they constituted.

The capabilities in question involved mainly the transformative manipulation of substances or their bearers; manipulations could be social, in the sense that they involved centrally conversations between different kinds of subjectivity-endowed beings, or material, in the sense that substances and agents, or substance-like agencies, thoughts/emotions, and tribulations, could be physically transformed without being treated as social interlocutors. Substance production – from felling the forest for gardening to preparing ritual substances and foodstuffs for consumption featured transformations of these various kinds. People of the Centre treated their dealings with cultigens as social relationships, in some contexts; they spoke of tobacco, coca, manioc, and chilies, in the form of cultigens in the garden or as prepared substances, not just as elements of themselves, but also either as divine parents and grandparents who had created human beings out of their own bodies, or as children in need of real people's care and sustenance. They were thus often addressed, cajoled, and otherwise dealt with as interlocutors in interpersonal relations.

People of the Centre rhetorically treated many of their manipulations – especially those men were responsible for – as esoterically violent, predatory movements and transformations of misanthropic thoughts/emotions, substances, and tribulations. Real people could make use of the transformative capabilities of the substances through their judicious consumption and other forms of incorporation. Like the substances they embodied, real people could burn, eat, attack with invisible claws, wound, kill, or blow away evil beings. The dark side of this matter was that improper substances in people could similarly burn, eat, spear, age, heat up, and kill their hosts, their substances or their organs, as well as the substances and bodies of those with whom the host interacted.

Some key dealings with substances and agents – including most of those that were women's responsibilities – were not themselves predatory; rather, they sweetened, purified, filtered, soothed, healed, nourished, or cooled body parts, thoughts/emotions, and other substances. Women's process of extraction of edible starch from poisonous manioc, for instance, did not involve death-dealing or the imagined destruction of any subjects.

People of the Centre portrayed many of their endeavours as instances of some use or another of transformative capabilities. Their descriptions of their food and ritual substance preparations tended to present these as processes in which some agent – water, fire, or some other subjectivity-endowed substance or object – killed, destroyed, or otherwise did away with pathogens and impurities in the original stuff, leaving only an uncontaminated, desirable essence. In their speech of felling they treated the felling and burning of the forest to make a garden as a human war against trees, or alternatively as a meal in which the deities of tobacco, axes, and fire all responded to the human demand that they 'eat' evil trees, transforming them into fertile ashes from which desirable substances would grow. Their speeches of healing to deal with diseases usually involved the use of tobacco paste and coca, understood in the first place to be the source and power of knowledge, and then to be predators that transformed the evil substances affecting the sick and placed them again in the animals that had originated them. They claimed that these animals then became easy prey for people and, thereby, nourishing meat. Finally, they produced masses of rhetoric according to which constructing a maloca involved numerous transformations of diseases and negative affects into elements of the house, and the 'domestication' of evil agents, such as the great trees that became house pillars or drums. According to mambeadores' metacommentaries on the speech of maloca construction, once it transformed them into a house, these elements became protective guardians that ensured the health and fertility of the inhabitants of the maloca. I will return in greater depth to these transformations.

People of the Centre's understanding of real humanity as perennially at risk of predatory attacks from inhuman beings, and of human capabilities as centred on predatory manipulations, translated into a profound ambivalence towards violence, hate, and anger. The latter were often mentioned as the most salient manifestations of animals' flawed thoughts/emotions; they were the object of many abstract prescriptions warning against their capacity to destroy life and relationships, and likely to be harshly criticized when actually made manifest. Anger, however, had a desirable, even necessary aspect: it was part and parcel of the dangerous predatory capabilities necessary for people to achieve the good life. Men and women, but more so the former, seemed to be obsessed with the idea of being capable of angrily killing, harming, scolding, or proscribing evil or threatening agents in the world, anthropomorphic or not. Men produced numerous moral self-portrayals and claims that pressed the point that they were awe-inspiring predatory agents.

Their understandings and practices in this regard constituted clear versions of the third element of the Amazonian package already discussed, namely, that for the making of bodies and generally for the achievement of social life relations of alterity were essential, in this case as a given background from which the substances of proper sociality were extracted violently; they also backed up the common claim – explained with exemplary clarity by Overing (1993) and Taylor (2001, 46) – that lowland South American cultures understand relationships with paradigmatic figures of alterity to be not only necessary, but to a great extent predatory.

## The Workings of Knowledge

The human capacity for predatory and other transformations was dependent on a privileged kind of knowledge. The capability and knowledge in question were supposed to be for the most part, though not exclusively, men's. The mambeadores stressed the great amount of knowledge they possessed, the authentically Muinane, Uitoto, or Bora, or clanic or patrilineal character of this knowledge, the propriety of their processes of acquisition of it, the legitimacy and effectiveness of their use of it, and the respect and fear others had of them because of it. Most of the People of the Centre I knew – men and women – produced, as well, numerous negative evaluations of other people, concerning the same issues. Both surreptitiously and openly they denied the amount, effectiveness, and legitimacy of others' knowledge, their good will, their formal correctness, and so on. They often found proofs of others' lack of knowledge and of their misdemeanours.

People of the Centre referred in Spanish to the instrumental speeches as *el conocimiento propio*, the 'knowledge of our own,' a term defined by its contrast with the speeches and other privileged discourses and techniques of white men. I should note parenthetically that most People of the Centre men possessed some 'knowledge of our own,' but by the time I did my fieldwork there were no specialized shamans alive of the kind Muinane people called *kakúmɨnaha* (sucking people), who were reportedly capable of extracting diseases from people through suction. However, some Muinane people did recognize certain known Matapí, Yukuna, Uitoto, Ocaina, and Makuna individuals to be specialized healers or sorcerers.

The different instrumental speeches pertained to numerous fields of endeavour and to different moments in life: the speech of life was deployed to fashion babies in the womb and to foster the growth of cultigens; the speech of healing was used to tackle disease and other tribulations; the speeches of felling, of burning, and of manioc were used at different stages in gardening; and so on. Many involved more or less formulaic utterances, which mambeadores understood to act in different ways to change some aspect of the world. My interlocutors made different claims about them: that they were the very speech of the creator deity sounding directly through the speaker; or that they were 'recordings' of the creator's words, akin to those registered in a cassette tape; or that they directed the attention of the creator deity to some transformation which people wanted him (or her, depending on the clan of the person telling the story) to carry out. Alternatively, they considered the spoken utterances themselves to be powerful, or somehow to harness the agency of substances.[1]

The manipulation of agents and substances was at times a matter of what I have called 'divine performativity,' where a speaking subject's performative claims name a state of affairs, and this state becomes real as an effect of having been so named, and where it is the subject's will that ensures the effect. Judith Butler uses the term ironically (1993, 12, 13), in an argument that questions radically the possibility of agents' wills autonomously carving out their meaningful effects in the world. Still, the term applies well in the case of People of the Centre's understandings of their own practices, where agents were supposed to have the capacity to bring about transformations in the world by means of naming or otherwise describing these transformations, and where the effects they named were supposed to come to be in virtue of the substance-empowered will of the subject that did the naming. A common example of such divine performativity took place during most evening coca circle rituals, which usually involved the recapitulation of the evils that had affected the community that day or could do so on the following one. Each of these evils was then dealt with in the mambeadores' rhythmic dialogues, which at some stage involved lists of statements, including self-referential ones about the statements' themselves, that claimed that these were effective and that they were sweeping away, blowing away, and proscribing these evils. Two different mambeadores in whose malocas I lived, Emanuel and David, also used to 'cool the land' in their nightly liturgies. They explained to me that the land got hot during the day because it was heated by the sun. This heat caused people to sleep restlessly and feel itchy. Their speeches to cool it at one point recited something like this:

It is now a cool land
  land of morning
  land of sweetness
  land of life
Nothing bothers the children
  the women
  the young men
  the young women
  They rest.[2]

When explaining this to me, Emanuel claimed that at that point in the ritual, the women and children could be heard to sigh, as they 'truly rested.'

*Óvɨkɨhi* (to aim), *mómonɨhi* (to name), and *ímijɨsuhi* (to name into good/beautiful) referred in Muinane to forms of talk that made things be as they had been named. An example was the practice of stating in a speech that the flesh of certain dangerous fish was in truth manioc. People of the Centre understood this to transform the original substance, pre-empting its more dangerous characteristics; the fish's pathogenic features were disarmed, because processed manioc was not pathogenic (see my discussion of sympathetic magic below). However, several of my coca circle interlocutors were explicit in saying that naming could be very dangerous, stressing – in a typical moral self-portrayal – that it was all the more dangerous when effected by knowledgeable elders such as themselves, empowered with tobacco and coca. Emanuel broached this matter after reproaching me one time for calling an airplane a 'fire eagle' (*kɨ́ɨjɨgai mogáje*), the term that some other clans used for planes. He said, 'Do not name it that way … that is why they fall and burn! Call it '*kámoga*' (canoe of the heights).'[3]

To produce transformations, the speeches often made use of what Frazer and Malinowski, early founding figures of anthropology, would probably have called 'sympathetic' or 'contagious' magic (Tambiah 1968, 186, 194) and Lévi-Strauss, 'magical thought' (Lévi-Strauss 1964, 30, 31).[4] Speeches often explicitly likened two objects, substances, or situations and then attributed some discursively privileged characteristic of one of them to the other; this characteristic was thereby *given* to it. For example, a healing chant for fractured bones described the speed with which a certain hanging vine, when cut, grew to reattach itself to the ground and set roots. When Lázaro explained this to me, he showed me one such vine that we had cut with a machete a few days before. Indeed, the tough vine had already produced some thirty centimetres of tender green shoot. At that rate, within a few days the vine would again reattach itself to the ground and spread out roots. The healing chant, as Lázaro described it to me, noted that speed expressly and matter-of-factly asked why the bone should be any slower in healing and setting.

This ties into the matter of semiotic ideologies, for again, such beliefs depended on a certain understanding of what signs and meanings were and of the kinds of agents that could produce them. In an 'enchanted' cosmos (Taylor 2006, 42) – and I would call People of the Centre's cosmos enchanted, in this sense – meanings in things include magic powers. 'Charged' objects in such worlds can affect persons and other things: they can effect cures, save houses from burning, stop lightning, and so on. They have this causal power that can bring about physical outcomes proportionate to their meaning. This is not a possibility in a naturalistic cosmos or in a semiotic ideology in which thoughts and meanings are purportedly only in minds, and where causal relations between things are independent of their meanings.

The use of sympathetic magic could be a form of performative manipulation requiring only a powerful will – that of a mambeador or a divinity – that imposed itself upon some material reality. I must point out, however, that in every case of it I witnessed in People of the Centre's communities there always seemed to be the alternative of imagining an intermediary agent who materially carried out the effect named. I often had the sense that they thought of this or that speech as a homunculus inhabiting a person's body or as some other material being. Alternatively, sometimes the speeches or references to the speeches seemed to treat the comparison between substances as a given formula, such that those who knew it could quote it and, thereby, compel the deity to carry out the healings. In such cases, it would have been more a question of persuasion that led to manipulative transformation, than a question of direct divine performativity. In any case, that the social manipulation of agents and substances was a central aspect of human capability made knowledge a field of much moral solicitude.

## The Moral Conditions of Knowledge

Muinane and other People of the Centre's self-depictions and critiques, as well as the speeches themselves and other discourses, tied together the morality and efficacy of individual's uses of speeches.[5] One axiom I found them to express was that if speeches were immorally transmitted, acquired, or deployed, they would not function well; if deployed in a formally correct manner and from a moral position, they would necessarily produce desirable results. Similarly, a general moral condition of knowledge was that it be used for a proper purpose, and conversely, such purpose could only be achieved if the necessary knowledge was deployed morally. However, whether a particular instance of the transmission, use, or acquisition of some knowledge was moral or not was obviously a question of interpretation and at times of negotiation. In any case, people produced numerous claims to the morality of their uses of knowledge, as well as many contestations of others' claims.

Ultimately, knowledge – namely, speeches – could only be gauged as 'true' (*míya-*) *a posteriori*, when it 'dawned' or 'made [something] be seen'; that is, when its effects became materially perceptible and beneficial.[6] Several mambeadores affirmed that the only 'true' knowledge was that which pertained to the cool path or path of life. This 'path' was that which led from the maloca to the garden. According to Pedro's explanation of this claim, it meant that the only worthwhile knowledge was that which was involved in the production of foodstuffs and ritual substances, and through these, in the multiplication of real people. True speeches led to material abundance, satiety, good health, tranquil community life, and demographic increase.[7]

In oft-repeated abstract accounts, a mambeador who had plenty of mambe and tobacco paste showed, by virtue of his possession of such substances, that his speeches had 'dawned' and that he was indeed a moral, knowledgeable person. Along similar lines, men and women of the Centre told me on different occasions that a woman who possessed a beautiful, well-weeded garden and who always had an abundance of foodstuffs available, to that extent showed that she, indeed, knew the counsels of the speech of advice and was a true woman (in Muinane, a *míyagaigo*). In abstract accounts, the existence of well-behaved, healthy children and grandchildren was also deemed evidence of knowledge dawning – producing desirable, material results. These abstractions were often concretized in evaluations of individuals.

Pablo and other mambeadores stated that a person could know every counsel of the speech of advice or a great many speeches of apprising, in the sense of having consigned them to memory, but if his knowledge did not dawn in well-behaved children, in the healing of diseases, or in the production of foodstuffs and ritual substances, others would claim that he did not really know, that his speeches were lies. So merely memorized recipes and speeches were not in themselves true knowledge; true knowledge was that which the individual had not only committed to memory but had, furthermore, made dawn.

Failures to make knowledge dawn were a matter of much attention and denunciation. Jonás's was a case in point: people claimed that he was very knowledgeable of speeches of apprising and that he was a pleasant man and a competent interlocutor in a coca circle. Nonetheless, they also claimed that his knowledge was false, for his very lifestyle of itinerancy and material poverty showed that his beautiful speeches had not dawned.[8] In another instance, Jafet likened David to jaguars and anacondas, who in a certain speech of apprising appeared as leaders whose speeches sounded beautiful, but were mere false appearance. They did not dawn, but instead led to death, hunger, and other tribulations for their people.

If moral knowledge was that which pertained to the cool path and, in general, to the production of real people, its spurious counterpart was sorcery. This was dangerous immoral knowledge that led to the destruction of people and communities, but which pleased those who lacked discernment because of its great destructive efficacy. Saúl told me a certain part of a speech of apprising that stressed the clear contrast between proper knowledge and sorcery; it followed a moral self-portrayal in which he claimed to reject the latter. The apprising went something like this:

> At First Time, some animals claimed that the creator's true speech was not true. They preferred to explore sorcerous knowledge, and collected substances for sorcery. Soon, however, they found themselves hungry and incapable of producing food. They sought the creator to beg him for manioc and other garden produce. He told them, 'Eat your sorcery stones!' They answered, 'Those stones do not bring satiety!' 'Then why do you use them at all!?' he demanded angrily. He then condemned them to a miserable life of scavenging and eating filth, and to be game animals for real people to eat.

Again, this mythical event highlighted that the proper use of knowledge was for production that led to satiety – a state of cool satisfaction – and derogated its misuse for the purposes of sorcery. Sorcery did produce results, but these were ultimately detrimental to the user.

There was an almost standardized autobiographical anecdote among men concerning their rejection of sorcery. I heard independent versions from Emanuel and Saúl, and then from several young Uitoto and Muinane men. They told me about their ignorant and innocent youth when they had been interested in hearing about or acquiring sorcerous knowledge with which to harm enemies. Each had asked his father or some other elder about this. The wiser elder had advised each overly eager youth against such deadly interests, which led to no production. And in each case, the elder had instructed the youth to 'look at where those who used sorcery ended up': invariably, in the myths and histories alluded to, sorcerers had died awful deaths and their lineages had come to tragic ends. I am not sure that these pedagogical events actually transpired in each of their personal histories; rather, I believe that oft-repeated stories such as this one, which involved interactions between stereotypical characters – that is, overly eager and ignorant youths and wise elders – reiterated key contrasts and associations of a vocabulary of moral evaluations central to people's accounts of themselves. Their frequent repetition and their moral plausibility made them an intimate part of their lives. What was important about them, after all, was that they were moral truths.[9]

Despite their condemnations of sorcery, it also had appeal for some people, especially men, and constituted an alternative for the self. Many men explicitly claimed, or intimated to me, that they could practise sorcery if they were so inclined. Eneas in particular made claims to being willing to indulge in such dangerous endeavours, if called upon to do so by the inimical gestures of others. This seems consistent to me with their ambivalence towards anger; attitudes towards sorcery, as with anger, were shaped by the aesthetic appeal of the image of a man capable of destroying or disabling all foes through radically efficacious esoteric violence.

Such moral and aesthetic considerations were a frequent feature in men's self-portrayals and criticisms concerning knowledge. They were premised on the agential character of the speeches, which were understood to be prone to anger, disgust, jealousy, and sulking, if mistreated. In such cases, morality in dealing with knowledge was a matter of treating it as an agent, respectfully and for purposes of expediency. In other cases, though, people's portrayals highlighted their own coolness, benevolence, discipline, and correctness in matters of knowledge, and bracketed the intrinsic agency of the speeches.

The formal correctness of deployments of knowledge was of singular importance. There was much rhetoric about the requirement of using speeches only when needed, and in the correct place, at the right time, and with the appropriate accoutrements. The claims could posit that the speeches themselves required it, as agents, or else they could simply highlight the virtuous orthodoxy of the person. One formal requirement of many speeches was that they be deployed in the form of dialogues. Individuals often emitted judgments of particular instances of speech deployment, or of their own and other's talents in this regard. Pablo, for instance, told me his son lacked the ability to 'give him strength' in dialogue; I witnessed one dialogue between them, and found that, indeed, the son lacked expertise as a what-sayer, merely answering his father with 'hmmms' rather than with the more varied repertoire or responses of an experienced interlocutor. This constituted an aesthetic problem, but it had implications concerning the efficacy of the speeches deployed, as well as the public evaluation of Pablo and of his son. People spoke critically about them, saying Pablo had not raised his children properly in that regard, and his son hadn't been attentive to the ways of the clan.

Another common moral claim of individuals was that they had acquired their knowledge properly: from the right elders, in correct circumstances, following the proper protocols, and so on. Moral obligations concerning transmission went both ways. Since the speeches themselves were sentient beings, and were tied to agential substances, their transmission and acquisition required care. Knowledge transmitted inappropriately could attack either giver or receiver, or simply sulk and cease to work. For instance, speeches could become resentful if not properly paid for with tobacco and could harm their original owner for not treating them as something dear to him. Knowledge acquired too quickly and in excess could madden young receivers, and it was the obligation of concerned elders to make sure they did not give others speeches carelessly.[10]

People of the Centre also made much of the ownership of knowledge. This was linked to the very nature of groupings and individuals, as represented in speeches of apprising but in much other rhetoric as well. The idea was that the Grandfather of Creation had created the different patrilines and clans and language groups in different ways, and given to each its strain of tobacco and its speeches. These were transmitted patrilineally, in the case of tobacco constituting the very bodies of members of patrilines and clans, who were thus consubstantial among themselves and, for that reason, supposedly similar in subjectivities, proclivities, and even vulnerabilities. Therefore, though many speeches and rituals were the same between different groups, some were unique to particular lineages and clans, because they addressed unique aspects of lineage-specific creation and bodily constitution. Ignoring such knowledge or preferring another group's knowledge were dangerous matters that could generate trouble or criticism for the unorthodox.

## Key Transformations

People of the Centre treated many of their significant endeavours conceptually as predatory transformations of evil or inhuman beings, often requiring a great deal of knowledge and hard work.[11] Some activities that men were in charge of, like everyday healing and hunting, were important but minor transformations that more often than not involved just individuals, a pair of siblings, or perhaps a nuclear family. They only sometimes required detailed shamanic knowledge. Other endeavours were treated as large-scale transformations that required a great deal more 'knowledge of our own' and work. The activities that condensed the most transformative rituals and the most intense social interaction, and which were deemed to be a man's greatest claim to an expression of effective knowledge and moral propriety, were the building and ritual handling of a maloca and the hosting of dance rituals. Women's knowledge and the transformations they effected were also matters of moral solicitude; most of these were imagined as endeavours that featured transformation but little by way of predatoriness.

*Gardening*

Cultivating and preparing substances were transformative activities with complex moral entailments, for they were, in the first place, part of the ongoing construction and maintenance of the person's body, affects, and capabilities; second, they were part of the human project of making new generations of real people; and third, they were a form of social interaction with subjects with bodies different from those of human beings. People of the Centre used gardening as a metonymical reference to moral endeavours in general, as opposed to unproductive, foreign, or sorcerous activities. It was part of a larger, cyclic and progressive process: food and ritual substances were the product of previous uses of food and substances, and the material pre-condition for further production. This was in turn essential to People of the Centre's explicit formal purpose of making new generations of people capable of perpetuating their ideally tranquil and uniquely admirable way of life.

People of the Centre practised slash-and-burn horticulture. Every year or two most couples felled, usually with others' help, a new section of rainforest, allowed the vegetation to dry, and then burned everything down to ashes. These ashes fertilized the ground, which was then ready for planting tobacco, coca, manioc, chilies, and numerous other cultigens. Gardens would be used for three to five years, and then, when lessened productivity and increased weeds made further cultivation less than worthwhile, allowed to go fallow. They did revisit old gardens over the years to pick fruit from planted trees that only really produced when a garden was already fallow. Abandoned gardens quickly grew into young forest.

People of the Centre treated, not only their own efforts in the garden, but also other processes, such as the desiccation and burning of the felled forest and the very growth of plants in the garden, which most Westerners would deem to be natural processes, as involving social interaction with various kinds of beings whom they referred to as forms of kin. Thus in their ritual speech of felling, the mambeadores addressed the tobacco, coca, the axe and machete, the summer, the sun, the wind, the fire, and the rain and asked, instructed, or otherwise persuaded these beings to help them with the different gardening tasks. In these speeches, the mambeadores presented themselves as the children or grandchildren of these powerful predatory beings and, as such, begged their protection and caring help, also promising reciprocity in the manner of proper younger kin. Thus the felling was portrayed to the Grandmother of the Axe as a chance to feed on trees; the dead vegetation was game for the Grandmother or Grandfather of the Summer to smoke, the burning was portrayed to the Grandmother of Fire as her prescribed meal of dry wood, and so on. Along with such imagery, mambeadores also described these processes as ones that involved the destruction of evil trees, itchy saps, hurtful vines, and, in general, of sources of bodily and social unease.[12]

Some also likened their relationships with the cultigens growing in their gardens to those between parents and children. Men and women attended to their own cultigens – men to tobacco and coca, women especially to manioc, chilies, and cool herbs – during their processes of growth; they weeded them, 'fed' them with the ashes of burnt weeds, and in some cases, carefully uprooted them and moved them to more fertile spots in their gardens.[13] The 'parental' aspect of these activities was not particularly obvious to me until the men spoke of them in the coca circle. Pablo told me that men had to refer in speeches to the different cultigens as 'children,' and instruct certain beings to help them care for them by pouring life-giving water on them, and inspiring them with breath, and feeding them with ashes. They also protected the plant children by instructing the wind not to blow too hard before they took root, and by proscribing or misleading any evil beings who wished to harm them. These speeches purportedly also protected flesh-and-blood children from a variety of threats.

My coca circle interlocutors knew well that cultigens would grow without speeches or ritual parenting for the couple's plant children;

however, it was equally clear that they could use this possibility in critical evaluations, attributing individuals' misbehaviours to poorly raised cultigens that merely appeared to be powerful materiality but were not true, capacity-creating, moral substances.

I recall walking across gardens and David, Pedro, or Pablo, or whoever happened to be my companion at the time, pointing out weeds or sickly crops and reiterating that their state was an indication of their owners' thoughts. The general claim was that the state of well-kept gardens corresponded to the knowledge and morality of their owners, much as healthy, well-behaved children did. In their own abstract accounts, gardens that did not thrive, and children who were sickly or misbehaved, manifested the ill-faring state, ignorance or confused thoughts/emotions of the owners and parents; people also treated this as a causal relation, making claims both to the effect that confused thoughts/emotions led to poor gardens and that unkempt gardens led to confused thoughts/emotions.

### *The Maloca and Dance Rituals*

Malocas were some of the most symbolically loaded objects in People of the Centre's lives. They featured centrally in speeches of apprising, and their very physical form was a necessary frame for dance rituals and for articulating patrilineal identity and relations. Numerous distinctions of worth among kinds of people were tied to the images of malocas. One old contrast – perhaps centuries old – established a hierarchical difference between the patriline that owned the maloca and the 'orphans' of other patrilines attached to it.[14] A related contrast that thrived while I was in the Medio Caquetá treated maloca owners as ideals of virtue – hardworking, generous, continent with their anger and desires, benevolent towards kin, demanding fathers-in-law, and mothers-in-law, esoterically knowledgeable, and dangerous to those intending evil against their people – and others as less endowed in these regards. They spoke of maloca owners and their wives as 'fathers' and 'mothers' of all who came to participate in dance rituals in them. Some individuals used these images – and their ownership of a maloca – to underscore their own superior morality and competences. On the other hand, individuals could also use the ideal link between great virtue and maloca ownership to stress the exceptional character of virtuous counterexamples. One man in the Igaraparaná pointed out to me in 2008 that he was indeed one of those who 'lived in a hut' as opposed to being 'people of maloca,' but that, even so, he had often proven in the past to be more competent and knowledgeable than maloca owners in the region, who often failed to behave properly or show wisdom. He clearly recognized the ideal of maloca owners' virtue and knowledge, but used this ideal both to portray himself as a surprisingly competent man and to question effectively actual maloca owners' ways.

Though throughout the twentieth century there were always people who had lived in malocas and knew how to build them, the fact is that after the rubber boom living in a maloca was the exception rather than the norm. People for the most part lived in woodboard houses that could house little more than a couple and their children, and perhaps a few others. In my experience, malocas were not uncommon – nearly every community I lived in or visited had one or more – but these were more often than not treated as a venue for cooking and rituals rather than as a residence. Maloca living, too, featured in claims and negotiations of morality, as some families that chose to inhabit their malocas made the case that they were, therefore, living as they should, in the more admirable fashion of their ancestors.

A man's decision to build a maloca in the Medio Caquetá was often a political and material risk. Building one required a great deal of hard manual labour, expertise, and food and ritual substances, and thus considerable support from the man's spouse, his brothers and other members of his patriline, and his in-laws and other patrilines. As among some other Amazonian people, like the Cubeo and the Trio, People of the Centre 'voted with their feet': helping somebody build a maloca was to some extent recognizing him to be a man of knowledge worthy of hearkening as a leader of his patriline.[15] There were endless discussions concerning whether particular maloca owners merited that kind of recognition, and whether the discussants would respond positively to invitations to build a maloca from this or that individual.

In myriad expressions, mambeadores claimed that the maloca and the dance rituals held in it protected people, rid them of their diseases, behavioural vices, and tribulations and ensured their multiplication, mainly by transforming substance-like thoughts and agencies. The reasons individuals cited when making public requests for help with building a maloca were, to paraphrase Emanuel, intentional understatements to the effect that there had been some population growth in the patriline already – an indication of knowledge and morality – and that therefore a bigger abode was needed. Emanuel himself had announced his intention to build his maloca claiming that his previous house had become tight because too many daughters-in-law had moved in. Others, said Emanuel, claimed that the house was too small and, therefore, became too smoky with the numerous bonfires burning inside, and that the smoke could harm the little children, and yet others claimed that the owner needed a place in which to sit with his sons to teach them. Emanuel also gave me a more esoteric reason for building his maloca, however: 'the spirit' had told him to. The message had begun with his suffering an unstoppable bloody diarrhoea. No conjuration or remedy had healed him, so he had taken a strong hallucinogen that he called 'forest tobacco' (*Virola multinervia*), in order to see what it was that was afflicting him. In his trance, the spirit of the forest tobacco had asked him, 'How can it be that an elder, the what-sayer of the cabildo, *mambe*s in a mere hut?' Emanuel said that the spirit had left without saying aught else, but that because he 'knew a little' – a typical self-portrayal of his to the effect that he possessed much knowledge – he had understood what it was that the spirit had meant: that he had to build a maloca. Once he had made the decision, the disease – which had been no true disease, but a prompt for this action – had disappeared.

The maloca constructions I witnessed and those I heard about required several great steps. For Pablo's maloca, as for others, people had to find and bring with them elements for the wooden structure. Then they had to assemble this structure into a skeleton of a house, in the very spot where Pedro's maloca had stood. After this, they had to go to the jungle and bring fifty or sixty large bundles of *puy* palm leaves, plus many segments of *chonta* palm. At home, they had to weave the *puy* leaves onto *chonta* palm planks to make 'combs' (*peinillas,* in Spanish), and finally tie these to the wooden structure to make the roofing. When this was finished, the main task was done and the maloca was ready. The insiders and the helpers could then prepare the maloca for the dance ritual that inaugurated it.

Each great task was supposed to be preceded by ritual dialogues between the owner and his men of the speech of tobacco – ritual partners from other clans – and Pablo and his counterparts did hold such dialogues. I gathered from Pablo's explanations, as well as from what I followed myself, that the dialogues consisted of the speeches of apprising and the speeches of maloca construction that related to the task at hand. These speeches focused on the origin of the materials, the ways in which they were discovered or made by the first mythical maloca builder, and the troubles he faced and successfully and unsuccessfully dealt with. Each narration was followed by the performative transformation or proscription of all evils, both those that the maloca was intended to pre-empt, and those that could threaten the workers during the execution of the task. They constantly reiterated that these speeches were true and that it was not people, but the infallible true tobacco, who spoke them.

One important and widely encompassing speech of apprising somebody translated for me at the time told of the origins of spurious, rejected malocas:

> First, the Grandson of the Centre (whose name and even number differed between clans) tried the malocas of fish: holes in sunk trees, under riverbanks, and so on. He found them unsuitable, and rejected them as improper. Then he tried out and rejected the malocas of earth: the lairs of agoutis and acouchies,[16] and the mounds of termites. He also tried and rejected the malocas of birds and then started to come closer to the proper human habitation. He made diverse huts of the kinds people make in their gardens or when staying out in the jungle overnight. Then he made a small, two-pillar maloca. He started trying different roofing materials, trying each kind of *puy*, noting their imperfections and then giving them names and rejecting them. Finally, he built a proper maloca with four pillars, and roofed it with properly woven *puy*.

The owner of the future maloca, the teller informed me, had to reject all the spurious malocas and *puys*, lest his maloca not become a proper house for human habitation.

The process by means of which objects from the jungle were transformed into important parts of the maloca or elements within it was called a 'bringing into the maloca' (*jáfévehi*, in Muinane); in other words, it was a process of domestication. According to several mambeadores, these objects were 'made to enter the maloca,' and thereby 'made to speak the speech of pain' (*áivojɨ́suhi)*, or 'transformed into headmen' (*kehésuhi*). They all converged on the sense that the previous evil predatory capability of these beings was transformed into proper predatory capability of the kind that did not harm the inhabitants of the maloca but, rather, defended them by capturing and killing extrinsic threats.

The most important elements of the wooden structure, on the basis of the emphases which People of the Centre made on them in their rhetoric, were the wooden pillars. In much rehearsed stories and anecdotes of experiences, these long, thick, hardwood trunks were carried with great effort through the jungle. Since childhood, boys were supposed to be constantly told that they had to become strong so that as men they could carry pillars for their fathers-in-law without faltering shamefully.

An instrumental speech stated that when growing in the jungle, the trees of the species prescribed for pillars allegedly hid jaguars, pumas, and other beasts and bragged about being unvanquishable leaders (*kehémɨ*) with power greater than tobacco's. The tobacco deity listened quietly when they said this, waited till they slept, and then chopped them down. He then made each one 'enter the maloca,' that is, he made it a part of the maloca. In doing so, the tobacco transformed them into true *kehémɨ* with the predatory capabilities and inclinations to guard the people who lived in the maloca from outside evil. Presumably, the speeches of the owner and the interlocutor were supposed to effect this very transformation every time a maloca was built.[17]

Similar transformations had to be effected with a great many other elements of the maloca: the *puy* palm leaves for the roof, the large paired wooden drums that guarded the maloca when its owners were gone, and the elements to make mambe. Pablo told me about a ritual dialogue along such lines that his father had held a few nights prior to a dance ritual, many years before, concerning the rafter above the door. In this dialogue, his father had named the rafter into a trap of the kind used to capture and kill large animals such as tapirs and jaguars. Any evil which stepped through the door would then trigger the trap, which would fall (invisibly) upon the miscreant, killing him.

A central aspect of the symbolism of the building was what I would gloss as the 'substantialization' of diseases, undesirable affects, and potential troubles and their pre-emption by means of transforming them into elements of the maloca. In somebody's meta-reference to these speeches, for example, the owner of the maloca could ask, 'Given that the pillar holds upon its back the weight of so much wood, and his back does not hurt, why should my people's backs hurt? I place that backache upon the pillar, who does not suffer from it. Why should it make me suffer, make my family suffer, when it is already there?' This preemptive capability of the maloca could also be applied to novel threats, which thereby became a harmless part of the building. Lázaro, to provide me with proof of his claim that he was knowledgeable and full of tricks, told me that when there was a jail sentence pending for kin, a speech could be used which would transform that jail sentence into a knot of the kind that tied several rafters together. How then, he asked, could the person be jailed, if the problem had already been transformed into a knot? And so on, different aspects and elements of the maloca either transubstantiated evil, pre-empted it or else guarded against it predatorily[18] (see figures 3.1 and 3.2).

Figure 3.1: A four-post maloca in Chukikɨ (2007).

The finished maloca's most important function, again, was to multiply people. Mambeadores noted in this regard its structural correspondences with the anatomy of a fertile woman, most particularly, in its womb-like interior and vagina-like door, which purportedly propagated the patriline of their owners and their guests. Marco provided an example of this structural homology between women and malocas, when, as an insider in Pablo's maloca's inaugural ritual, he carried out a preparation for 'deflowering' it. He took scissors and cut the messy *puy* palm leaves that framed the door, making it a clean-cut square. He made a joke about giving 'her' – the maloca – a (pubic) haircut. Lázaro also cited these correspondences when telling me about speeches to help women give birth. One such speech that he described invoked the fact that the maloca's door-*cum*-vagina was penetrated by numerous people in one long line at every dance ritual and that the same line left through the same door. Somebody elsewhere had compared the initial entering line to a penis, which, in the case of a new maloca, deflowered the door which had remained sealed till just prior to the ritual. Lázaro reiterated this and added that the line of dancers coming out of the door in the final song of the dance ritual constituted the 'birth of

Figure 3.2: Upon the death of an old Muinane man of People of the Grub, his sons set fire to his old two-post maloca, in Chukikɨ. Afterwards they planted tobacco in the ashes (1998).

people.' The dance dramatized its own desired effect: the multiplication of people through reproduction. Lázaro's point, however, and one he stressed explicitly, was that despite the numerous legs, arms, and dancing poles that went through that door and which could potentially snag, the door never hindered anybody's exit. People were never stuck at that point. The birthing invocation demanded, 'Many people go out the door of the maloca together, in line (in dances), carrying poles, and yet none get stuck. Why should my child be stuck?' The invocation purportedly pre-empted that possibility.[19]

Dance rituals, in general, were great transformative events as well, organized as transactions between different lineages and clans. There were different kinds of dance rituals, each with different mythical origins and constituting transformations of different evils into life-giving, healing, enjoyable substances, actions, and thoughts/emotions. Each lineage was entitled to carry out some rituals and not others. All the dance rituals featured reciprocal exchanges between the lineage hosting it and its visitors. In some, the hosts would provide guests with cooked foods in exchange for game; in others, they provided game in return for unprocessed fruit. In every kind of dance ritual, however, people were supposed to benefit from eating and drinking wholesome stuffs and from using ritual substances.

These rituals constituted a large-scale version of the predatory and other transformations of the kind seen in everyday hunting and healing rituals and food preparation. Dance ritual owners would send *ímogaibɨ*, dollops of tobacco paste wrapped in *puy* leaves, to their men of the speech of tobacco as an invitation to their dance rituals. The men of the speech of tobacco would distribute the paste among their own people, whom it would enlighten as to the nature of whatever tribulations they and their communities were suffering. I recall when Pablo prepared the *ímogaibi* to invite people to his first dance, his conjurations over the tobacco paste demanded that the tobacco make all envies, all anger, and all disease fall as game. The claim was that the tobacco paste would hunt down the animalistic causes of these tribulations, in such a way that all the hunters had to do was go out for brief walks to find their prey, ready to be plucked like fruit. All diseases and social tribulations were thereby removed from human beings and transformed into nourishing, delicious meat.

Dances were salutary in a number of other ways. First, people consumed manioc juice, chili paste, and other substances of women that cooled, sweetened, comforted, and healed. Second, they involved riddles concerning the mythical origins of diseases and, so, tested the hosts' knowledge and offered learning opportunities, though, on the other hand, they could also make a host look ignorant and embarrass him. This offered endless fodder for my interlocutors' moral evaluations, who all had several good stories about successful and catastrophic dealings with riddles. Finally, dances featured, among several kinds of songs, some that explicitly criticized the host patriline or its members for their laziness, stinginess, ugliness, incompetence, despotism, and other flaws or misbehaviours. David and others explained to me that such songs were an important resort – in some cases the last one – for correcting miscreancy. Their virtue lay in part in that they were frank and helpful, while critical talk in the absence of the person being named could cause the latter, or his or her family, to fall sick.

### *Emanuel's Necklace and the Transformation of Evil*

Emanuel's autobiographical anecdotes constituted excellent and highly reiterative examples of People of the Centre's accounts of knowledge, predatory transformative capabilities, and morality, and of how these featured in people's understandings and representations of self. One of his most rehearsed stories concerned the process of transformative domestication that resulted in the creation of his tooth necklace. He explicitly treated the events involved in this process as profoundly formative of his subsequent characteristics and lifestyle. He often reiterated that in the past he had been an angry man, always picking fights and drinking too much alcohol:

> I used to treat my wife like I would an animal, and one day my father called me to the coca circle and said to me, 'You are an animal! Leave!' But I withstood his scolding, and stayed. He also said, 'People will gape at you … and I will eat you.'[20] I answered, 'Since when are people to be eaten?' He made me stay awake for four nights, and on the fourth night he explained things well to me. He said 'Because I love you I said these things to you . . . but it is not to you that I said this, but to the one who has you [that is, the animal or animals inside Emanuel] . . . Someone else who did not love you would have let you continue thus, evil, until you met a real man who would kill you.' That night he showed me how things were.[21] I saw a muscular man, big and strong, and I blew on him and he disappeared. I saw many men, well painted, with tooth necklaces . . . scary people, but they disappeared too. Then I rested [healed].

Emanuel described how thereafter he started killing off the animals who had caused him to be violent, angry, jealous, and a drunkard and whom he'd perceived as people when in trance. He collected their teeth or 'weapons' for a necklace: there were tapir molars, peccary tusks, anteater claws, a giant armadillo tail sheath, and some jaguar, puma, and ocelot canines. Though he told me this many years afterwards, he claimed that he still had to kill an eagle to put its claws in his necklace. He told me he said the following to his necklace: 'When you were animals you used to claim that you were fire, the sun, rocks, and thunder[22] . . . but not anymore. Now you are truly people of the painful speech, and *kehémɨ* [powerful headmen and guardians]. Beforehand you used to skulk in hiding . . . with me you now show yourselves to the people.[23] These [Emanuel's children and grandchildren] are now your grandchildren.'

Emanuel explained that the spirit of each animal whose teeth he had added to his necklace had become domesticated. He explained to me that when a tooth came from a male animal, it had to be named as a 'coca picker'; when it came from a female, it had to be named as a 'plower.'[24] They thus became morally discerning agents able and inclined to participate in real people's predatory transformations. The teeth in his necklace had been evil 'axes' when animals had borne them, but in being wrested from the beasts and transformed into a beautiful necklace, they had become predators who worked for Emanuel, killing purveyors of disease and negative affects.

Emanuel added, generalizing in the present tense, that when there was some disease affecting kin or the community in general, 'one sits with the necklace and addresses the disease: "Here it is [the necklace]! Is it that you wish to accompany them [the teeth]? But beware! It is tiresome for them! They have to slash the forest, pick coca, and toast it!!"' On one occasion at Saúl's maloca there was a loud explosion in a bonfire, and it seemed to Emanuel to signify some threat. He addressed the

Figure 3.3: Mariano Suarez, a Muinane man of People of the Wooden Drum, asked me to take this picture of him wearing his tooth necklace in Chukikɨ (1998). The necklace also featured anteater claws and bird beaks. 'It still needs eagle claws, to be complete!' he told me.

teeth in his necklace, as a form of threat indirectly addressed at some agent involved in the explosion: 'Look! There is one who wishes to join you in my necklace!'

The events in question were clearly important to Emanuel's understanding of himself. In telling them, he reproduced a succession of event-types I heard at other times, according to which at a certain point a male protagonist had a misguided (inhuman) perception of others that led him to violence or some other antisocial action. Then, the person came to realize this was not truly his own speech but that of several evil animal and jungle spirits. Emanuel's stories converged with others in that the protagonist at some point achieved a privileged form of vision and saw the evil beings that caused his or her troubles, addressed them or blew upon them, and thereby killed them or transformed them into animals that could be killed. In a typical narrative denouement, Emanuel, thereafter, killed and ate most of them. His making a tooth necklace out of their 'weapons' was something few men did, but as a story event it would by no means be unfamiliar to other People of the Centre. Finally, the transformations in question, including the removal of extrinsic sources of evil, resulted in the protagonist's renewed judiciousness and capacity to rest (see figure 3.3).

## Hierarchies of Capabilities

The talk I heard from both men and women concerning women in relation to the *conocimiento propio*, stressed that they did not have the capacity for it. There was relatively less interest in their predatory capabilities or possession of dangerous knowledge. Lázaro did tell me that in the past some women who licked large quantities of tobacco paste became esoterically perspicacious and capable of dealing with the more dangerous threats. By the 1990s, however, there were none such, according to Lázaro himself. Adaliah, an Andoke woman, may have been an exception in this regard: I heard Muinane and Nonuya men and women talk admiringly about her knowledge of esoteric and traditional ways of different People of the Centre, and according to Juan Echeverri (personal communication), the men in her own community would turn to look at her for confirmation when making particular claims about the nature of esoteric matters. Nonetheless, even there it was the men who were charged with speaking as experts.

The genders provided each other with gender-specific goods and with services that enabled the other to work. For instance, men felled gardens, which women required in order to grow manioc; women made manioc bread and manioc starch juice, which men needed in order to conduct rituals. These and other practices constituted an imagined cycle in which the genders' responsibilities were complementary. Women's knowledge and production were recognized and explicitly valued in cosmological terms: without women's cooling contributions to existence, so the argument went, men would burn up. Furthermore, men and women stated that men 'multiplied' themselves and reproduced their lineages through women's bodies. This cycle of complementarity between men and women, which men sometimes treated as a matter of equally necessary gendered contributions, nonetheless, seemed to me more often than not to be inflated on the male side. In their accounts of key historical moments or of rituals, people tended to remember as most salient men's successes and failures. Women's knowledge, capacities, and hard work were also, of course, a matter of evaluative solicitude and remembrance in the form of moral portrayals and critiques, but were more likely to be glossed over or ignored and a focus of somewhat less general interest and talk.

As for age differences, older people were supposed to possess greater knowledge and abilities than younger people, owed the latter care, but were in turn owed obedience, respect, and deference.

People of the Centre's understandings of the cosmos, their accounts and deployments of knowledge and substances, their valorization of predatory capabilities and expressions, and the patrilineal corporativity and virilocal post-marital residence these practices were tied to, entailed that adult men were usually in a stronger position than juniors and women to be hearkened to. They could therefore push or impose their desires and interpretations of events, in cases in which these conflicted with those of juniors and women. Since these practices also shaped people's understandings of themselves and of their interactions, and established what mattered to them, they helped reproduce these differences between genders and between people of different ages.[25]

# 4 The Substances of Humanity

People of the Centre's accounts of substantial composition of persons constituted a clear version of the Amazonian package: first, social life among them centred on the production of human bodies on the basis of substances; secondly, the substances – independent, subjectivity-endowed agents of divine origin themselves – were key figures of alterity in need of transformation in order to become kin and elements of consubstantial human bodies; and third, the context for this was a perspectival cosmos, within which the affects, inclinations, and ways of life that the substances incarnated were judged and placed in a hierarchy of worth.

Perhaps People of the Centre's most straightforward claim concerning the nature of the link between cultivated substances and human beings was their frequent postulation that they *were* tobacco or juice of tobacco; at times, they claimed, as well, to be the juice or starchy essence of manioc, coca, chilies, and herbs. They averred that the key substances were constitutive of the very flesh of human beings, or represented these substances rather as homuncular forms somehow stationed inside human bodies. Their rhetoric about social life dealt incessantly with the production, distribution, and consumption of substances and with the entailments of this for their bodies, behaviours, and thoughts/emotions.

Many of their cosmogonic and cosmological speeches of apprising – narratives focused on the origins of foodstuffs, ritual substances, and tools, on the embodiment or first manifestations of human capabilities, and on the failures of spurious versions of these substances – described the cultigens as featuring human bodily shapes, and as growing, talking, walking, and behaving in recognizably human, if at times dramatic, ways. In the speeches of apprising, as well as in other talk, these substances incarnated capabilities and subjectivities – I would call these perspectives – that narrators portrayed as clearly worthy and admirable. Their humanity, however, was not that of members of the human species; they were divine alters that had to be lovingly cultivated and processed in order to become available as literal consumable substances.

According to the speeches of apprising and to people's explanations of or references to them, the ritual substances and the tools and protocols for their formally correct cultivation, preparation, and consumption were given to each lineage and clan by parental divinities or mythical heroes. Since then, each people knew how to make use of their own substances' often violent capabilities and to cool them, preempting any harmful effects they could have on the consumer. However, misappropriation of the substances – that is, their consumption or use by the wrong person, in the wrong circumstances – could always turn those substances into poisons. I must have heard People of the Centre bring up this image dozens of times, when they framed others' actions and tribulations as misbehaviours and misfortunes caused by the capabilities of misused substances that had turned against the consumer, causing them madness, anger, a range of diseases, and even death, much like the effects of the substances of animals.

In these and myriad other ways, People of the Centre deployed substances and rhetoric about them and about the material aspects of their production and consumption to claim or refute that individuals or groups of people behaved in the proper fashion kinspersons should, that they were people with whom it was pleasurable or even healthy to reside, that they were productive, that they were knowledgeable and competent, or that their thoughts/emotions – especially their anger – were human. They cited the image of the morally determinant composition of persons in their quarrels with each other, a variety of rituals, their practices of livelihood and of social organization, and their accounts of the counsels children should receive, among other activities.

## Substances and Gender

The key substances were gendered, as was the social division of responsibilities for dealing with them; furthermore, the bodies of men and women differed slightly in their purported substantial composition. All were made of tobacco juice and manioc starch, but women were more thoroughly imbued with water and cool herbs, and only adult men's bodies could be made of coca. The attributes of the gendering substances that constituted their bodies, and of those they were responsible for, corresponded coherently with each gender's obligations and with the emphases in moral evaluations of them. Men's cultigens were understood to kill flesh-and-blood animals and other kinds of beings as part of men's protective endeavours, and how properly manly and admirable a man could be was tied to his predatory capabilities, where even his expressions of cool calm at some level depended on his predatoriness. The substances that were women's responsibility – manioc, chilies, peanuts, yams, maize, pineapples, and the medicinal cool herbs – for the most part quelled hunger, quenched 'false fires' (fevers, jealousy, anger, and other tribulations), cooled and sweetened burning hearts, and generally brought comfort and satiety, but did not usually kill. People of the Centre's abstract accounts of what constituted a good woman centred on the claim that she fed good stuff to her children, husband, and parents-in-law, nourishing and cooling them.

Again, while accounts of the contributions of substances to existence often stressed their complementarity and, therefore, that of the genders, there was also considerable room for making this complementarity hierarchical. If the amount of sheer talk about the matter was significant, then People of the Centre admired less the capabilities metonymically tied to the various kinds of manioc and cool herbs that women produced than they admired the more radically predatory agencies tied to men's tobacco and coca and women's chilies, at least as far as moral self-portrayals were concerned.

Another important contrast in talk about men's and women's cultigens was that the latter were not assumed to constitute the bodily basis for lineage, clan, or language group differences. That is, unlike their tobacco, which men of a particular lineage would claim was uniquely their own, determinant of the kinds of persons they were as members of that patriline, and different from the tobacco of other lineages, manioc and other cultigens of women were not tied to particular patrilines. On the contrary, women imported and exported them to and from patrilineal settlements as they married in or moved out. They were, thus, likely to have in their gardens manioc from seeds acquired from their mothers-in-law, mothers, sisters-in-law, and others.[1] Manioc was therefore a substance more or less shared by real people in general.

## The Substances of Men

### *Tobacco*

The most salient ritual substance for People of the Centre, in so far as it was the one they spoke about the most in accounting for moral matters, was tobacco. Men, women, and sometimes children consumed the latter in the form of paste, known as *duuta* in Muinane and *yerakɨ* in Uitoto, mixed with salt extracted from plants. It was a strong substance with a potential for very noticeable physiological impact. I always licked it carefully, but still managed to make myself mildly dizzy with it every once in a while. Consumed in small amounts – the equivalent of a small pinch of the sticky stuff every ten to fifteen minutes or so – it was supposed to help people stay awake; in my case, I never knew whether it was the tobacco or the mambe helping me do that. In slightly larger quantities, tobacco paste could make a person dizzy to the point of toppling over or passing out, vomiting, and reportedly, as David loved to rehearse, even defecating upon themselves. People of the Centre called this *emborracharse*, the same term in Spanish for getting drunk.

Their use of it as a symbol, more often than not, was part of a number of social organizational and ritual practices and institutions that tended to reproduce a view of existence that attributed greater capabilities, relative importance, and authority, to men than to women (pace Overing 1986; Belaunde 1992; Echeverri, personal communication). Perhaps most importantly in this regard, tobacco, the quintessential constitutive substance of humanity, was transmitted via male lines only. As discussed previously, it was understood that what made people kin was first and foremost that they were made of and regularly consumed 'the same tobacco juice.' 'Tobacco juice,' I should note, was also the term for semen. People of the Centre also tended to attribute to tobacco virtues they particularly valued in men.

Despite the undisputed patrilineal nature of the transmission of tobacco, there were differences between clans and language groups concerning the gender of tobacco itself: for some, the sweat-*cum*-seminal substance of the Grandfather of Tobacco was the origin of the Land of the Centre, of rivers, and eventually, of people. For others, the tobacco deity was the Mother upon whose shoulder the creator god created the land and placed it. In the myths of at least one Muinane clan – the People of the Cumare Palm – the creator deity made the first man out of tobacco paste and other substances, and brought him to life by blowing tobacco breath into him. These differences between clans and language groups among People of the Centre required them to be diplomatic in their conversations with each other on cosmological matters, but did not seem to entail noticeable differences in their understandings of the constitution of bodies, their relation to morality, or the relations between gender and kinship.

Many of their protocols for the preparation, distribution, and consumption of tobacco were similar among the different clans and language groups of People of the Centre and reflected its character as a life-giving substance and vehicle for knowledge. The most common form of tobacco sharing was the interchange of tobacco paste containers which took place whenever men wished to greet each other with some formality or sit together to speak in a coca circle. Muinane men referred to these tobacco containers as *jɨ́ɨbogo nejéyɨ* (apprising cumare nut) or *nejéyɨ*. In the past, they used to be made out of a *nejéyɨ*, a cumare palm seed, which they hollowed out into teardrop-shaped containers, about ten centimetres from top to bottom and with three small holes for access to the paste within, with a thin twig or carved monkey-hand bone. The term 'apprising' (*jɨ́ɨbogo*) was linked to the tobacco paste in the container because it was supposed to provide the person who consumed it with proper thoughts/emotions and the capacity to learn, remember, and discern and to counsel and apprise him or her concerning dangers. People furthermore said that tobacco awakened the consumer to full vigilant awareness, making his – or more rarely her – body sensitive to the presence of threatening evil through tingling sensations in the skin and back, or through his toes, which felt the earth much like the tobacco plant's roots did. Depending on the expertise and knowledge of the consumer, the tobacco also provided a privileged sight, especially in the coca circle: the person could see evil substances or objects in people's bodies, hidden animals and past and future events, among other normally invisible things.[2] In the 1990s, when I carried out most of my fieldwork, many men had small plastic flasks for their paste, but Muinane men still called them '*nejéyɨ*.'

Men also provided tobacco for others when they 'invited' each other to their dance rituals by sending palmleaf-wrapped dollops of tobacco paste and prepared bowls of diluted tobacco paste to keep in the coca circles for people to dip their fingers into and lick during the rituals.[3]

People of the Centre's talk about tobacco reflected their understanding of and interest in predatory capabilities. Whatever the differences between clans, mambeadores' narratives converged in their emphasis on the appearance of fragility and the need for care of the tobacco plant, but also on its invulnerability and capacity to kill. The practices and discourses concerning nearly every stage of the cultivation, preparation, and consumption of tobacco alluded to the fact that tobacco preyed upon animals and other inhuman beings, or escaped their predations. The capabilities that people purportedly gained from the use of tobacco corresponded to this emphasis: they allegedly became capable, despite their own initial fragility, of dealing effectively and in an esoterically violent fashion with anything that would cause them harm. My perception was that men's depictions of tobacco as a clairvoyant, efficaciously violent, scolding agent revealed their admiration for these qualities and their aspiration to feature them.

The virtuous features that people stressed involved such things as becoming invisible to the enemy, much as the tobaccos' tiny black seeds were invisible once they were spread out upon the dark ashes of a recently burnt field. Speeches of apprising, I heard, spoke of the how the growing tobacco plant managed not to be killed by animals that insisted upon attacking it, but instead itself somehow killed ever larger and more powerful beasts and ate them. Emanuel said that for this reason, tobacco could kill and consume any creature without being harmed. Tobacco was washed and boiled, all the pollutants upon it removed, but yet it itself only became stronger and purer. Once cooked, the thick paste was ready to be mixed with vegetable salt. The latter was extracted from certain palms and plants in a process People of the Centre portrayed as the predatory transformation of itchy, thorny, slimy, poisonous, ill-willed plants and their animal inhabitants into a tasty, life-giving substance, by means of fire and water. These protocols and activities were all available as images for mambeadores to use in speeches in which they identified themselves with tobacco and, thus, gained its admirable features.

My coca circle interlocutors reiterated to me that throughout the process of cultivating the tobacco and preparing it for consumption, the mambeador who owned it was obliged to care for it and ensure its proper character. This involved fertilizing it, in some cases replanting it, but also using speeches to nourish, protect, and shape it. Emanuel explained to me that proper tobacco had to be cared for through speeches in which the mambeador raising it listed the names of the kind of tobacco it should be: tobacco of life of the Centre, cool tobacco, tobacco of apprising, tobacco of enlightenment, tobacco of wakefulness, tobacco of dazzling,[4] tobacco of heart-making, tobacco of eye-making, tobacco of walking, tobacco of seeing, tobacco of searching, tobacco of illumination, tobacco of speech-making, tobacco of satiety. Emanuel's claim was that thus named in effective speeches, the tobacco became a life-giving substance that cooled people and provided them with moral, sociable discernment and predatory capabilities. It thereby enabled them to produce an abundance of foodstuffs and ritual substances. The tobacco made people alert, vigilant and esoterically clear-sighted, so that evil beings would not be able to creep up on them unawares and make them misbehave or become ill; it apprised people of the speeches necessary to deal with those agents, and refashioned their eyes and hearts so that they would be strong and perspicacious in their dealings with evil. The tobacco also made people blindingly brilliant to the eyes of ill-willed animals and, furthermore, hunted the latter and other evil beings down when deployed in healings, dance rituals, and generally in instrumental speeches.

The mambeadores' speeches to raise tobacco also required rejecting undesirable 'tobaccos,' some of which were garden weeds, but many of which were simply corrupt but perceptually indistinguishable versions of the tobacco plant or paste itself – a reiteration of the focused interest of People of the Centre in the possibility of impostorship and deceptive appearances. These tobaccos included, among others, tobacco of confusion (or of mistakes, or of misguidance), tobacco of itchiness,[5] tobacco of madness, tobacco of corruption or of obsession, tobacco of intoxicated confusion, tobacco of animals, meat-eating hunting tobacco, tobacco of sorcery, tobacco of war, tobacco of opacity, tobacco of lies, tobacco of fire, tobacco of not seeing, tobacco of fever and diarrhoea, and tobacco of animal sorcery. Some of the tobaccos rejected related negatively to awareness and knowledge, much as the true tobacco related to them positively. Thus, they produced confusion, sightlessness,[6] madness, obsession/corruption, and itchiness or sexual fixations, all of which could make people vulnerable, deprive them of moral discernment, and keep them from proper endeavours. Others brought about dizzy intoxications that did not benefit the consumer or his or her kin, and caused people to lie, hate, and destructively attack other people with their bodies, their speeches, or, in the worst cases, with sorcery. Still other tobaccos caused people to be lazy and unwilling to fulfil their obligations. Some also caused diarrhoea, fever, and other diseases.

Several mambeadores explained to me that failure to reject any source of evil which the speeches of apprising linked to a particular problem, enabled that particular evil to slip in through the 'gap' that the invocations did not plug. In the case of tobacco, it could potentially become an evil tobacco of a kind that was not explicitly rejected. As such, it could do great damage to individuals and to groups.[7] If evil tobaccos engendered evil behaviours, the converse was also true: an evil behaviour could in some cases damage proper tobacco, transforming it into one of the rejected tobaccos. The availability of this panoply of possible causes of misbehaviour or misfortune offered considerable leeway for different and mutually contesting evaluative accounts of particular persons or instances of action.

Despite its death-dealing predatory capabilities, tobacco was cool and ideally only became manifest as ferociousness when dealing with evil. According to the mambeadores, the thoughts that tobacco generated were mostly peaceful and serene; they made people feel love and compassion for kin, and the willingness to support and care for them. In part this was because kin were consubstantial. Pablo explained to me on one occasion that he and the members of his clan had been bred and raised by elders who used tobacco paste made from the clan's supposedly single strain of tobacco plants, in the numerous processes and rituals involved in making, rearing, and protecting children. 'They [the members of one's patriline and clan] are one's own body . . . they are made with the same tobacco with which one is made,' he told me. To care for one's clanspeople, he said, was therefore to care for one's own body.

The consubstantiality of kin and co-residents was tied to individual and communal tranquillity, one of the purposes and manifestations of a proper lifestyle. Because substances were linked to thoughts, this consubstantiality entailed, ideally, that kinspeople all 'had the same thoughts' and could collaborate without contradictions or contestations.[8] References to the threats of evil or even merely foreign substances indicated that 'speaking with other tobaccos' led to dissent, contestation, and other tribulations which were detrimental to a tranquil lifestyle. This was also true within the individual, and not only between individuals. I heard men and women among People of the Centre describe as extremely undesirable situations in which a person kept 'thinking one thought and another and another.' This was a description of people experiencing an anguishing confusion of simultaneous thoughts or desiring contradictory things. In their accounts, this situation could stem from the consumption of improper or alien tobacco or other substances, or the use of speeches of different clans or foreign peoples; presumably, these brought about different and contradictory motivations.

I heard individuals produce rhetoric on tobacco-based consubstantiality in hortatory discourses demanding unity among Muinane people, or among People of the Centre, and at another level, demanding a more general philanthropy (love of humankind) based on the sameness of all humans. In several meetings which brought together different language groups from the region, the elders reiterated that they all had the same hearts, made from the same tobacco. The same understanding – that tobacco constituted persons – could be used for the opposite purpose, to stress distinctions between groups of People of the Centre. I remember Pablo telling me proudly in the privacy of his coca circle that his father had been the only Muinane elder who had not lost the seeds of his clan's strain of tobacco at the time of the rubber holocaust. Because of this, Pablo claimed, he, his siblings, and his children were made with the same tobacco of his clan's ancestors, while other Muinane clans depended on whatever tobacco their clans' survivors had managed to get after the genocide.[9]

Mambeadores vacillated between making tolerant claims to the effect that each people had received a different form of tobacco with which to make its people, and more critical, segregationist and hierarchical claims to the effect that the tobaccos of other lineages, clans, or peoples were morally suspect. Some Muinane elders claimed to be very suspicious of the tobacco pastes made by their Uitoto and Andoke neighbours, for example, and Saúl claimed marihuana – the tobacco of madness – had been rejected from the Land of the Centre and given to white men. Some insisted that touching the tobacco raised and prepared by other peoples could cause one's tobacco to be resentful and to make trouble. David's lineage in particular was criticized in songs and gossip for using a tobacco other than their own; the critics' cryptic references here were to David's and his brothers' tendency to sing in their mother's Bora language rather than their father's Muinane, and to do certain things in ways other Muinane people claimed were not really Muinane.

Wagner (1985) states that anthropology addresses the differences vis-à-vis others by inventing a 'culture' for them, even though they do not think of their ways of life in terms of culture. It occurs to me, perhaps whimsically, that People of the Centre's own accounts of differences between peoples and between ways of life – their 'anthropology,' so to speak – inquire after others' tobaccos, rather than their cultures. They invent tobaccos and the bodies they constitute, for themselves and for others, as incarnations of affects and ways of life, and produce hierarchizing moral evaluations of these in terms of distinctions between tobaccos.

*Coca*

Despite tobacco's greater importance in the speeches of apprising and as a vegetal metonymy for the different patrilineal groups, mambe rather than tobacco use was the more radical marker of gender and age differences. Only adult men consumed mambe, and only they sat in the coca circle. The consumption of mambe marked men's full achievement of adulthood, in a way tobacco paste – consumed by all – did not. Mambeadores stated that women should not mambe because they were intrinsically cool and wet, and had to protect themselves against the dryness of the coca, in order to be able to bear children.

The coca plant from the leaves of which mambe is made in the Northwest Amazon is the same species used for the fabrication of cocaine for illegal trade, and, indeed, the region where I worked was an important source of cocaine base in the 1980s. Cocaine features a much more concentrated proportion of the alkaloid in the plant than mambe does and, furthermore, has a great number of other ingredients put together in a complex industrial process. Mambe is by comparison very mild stuff. I consumed the latter every day I spent in the Medio Caquetá without ever developing symptoms of addiction, habituation, or withdrawal. It was a pleasant, mild tasting green powder, excellent for regular digestion, and the strongest effect it ever had on me happened once when I consumed a lot of it throughout the day; in the evening I felt particularly energetic, creative, and smart. Again, this only happened once.

The standard procedure for the fabrication of mambe involved harvesting the coca leaves and then toasting them on a flat metal sheet or else in a clay pot, above fire, stirring them constantly for half an hour or so. Once crisp and brittle, the leaves were pounded into a fine powder in a hollow wooden cylinder. The powder was then mixed with a few handfuls of ashes of burned *Cecropia* leaves.[10] The mix of ashes and coca powder was then put into a fine cloth bag and carefully shaken so that the finer particles would sift through and drop into a container.

This finer powder was the mambe that men consumed. Whoever did the sifting would distribute mambe among the men seated in the coca circle, summoning each one to come over and receive a spoonful or two, sometimes following an age hierarchy from older to younger.

In my experience, two out of every three or four nights one or two men in each settlement would make mambe, either alone or with the help of siblings or neighbours, and all would sit in the coca circle to converse; they would talk about the events of the day, or make plans for the following day, and every so often would deploy their more formal, rhythmic instrumental speeches to heal somebody or to prepare themselves and the cosmos for some activity or event.

The whole process of coca cultivation, preparation, and consumption was rich in allusions to morality. Coca, like tobacco, was a person in itself, and so people had to deal with it carefully and respectfully so that it would, indeed, fix knowledge and discernment in mambeadores' bodies, and generate bodily well-being. The harvesting, for instance, had to be effected with what seemed to me to be a fine balance between vigour and care; the harvesters could be neither lazy nor hasty. They made much emphasis on the purifying aspect of the whole process of the mambe: ideally, only the desirable 'starch' of the coca – the pure material essence – made it into the mouth of the mambeador. The pollutants, 'bones' (veins), and other useless aspects of the material leaves were removed and destroyed or thrown away.

As with tobacco, mambeadores produced much rhetoric and numerous prescriptions concerning rules and etiquette for the production and consumption of coca. Muinane men narrated for me several speeches of apprising that concerned the origins of the processes of preparation and consumption of mambe. Different versions of these described the trials and errors of various First Time characters to pinpoint the right plant source of mambe and to develop the tools and processes for preparing it in a truly human fashion. Along the way, they tried out different 'cocas' and protocols for their preparation, and all except a couple were rejected as fit only for animals. The speeches of apprising also described the development of the tools and ingredients for mambe as the products of predatory transformations of evil beings.

In People of the Centre's portrayals, a young man's initiation into mambe was a highly ritualized affair. Many men, however, told me that they had started to mambe 'just so,' 'out of a whim,' 'behind my father's back,' rather than through a proper initiation. This was an almost standardized self-portrayal, part of a common narrative frame according to which youths were ignorant, and the speaker in his present stage more knowledgeable and discerning. Though I never witnessed a 'proper' initiation, and know that for the most part these did not take place at all, David and others spoke of them in the present tense, in terms that stressed the moral requisites and entailments of mambe use. These idealized events in theory took place when a father noticed that his son was strong and judicious enough to take on the responsibilities of being a mambeador. After some months of preparation during which the youth would ready his own garden and learned to fashion baskets, sieves, and other tools women needed for their own tasks, his father would sit him in the coca circle, give him his first spoonful of coca, and then give him what my interlocutors called 'the coca circle course' (*el curso de mambeadero*, in Spanish). It began with the warning that mambe was jealous and demanding; the youth who *mambed* would have to fell the forest and work hard to produce substances, and he would have to sit in the coca circle for long hours every night protecting his people, and this would keep him from resting and lying with his wife. This was not for weak, lazy, or wanton men!

Over the next few days, weeks, or months, the father would teach the son the counsels, prescriptions, protocols, and speeches of apprising pertaining to the origins of tobacco and mambe, and to the origins of the initiate's own lineage and clan. The course was geared towards the youth's acquisition of a wife and to their procreation, so he was supposed to learn, as well, the speeches of apprising and incantations necessary for healing and protecting his future wife from the particular diseases that threatened women and, also, those that told the origins of the diseases that affected children.

My interlocutors stressed greatly that the initiation into mambe was a dangerous time for the youth. He had to control carefully his endeavours, bodily position, movements, thoughts, and speech, for whether these were appropriate or not, they would become fixed in his body. Evil beings, aware that the youth was in the process of becoming a capable producer, a mambeador, and a killer of evil agents, would try to distract the youth with sensations or thoughts/emotions of anger, envy, sexual desire, heat, or itchiness; their purpose was to induce him to misbehave and, thereby, to keep him from becoming a knowledgeable, well-set person.

Several mambeadores independently told me speeches of apprising and other stories that they said were supposed to apprise youths of behaviours they had to avoid during their initiation. As with the speeches about tobacco, those about coca described spurious versions of it that brought about immoral subjective states; individuals also cited these stories to frame virtuous and flawed behaviours. One important speech of apprising Muinane mambeadores told concerned the Anaconda of Food (*Máchúta búha*), sometimes presented as a sage, sometimes as a powerful and dangerous being who, nonetheless, could not live properly. Episodes of this speech, often narrated piecemeal, described how different kinds of forest beings – still shaped like humans during First Time – would come to the Anaconda's home. Prior to each visitor's arrival, the Anaconda would suffer some discomfort or would misbehave in a different fashion. The visitor would then arrive, and the Anaconda would know that at that point that his suffering and misbehaviours had been generated by the visitor's mambe. He would then perform a sleight of hand in order not to mambe what the visitor offered, but rather to make the visitor mambe him or herself. The visitor would then suffer and misbehave in his or her unique fashion. The Anaconda would then scold it and banish it, and state that the beast's coca would forever be flawed and generative of the thoughts/emotions and ways of life of the beast in question. Many episodes in this speech focused on the protocol of the mambe, and yet others on the diets and behavioural restrictions which different animals violated and which explained their undesirable final anatomical and behavioural characteristics. The animals became set with their flaws and evils. Thus the small anteater (*Tamandua tetradactyla*) would forever mambe coca of sleepiness, which it would also deploy against people to make them lazy and slow; the coati (*Nasua nasua*) would forever mambe coca of jealousy and anger; and the large anteater (*Myrmecophaga tridactyla*) would always be vulnerable to great rage generated by its mambe. And so it was with other kinds of beings, whose ways were characterized by the desire to attack others, laziness, sleepiness, bad temper, adulterous or incestuous or obsessive sexual desire, jealousy, and so on, but also diarrhoea, bloated stomach, and other bodily tribulations, which they sometimes succeeded in transmitting to people.

This story was supposed to be a detailed barrage of counsels, meant to keep the young man's body disciplined, so that it would set with the correct posture, habits, and thoughts/emotions.

*A Moral Exemplar*

People of the Centre very frequently brought up the image of the knowledgeable mambeador, seated in an unwavering posture, his cheeks tightly packed with coca, 'rooted' in his place, attending single-mindedly to moral, esoteric matters in the coca circle and effectively defending himself and his people from evil.[11]

This image, which cohered and often coincided with talk about patrilineal corporativity and consubstantiality and virilocal postmarital residence, was for them one of the most seductive ideals of masculine personhood. In talking about sitting firmly, several mambeadores brought into account a connection between a mambeador's life process and the tobacco plant's. Both started life as vulnerable beings: the tender young tobacco plant that first sprouted from the ground was still fragile and loose, and any breeze could uproot it; similarly, a boy or recently initiated youth could easily be swayed from the 'path' of proper development and become flitting, undisciplined, weak, and inconstant. With time and proper care, however, both the mambeador and the tobacco matured. Mature tobacco had deep, strong roots; no wind could uproot it.

The Nonuya man who best explained this to me extolled a slightly different but equally ideal image of a mature mambeador who had a tobacco 'tree' rooted in his abdomen; it was this that kept him firmly rooted at the moral centre of his world, the coca circle. Such a man featured a keen awareness of propriety and impropriety, and had the strength, the control, and the presence of mind to reject all temptation to misbehave and violate the prescriptions of his forefathers. He recognized which knowledge belonged to him and his people, and which belonged to others. Unlike a flitting youth, the 'wind' of white men's or other people's knowledge did not unseat him or seduce him into forgetting his own. (See figure 4.1.)

That men and women tended to find the highly aesthetic picture of a man sitting firmly in a coca circle to be an ideal of agency seemed to me to be evident as well in their use of the term 'to sit' as a common metonym to refer to a person's – a man's, but also sometimes a woman's – judicious reaction to important challenges. Numerous times I witnessed speakers producing a certain gesture to accompany this metonymic reference: they would half-sit in an imaginary seat as if with elbows solidly planted on their knees or thighs, hands close to but

Figure 4.1: Segundo, a Muinane man of People of the Pineapple, begins to mix pure tobacco paste with salt in Chukikɨ (1997).

not touching their heads, and tighten their arm muscles in a quick, visible gesture: a recognizable semblance of a mambeador (see Londoño Sulkin 2006 for a more detailed discussion of this).

## The Substances of Women

### *Manioc*

Manioc was the main staple of the diet of People of the Centre and of surrounding groups. They related the production and consumption of manioc with their subjectivity, their agency and their identity, much as they did with other key substances. The proverbial 'true woman' or 'woman of satiety' was a very hard worker who therefore always had at hand an abundance of delicious food and drinks, and who would provide these to her kin and visitors with solicitude. Men and women referred to manioc and manioc products as the main evidence – the material manifestation and the main source of a woman's moral thoughts and agency. Sara spoke to me about this:

> 'A woman's strength is *manicuera* [sweet manioc drink], the chili pot, caguana [manioc starch drink], manioc bread, and peanuts. If visitors arrive and one does not have these things, one is weak. What will one offer to the people? If one does not have these things, people may say, 'The people from that maloca do not greet anybody, and do not offer even water! How is it that a maloca woman can do thus?'[12] One has to offer whatever one has. My grandfather told me that when a person arrived angered and hot at the maloca, they used to give him manicuera, and that sweetened his heart. When a woman offered people manicuera, they would say 'This is a true woman . . . she makes our hearts cool.'

Sara thus effectively highlighted the centrality of these substances as material evidence of women's morality. The other side of the coin was the frequent gossip about this or that lazy, stingy, inhospitable woman who would not attend properly to visitors, or who would hide chili pots, game, or fish upon hearing visitors docking at the port, in order not to have to share.

Though the processes of cultivation and preparation of manioc were mostly the responsibility of women, men also contributed with what Pablo called 'the speech of the manioc plant.' In his performance of it, Pablo started (and ended) by claiming that this speech and the speech of tobacco were one and the same speech – they were powerful, and were all directed towards the multiplication of humanity. His speech of apprising told of several gigantic evil manioc plants of the First Time, the distant mythical past in which evils were too great for humankind to deal with. These enormous plants bore all kinds of bitter, irremediably poisonous, evil maniocs and other fruits of animals, and caused hunger, war, madness, and other deadly tribulations to the people who lived at the time. These 'manioc trees' were finally vanquished by heroes bearing metal axes, and humankind had the chance of receiving the proper, harmless, and nourishing stuff from the mother of satiety. Pablo ended his liturgy with an invocation that noted that the false maniocs had been rejected and destroyed and that the manioc he required was the true manioc, the proper food of real people to which no other being should have access.[13] He led me to understand afterwards that these speeches would ensure a smooth-running material process: an easy, fruitful harvesting day in which nobody would get injured, as well as manioc that would be easy to grate and would yield much starch.

As in their talk about many other rituals, People of the Centre reiterated that the speech of manioc plant also ensured a community's good life. By rejecting or transforming false maniocs in the form of actual tubers, it did the same with the substances of the emotions of people.

Much like People of the Centre rhetorically linked men's good thoughts/emotions to their tobacco and coca plots, so too did they link women's thoughts and health to their manioc plantations. According to the counsels, they had to keep their manioc from being smothered by weeds and, on occasion, fertilize the plants with the ashes of burnt weeds. Furthermore, they had to cut and replant their manioc regularly to keep it fresh and young, for its aging and thickening would make its owner old and pain-ridden. Manioc rarely got old – a key symbolic image – simply because whenever it started to show its age, people would cut it up into sections (cuttings which People of the Centre referred to as *semillas*, 'seeds') and then replant these. Out of the old 'seed,' a strong, healthy new plant would grow. Manioc was, thus, eternally being healed and rejuvenated, and with it the woman who owned it would be healed and rejuvenated.[14]

People of the Centre treated women's gardening activities as both requiring and creating properly formed bodies. These were produced by means of dietary practices of the parents and of the child, of watering and other rituals, and of girls' own bodily care and discipline during adolescence. For instance, a counsel warned each girl to work assiduously in the garden, without sitting to rest on tree trunks, for the latter were the sun's penis; should she sit on it often during their malleable first days of work, she would become and forever remain wanton and lazy. The terrible consequence of this that the counsel warned against was that no man would take her as his wife, or if such a man did take her, his disgusted parents would soon return her to her own parents.

A woman with her husband and children sometimes sufficed for planting manioc, but several times I contributed to work parties summoned to help a woman plant a new garden; in the latter cases, people contributed some seeds from their own gardens. The women who owned the gardens in each case gave general instructions to the others concerning where they were to plant the seeds. They provided food and drink for the workers, and their husbands provided tobacco paste and mambe. People expressed much enjoyment in such events.

Manioc harvesting was also strenuous work, and women did most of it. Some of the tubers were deeply rooted and pulling them out of the ground required a strong back indeed. Usually the harvest occupied women for only a couple of hours, a few times a week. The tubers were packed carefully into the baskets so that they would be comfortable to carry. It was concerning the process of packing these baskets that I heard women refer to manioc tubers as their children. They claimed that even the small, apparently worthless tubers should be brought home for processing, for otherwise these would remain behind crying and would keep their siblings' starch for themselves. One woman stated that to leave these little tubers behind was to abandon one's children, and what kind of woman would do that?

The preparation of manioc products took up much of women's time. Most of the many variants of manioc used by People of the Centre were poisonous and so had to be processed carefully to avoid intoxication and even death. The emphasis of the rhetoric, however, was more on its final purity, nourishing harmlessness, and life-giving attributes. The resulting foodstuffs were deemed to be able to quench false fires such as fevers, anger, jealousy, and so on.

The methods of preparation were very similar among the People of the Centre and other groups beyond. One way in which they prepared the manioc was by fermenting the tubers in a pond or barrel, peeling them and beating them into a mash in a trough, and then compressing the mash by wrapping a long, flat band of interwoven bark strips (called *gádámehu*, in Muinane, and *tipití* or *matafrío* in local Spanish) around it and then hanging and twisting the band in such a fashion that it wrung out the rest of the poisonous liquids. The almost dry dough was then pounded into a fine powder in a wooden trough, after which it was ready to be placed on a manioc bread plate and cooked into the form of what they called *casabe seco* or *casabe uitoto* (dry manioc bread or Uitoto manioc bread) in Spanish, or else to be toasted as *farinha*, a granulose manioc flour. The method of manioc processing that Pablo, Lázaro, and Elena considered to be properly Muinane involved first peeling the fresh manioc and grating it on wood and metal graters fabricated by the men. The wet mash was then processed to separate the starch from the pulp, by means of the *nitiiba*, a concave disc (of about seventy centimetres to one metre in diameter) woven out of flat strips of the bark of certain plants. The grated mash was placed on it, water was poured over it, and with vigorous movements the women mixed water and mash. The finer starch, dissolved in the water, sifted through the weave and into a container. The women then waited till the starch settled at the bottom, and poured out the poisonous water to be discarded or used in other preparations. The pulp was disposed of, usually, or else small amounts of it were mixed with starch and used in manioc bread preparation.

Muinane men seemed to attribute particularly strong efficacy to the image of the precipitation and desiccation of the very pure starch. This image was their model for the process of generation of a child in its mother's womb, but they also understood their deployment of this image as being generative. As determined by the speech, the father's semen precipitated and dried – like manioc starch did – in the wholesome warmth of the maternal 'cup of life' (imagined as a small drinking gourd inside the womb), until finally it took the shape of a child.[15]

An important manioc concoction was the caguana, the manioc starch drink, which was prepared by mixing manioc starch with very hot water and beating it. The resulting drink was thick and white, and on several occasions mambeadores quietly called to my attention its visual similarity to semen and that, like semen, it was a very pure, invigorating, fertility-creating substance. Several men and women represented their dance rituals to me as having the specific goal of getting everybody to drink masses of caguana, which would make its drinkers healthy and fertile. Men and women stated that the wife of a maloca owner, the true woman of painful speech or woman of satiety, never lacked chili broth, manioc bread, and especially, caguana with which to feed and refresh her people and any visitors.

Manioc bread, whether made out of pure starch or fermented dough, was the other essential manioc preparation. It was usually a thin, flat, round loaf of about fifty centimetres in diameter, cooked on a ceramic plate above the fire. It was the staple of the daily diet of People of the Centre and the quintessential food of real people, the 'real food' that any true woman was always supposed to keep available to feed her family and guests.

Manioc bread's humanity-defining nature was reflected in a speech of apprising David told me, in which evil beings attempted to feed a human carcass to other humans, making it appear to the eyes of the latter like an agouti carcass. One woman distrusted the meat bringers, and instructed her children to wash the meat in the river and to inspect the contents of its guts. The children found pieces of manioc bread in the intestines and, in that manner, discovered it was actually the carcass of a real person, and the visiting hunters were actually predatory ants – a kind of 'jaguar.' The great danger there concerned perspective: again, as in much of Amazonia, the kind of being one was, was determined in part by what one ate. Eating the manioc bread fellow members of the human species ate made one human like them, as did eating an agouti. However, being tricked into eating a fellow real person – even one disguised as an agouti – could make one an inhuman predator.

Yet another manioc preparation was the very sweet drink called 'manicuera' in Spanish, made out of a particular variety of manioc with the same name. Manicuera, more than other substances, constituted women and cooled and sweetened the hearts of men and children, which could be heated and made angry by other substances and by the sun. Lázaro explained manicuera's healing properties in part by reference to cool water and its impenetrability to disease-bearing substances and beings: 'The manicuera is entirely water . . . how then can disease enter into it?' He stressed that people should always be cool inside, like the manicuera, even in hot milieus. According to the mambeadores, the cool speech of manicuera constituted a pleasurable sense of calm and well-being, and when expressed, brought the addressee tranquillity and relief from anger and haste. The person imbued with manicuera felt no harried haste, but no laziness either. Anger could not touch him or her and neither could itchiness and confusion.

### *Chilies*

That women's inclination and obligation were ideally mostly oriented to nourish their kin did not imply that they did not participate in protecting them; nor did their sweet, wet bodily composition necessarily mean they or their substances could not 'hit hard.' Their chilies were an example of a substance of women that could cause ill-intending beings serious harm and pain.

People of the Centre grew a variety of kinds of chili, and used these in many ways. They were an essential component of the ubiquitous chili pots, broths made from meat or fish boiled in manioc juice or water with chilies; they were also cooked into chili paste, or smoked, or toasted and powdered. They were eaten in all of these forms, or added fresh to any broth. In most meals, the people sat around the chili pot, broke off pieces of manioc bread, and dipped it into the broth. If there was plenty of fish or meat in the broth, they would take some out; otherwise not.

Men and women valued women's ability to prepare a variety of delicious chili pots, manioc breads, and other foods and were critical of those who lacked it. Before leaving Lázaro's and Elena's house to move in with Pedro and Sara, Elena and her children humorously prognosticated that I would have a terrible time over there, for I was used to the delicious, changing fare at their place, but would suffer with Sara, whose cooking was unvarying and boring. Fortunately, this did not turn out to be the case.

Men and women would also on occasion light dried chilies to generate smoke to be smelled, and men would wrap them in tobacco leaves and smoke them as cigars; the smoke purportedly terrified and tormented evil beings into abandoning the bodies of those who subjected themselves or others to chili smoke.

Chilies, Pedro told me, belonged to women. He explained that they were hot because of the sun that shone upon them and entered them. Like chilies, women got red-faced working in the garden under the sun, and they too got hot and therefore sometimes scolded. Nevertheless, he said, women were counselled to consign the heat and anger they received from the sun into their chilies, and not direct it against their husbands and children. He explained that women used chilies and fire to transform any filth and sources of disease that remained in meat, fish, and other foods they or the men brought home. He claimed that the chili pot 'ate' the left-over, unpleasant blood-taste of the game or fish and, along with the fire, it transformed the 'bite' or 'pain' of different kinds of ants and edible insects added to the broth into a pleasant, spicy taste.

Women's chili pot had a predatory and salutary aspect, as well as a nourishing one. Sara stated that when people ate a lot of chilies, their bodies became spicy hot; diseases would approach, find such bodies painfully inhospitable, and wouldn't enter them. She then rectified: 'The *heart* must be cool, but the body spicy hot. People in the past did not have any drugs, but still they did not often become sick. Perhaps it was the chilies.'

Chilies' link to thoughts/emotions was made evident in dance rituals. Pedro explained this to me:

> Chilies are war. They cool people, but heat up and kill animals. When there is a large harvest of chilies, women make *kíígai* [a strong chili broth

> reduced to a paste by means of a long cooking process; it is known in local Spanish as *tucupí* and in Uitoto as *yomaki*]. Then they add a basketful more of chilies, and put meat, *kííta* ants, and grubs of the kind that cause stomach ache into it. The *kíígai* eats all this, transforming the diseases and stings. Then it is called '*dúúmoba*' [meat eater]. The woman's anger becomes extinguished, because it is all instilled in the *kíígai*. Then when there is a dance, the maloca's leader says, 'Women! *Now* show your anger!' And they fight with all comers, with chilies. That is why the dance is called 'war.'

I never witnessed this 'war,' but according to Pedro, women used to brush very strong chili paste on the mouths of guests, in particular of those who sang critical songs addressed to them. Some such songs – a standard and necessary element of most dance rituals – openly accused the maloca's women of being angry, stingy, inhospitable, lazy, or ugly. Women could retaliate with chili paste, showing that they were productive and therefore moral individuals. Such 'war' benefited both them and their critics. They were freed of the weight and threat of *hidden* and therefore very harmful criticism, and the singers were made healthy by the chili paste.

Sara told me that when a woman's *kíígai* was hot, others said 'This woman is angry in truth! She is [spicy] hot, like her chili pot!' On the other hand, if her chili pot or *kíígai* were not hot, people scorned any anger she showed, saying 'How can you claim to be angry, when you do not have hot chilies?' or 'Your anger is empty ... you have not "shown" yet!' That is, she had not proven with literally substantial evidence that she had proper thoughts/emotions. This was a narrative people could use to make the case that a woman's hot chilies showed her anger to be based on true substances or moral thoughts/emotions, and it was, therefore, defensible as a rightful anger, or one that resulted from moral activities such as working hard under the hot sun. On the other hand, the narrative was also widely available for use in pointing out the purported lack of moral substance of a woman who was bad tempered, but whose chilies proved to be few or mild. Others could point out her scolding or her incensed gossip as the empty, fruitless speech of a lazy woman who had not worked as much as she should have.

As with tobacco, coca, and manioc, People of the Centre also used images of true and spurious versions of chilies in their evaluative accounts of subjectivities and actions. Pedro mentioned in particular the 'chili of the coati,' which were real plants that produced chilies of different sizes and colours. Some were large, some small, some red, some purple, some green. He added that the speech of this chili was rejected because it was as inconsistent as the fruits' appearance: at times it was cool, at times hot, sometimes good, sometimes bad. Referring to what I would call equanimity and consistency, he noted that proper speech that stemmed from true substances was always 'the same,' much as true chilies were always bright red and of regular shape and size.

*Cool Herbs*

Another kind of substance that was the responsibility of women were the so-called 'cool herbs.' Lázaro and Elena both affirmed these belonged to women, and it was their responsibility to plant them and care for them. However, I only witnessed men making invocations upon them to make healing concoctions. These herbs – known as *sɨ́ɨ́kuje, kátɨho, gañíírraba, gaakába, nɨɨbɨmɨ*, and *dúúmoho* in Muinane[16] – were paradigmatic of all that was cool, gentle, sweet, and serene. Mambeadores highlighted that they were wet, like the manicuera, and like the manicuera, the sun could burn hot upon them but still they remained cool and sweet inside. They were 'mothers' or 'grandmothers.' Two of the cool herbs were understood to be male: *kárefiku* and *bakúhono*. These herbs spoke mainly within women, generating the thoughts/emotions that made them nourish and cool their husbands, fathers, fathers- and mothers-in-law, and children.

People of the Centre used the cool herbs in different ways. *Kátɨho* was used to paint bodies or parts of bodies black, while most of the others were used as ingredients of infusions to be drunk or to be used in bathing. Among the prescriptions of the speech of advice, one counsel instructed women to bathe their bodies in *sɨ́ɨ́kuje* after a day of work under the hot sun, to cool their bodies down. Another counsel instructed them to bathe themselves with 'the grandmothers' so that anger would not affect them too much. They were also to bathe their little children with these herbs before laying them to sleep in their hammocks, to soothe them and ensure that they slept well. The cool herbs, in general, could be used to counteract the aromatic or pungent odours of certain forest plants, as well as the sickening stench of certain rotten animal carcasses. Ariel informed me that unwittingly smelling any such pathogenic odours could cause people headaches, sore throats, dizziness, or mad behaviours; the sweet aroma of the cool herbs, crushed in the hand or seeped in water and then breathed in, removed these pains and troubles. *Kárefiku*, for one, and perhaps a few of the others, could also be dried and smoked.

Emanuel once told me a speech of apprising that seems to me to have spoken eloquently about People of the Centre's understandings of what might be called character, and about the virtues of women's substances. The myth in question concerned the *gáákába*, a herb that people said watched over the manioc in the garden, making stamping sounds to scare off the agoutis that pillaged the manioc tubers and frightening passers-by.[17] The following is my summary of it:

> There was once a child whom the animals were trying to sicken and corrupt. They would give him sticks and have him hit them with it; they would teach it to bite them and pinch them. They also wrapped him in their own itchy carrier cloths. The child became very troublesome. He cried constantly and hit others with his stick. His mother tried to make him sleep, to no avail. One of his grandmothers, the cool herb *Gaakába Mógai* (woman of *Gáákába*) perceived this and came to help. She told the mother, 'Your whole body is like thorns and itchy fuzz to him … I will paint you.' The *Gaakába Mógai* made an invocation upon some *kátiho* paint and painted the child's mother with it, healing her. When the child wanted to play with his stick, the grandmother took it from him and placed it in the rafters of the maloca above the door. She told him, 'I will take care of it for you until you are a grown man.' [At this point in the narration Emanuel emphasized that one should never give children sticks to play with, because they quickly learn to hit and spear people with them]. She then cooled the child down and sweetened his heart by giving him a gourdful of manicuera. She also got rid of the itchy carrier cloth in which the animals had wrapped him, by covering him with *kátiho* and anthill cotton. The child and the mother then truly rested.

This speech treated the child's misbehaviours as the product of evil being's own purposeful elicitation of such misbehaviours. These then became set in the child's body. His bad temper and violence were also tied to sheer bodily discomfort, exacerbated by a mother that felt to him anything but motherly and comforting. Through the action of the cool herbs and manicuera, the child's heart was cooled and his violent desires and physical discomfort made to disappear.

## Negotiating Morality in Terms of Substances

I witnessed an interesting negotiation of morality in terms of substances while doing my first stint of fieldwork at a Muinane community in 1993. Lilith, who must have been around forty years old at the time, announced that she was convoking a drinking bout. She had prepared a large vat of starchy plantain drink, and people would pair off and give each other gourdful after gourdful of the stuff in a contest to see who could drink the most. As we headed towards the maloca to participate in the event, David, the leader of that community, explained to me that several weeks earlier he had thrown at Lilith's doorstep a wild pig he had shot, saying to her, 'There's your gossip.' I inquired into the affair and gathered that Lilith had been talking critically about another woman in the community, and this had generated some tribulations. David's gesture of giving her the pig with the claim that the carcass was her gossip was a complex challenge and insult, as well as a purported favour. It basically framed her talk as destructive gossip generated by the antisocial substance of a wild pig inside her and her as susceptible to animalistic thoughts/emotions. David appeared as an esoterically efficacious killer who had transformed and removed the substances inside her and violently reconsigned them into the animal.

By killing the pig and giving it to her, David had purportedly healed Lilith of her antisocial, ultimately inhuman, gossiping ways. She was, thus, obligated to reciprocate with the product of her own hard work. By working hard and successfully on a nourishing endeavour, and producing a tangible, consumable substance, she showed she had proper corporeal substance – after all, it made itself manifest in her productivity – and, therefore, her talk was not empty bluster or animalistic sabotaging of community life.

As a newcomer to the field – and one painfully bloated after numerous gourdfuls – I did not take care at the time to follow up on the interactions between Lilith and David, or to attend carefully to the moral implications people probably drew from details of what happened. From participation in other more or less similar events in which the moral quality of personal substances were questioned and defended, I gather Lilith could have said that she had plantains, a nourishing substance, and those were in themselves proof of her hard work and morality. There had also been room for her to turn tables on David; should he have found himself full before she did and unable to swallow any more of the drink she proffered, she could well have scornfully told him not to challenge a real woman, when he himself could not deal with her response.

Amy McLachlan, addressing the sensible sweetness of women's substances as a central symbolic form for People of the Centre, writes poetically that in the resguardo (indigenous reserve) in Leticia where she worked,

> entanglements with life ... were not always pleasurable and 'sweet'. There, especially, relations between non-kin women are often negotiated through the idiom of taste. Provoked by rumors that her husband, Juan Jose, had been visiting a neighbor's daughter during nocturnal hunting trips, Rosa had been feuding with the girl's mother, Lucia. Yet given the delicate balance of emotions in her house, she had avoided complaining to her husband and had reacted to his friends' teasing innuendo by clenching her jaw and swallowing her pride. When Lucia and her husband, Paco, held a *minga* (work party) to clear a new *chagra*, Rosa insisted that she had too much work in her own *chagra* to spend the whole day in their service. When an exhausted Juan Jose returned late in the afternoon, carrying a plate of rice, fish and *cassave* – Rosa's portion from the *minga* – she took a resentful bite and announced: 'Hm! Ni tiene sal! y mira que el arroz está sucio,' (Hm! It doesn't even have salt! And look, the rice is dirty!) setting the plate aside in anger and disgust. The food sat uneaten until the next morning when it was sent flying to the chickens, seemingly along with Rosa's anger from the day before. (McLachlan 2010)

Men too sometimes questioned each other on the basis of their possession of substances, and several men reported to me on instances in which they had snubbed others who had spoken authoritatively but yet did so without having tobacco paste of their own production at hand.

## Substances and History

People of the Centre's way of life depended on the material availability of the forest, rivers, and gardens, and it involved practices of direct manipulation of game, cultigens, tools, and other available objects. It also involved the consumption of substances that had sensible effects upon bodies: they tasted and smelled, and they had the effects of variously sating, awakening, inebriating, and causing pain to those bodies. These material accoutrements of their lives featured centrally in their narratives and other symbolic forms. Their social organization – who they lived with, who they married, and how they organized themselves to work and otherwise conduct their daily lives – was similarly a material product and condition of their form of life.

Materials are subject to myriad historical vicissitudes, making the human ways of life contingent upon these materials' chance affairs (see Manning and Meneley's 2008 discussion of this). In time, things happened to People of the Centre's gardens: they regularly became less productive and more saturated with weeds, or more unexpectedly, they flooded, were raided, or suffered drought. In a cosmos where such events were deemed meaningful signs, they impinged upon persons' understandings of themselves and their relationships with each other. People could make the case that a certain man was or was not knowledgeable or a woman more or less generous, depending on their harvests.

Greater, unexpected changes in material affordances changed life all the more with the arrival of metal axes via long-distance trade with Brazilians in the second half of the nineteenth century, as Echeverri (1998) shows. Axes enabled People of the Centre to make much larger gardens in shorter time and with less dependence on extended groups, which likely enabled men to work less to fulfil their gardening responsibilities and to produce and consume more tobacco and mambe, while women had to work more to deal with the suddenly larger plots. This may have altered gender relations, and it certainly changed the implications of social hierarchy, as they began to trade orphans and other vulnerable members of their communities for axes and other manufactured goods.

Pablo's story about having been the only Muinane-speaking clan to keep its own tobacco alive during the rubber holocaust similarly underscores the material vulnerability of symbols to contingency. For a number of years, many People of the Centre were enslaved to the point where communities could not easily keep full-fledged gardens or were forcibly transported away from their gardens. These key symbolic substances depended on people having the time, available land, and seeds to cultivate them, and lacking these material conditions, they had to do without. Fortunately for several of the Muinane clans, Pablo's father and uncle had saved plenty of tobacco seeds and had replanted, and in the years following the holocaust provided some to others. This story was a resource for Pablo and his siblings in underscoring their own virtue with claims to the effect that only they among all the Muinane clans consumed tobacco that was originally their own. This particular story was not widely picked up by People of the Centre, in general, but that substances were tied to patrilineal origins was very much a matter that People of the Centre attended to with evaluative intent.

Other economic processes also generated new associations and important distinctions for coca. In several boom-and-bust events between the 1970s and the early 2000s, a number of People of the Centre made gardens larger than they ever had before, dedicated exclusively to growing coca for cocaine. They began to define traditional mambe productive and consumptive practices by contrast with the practices required by the cocaine trade, and new ways of being suddenly became materially possible: that of the man, woman, or couple pragmatically engaged with becoming affluent and interacting with new kinds of outsiders – small mafia bosses – while daringly engaged in an endeavour they knew to be deemed criminal by some (not all) representatives of the nation-state. Several mentioned to me that they knew cocaine to be a maddening substance and the coca it came from to have been corrupted; therefore, they had kept their plantations for *mambe* and for cocaine apart. A few contrasted their own traditionalistic respect for the coca plant with other's corruption of it in the cocaine trade – so *not* being a drug trade coca grower became a marked moral alternative.

While doing fieldwork, I also met specialized fishermen in Araracuara and Puerto Santander who did not have their own gardens and who, therefore, had to buy their mambe if they wanted any. The transactions in question appeared to be a matter-of-fact sale of a commodity that people engaged in easily; however, some mambeadores in the communities commented on how that was a corruption of the coca, for the buyer was not engaged in the permanent production of this essential substance, as a mambeador should be. This was potentially harmful to the consumer and to the seller, should the coca resent this unorthodox process of acquisition. Again, this narrative was clearly available as a symbolic resource with which to explain misfortunes and judge the characters of fishermen and others who did not have gardens.

Another important material change of the twentieth century was the new availability of the narratives and practices of the various kinds of missionaries – Catholics of different orders, and Summer Institute of Linguistics (SIL) Evangelicals – who arrived among People of the Centre as of the 1930s. One day, Jonás – who had received some training to be a missionary – mentioned to me that an Evangelical Protestant missionary had once questioned him for carrying a cross, pointing out that it was idolatry to treat a piece of carved wood as a manifestation of God. Jonás told us he had agreed, but he had said that, nonetheless, the cross made him feel closer to God. He added that the same applied to tobacco and coca. He gestured towards his flasks of tobacco paste and mambe, and said that tobacco and coca were merely plants, but having the substances at hand and consuming them still made him feel closer to God.

My notes on this became, suddenly, matter for deeper consideration when I read Keane (2003 and 2010) on Protestant missionaries in Indonesia, and how worried they were about the relationship between immaterial spirituality and material manifestations; the former, to be virtuous, had to be independent of a material world of causation, and capable of judging it. The independence of a purported domain of spirits, thoughts, or ideas from that of materiality – a dualism which Jonás's missionary's question seemed to be citing – would seem to me to be necessarily at odds with People of the Centre's emphasis on the substantial sources and nature of thoughts/emotions, and with the personhood of nonhuman and inhuman kinds of beings.

Jonás was amalgamating the tobacco and Christian deities – something People of the Centre sometimes did, self-consciously – and considering that perhaps tobacco and coca were not 'really' divine or even persons at all; but was he in the process objectifying his own thoughts in a manner that did not treat these as substantial in origin and nature? Perhaps the Protestant voice that he was animating led him to question the nature of thoughts/emotions and other subjective experiences, and even of what constituted a candidate for agency. Over the years, however, Jonás more than most of my informants provided me with examples and explicit explanations of subjectivity that seemed to take for granted its own materiality or links with substances. In 1993, for instance, it was Jonás who interpreted a certain dream I'd had as a warning of impending tribulations. When I asked him who it was who was forewarning me, in this fashion, he answered with some impatience, 'What is it that you lick, then!' He was telling me that it should have been obvious to me that it was the tobacco paste generating those dreams, apprising me of matters to happen. As an aside, I will add that when Jonás left the coca circle on the occasion in which he spoke of tobacco as a mere plant, Pedro quickly noted that Jonás should not have spoken thus; such claims would upset his own coca and tobacco, and these would then cease to work for him.

Catholic missionaries had been around in greater number and for much longer than Evangelical ones, and I believe the former's more enchanted world conceptually clashed less with People of the Centre's semiotic ideology, with its attributions of personhood and intentions to animals, plants, substance, fishhooks, and much more in the world. Nonetheless, there clearly were voices in the region proselytizing a different account, generating a reframing of the consumption of tobacco and coca as 'traditional' religious practices that somehow were 'cultural' equivalents to the Catholic sacraments of eating the wafer and drinking wine. Indeed, I found that some people framed their own continued consumption of tobacco paste and coca as expressions of a virtuous commitment to tradition in the context of much noted and ostentatiously regretted loss of 'authentic culture.'

To summarize, People of the Centre treated substances as the constitutive elements of bodies, and the production of such substances and bodies by means of various transformations as a central project in human existence. Their narratives and other discursive practices concerning these matters stemmed from and shaped their understandings and practices of gendered, moral personhood. However, the very materiality of these substances and of the webs of symbols that gave them meaning entailed that they were subject to contingency and, thus, to historical change.

# 5 Virtuous Relationships and Social Organization

## Tropes of Relatedness and the Need for Others

In People of the Centre's version of the Amazonian package, real persons endowed with competence and moral acumen were the product of social processes of production of proper bodies out of key food and ritual substances. Their accounts of these processes linked social organization with virtuous bodies and affects. Ideally, these processes required proper interpersonal relationships, and took place in cool (mainly patrilineal) communities of residence that in cyclical turn were the collective achievement of real persons who were motivated by loving care, generosity, and discernment that originated in key substances. They spoke of such cool communities and of the appropriate interpersonal interactions between them in terms of figures of bodily relatedness: like bodies, made out of like substances, experienced and acted upon like thoughts/emotions; their bodies were comfortable in each other's company, they felt love and the inclination to care for each other, and their thoughts were so like each other's that there was no contestation. Nonetheless, they also recognized personal uniqueness, necessary differences between persons and between kinds of persons, and the indispensable complementarities among these. Finally, the production and maintenance of bodies and communities depended on ritual interactions between different patrilines and clans.

They deployed several key tropes that highlighted the mutual indispensability and complementarity of members of kinship or coresidential groups. One such trope I heard from David, who told me about leaders who spoke of their people as a body, likening each kinsperson to a body part according to his or her consanguineal proximity and relative importance as a contributor to the leader's community-making endeavours. Thus, when a grandchild was sick or in trouble, such a leader would claim that his fingernail was hurting. This trope highlighted, on one hand, the consubstantial unity that implied intersubjectivity or empathy and, on the other, the leader's capacity to get his community to produce for him. David himself compared the members of his community to his body, of which he needed every part in order to be well and work.

On two occasions I witnessed how different maloca owners deployed another trope that similarly stressed mutual dependence. Each one addressed his community with a discourse that likened the group to the physical structure of a maloca. David called attention to the wooden pillars, rafters, walls, and other components of the maloca. It had *all* these different parts, not just some of them. How could a maloca lack any parts? he asked rhetorically, underscoring the senselessness and undesirability of such a lack. The trope clearly expressed the sense that the community needed all its members for support, but also hinted at organizational hierarchy: David himself was like a maloca's 'heart,' or like its front pillars, and the others, depending on their gender and distance in the reckoning of kinship, were rafters, walls, roofing, and so on.

The general message which these tropes conveyed was that to deal with the threats of evil agents, to produce the abundant foodstuffs and ritual substances needed to live well, and to achieve the all-important goal of procreating effectively, people depended on mutual support among leaders and their communities, spouses, co-residents, and patrilineal groups. Men depended on food, substances, and services provided by women, and vice versa; couples provided food for other couples; and many rituals required dialogues for which men required partners from their own patrilines and from other clans. Men and women also stated that working together with others was simply more fun; women told me that several of them working together grating manioc for a dance ritual would make short shrift of this enormous task amidst much talking and joking, making an otherwise taxing and tedious job seem easy.

The normative recognition of mutuality and necessary complementarity was crystallized in the Muinane formula: *'Úro' mónótatɨhi* – We are never to say 'I alone.' Pablo and Emanuel explained that people should never claim to have achieved anything by themselves, not even those tasks they had carried out without the help of other people. Rather, they were always to claim that things had been achieved with the help of the Creator or the Grandfathers and Grandmothers of the Axe, the Summer, the cool herbs, and others, and in the case of youths, through the ritual mediation of the elders. Otherwise, they said, these beings would say, 'If that is so, let us see how well you do on your own next time!' and would abandon the proud braggart to his abilities. This emphasis on the need for others, I should note, offered a symbolic resource for a common moral self-portrayal – people underscoring their own competence or hard work by pointing out that they had indeed carried out alone some tough task for which, for the most part, the collaboration of several was expected.

My interlocutors linked the need for support to the importance of convivial virtues, such as productive competence, a stable good temper, generosity, respect for others, good humour, helpfulness, and willingness to defuse or 'cool' conflicts. David, when comparing his community to the structure of his maloca, also stressed, on that occasion, the need for the peaceful cohabitation of all involved. He demanded they look at the different parts of the maloca and note that though these elements lived in close proximity, they never bickered or came apart. He asked then – in a formulaic type of question meant to reject, with esoteric effectiveness, the scenario described – how it could be that his own people could bicker, or come apart, if they were like the parts of a maloca. This claim also served to remind listeners of the well-known moral reprehensibility of bickering among close kin.

Like David, others too made explicit their awareness that one of the threats of situations of social conflict inside a community was the dampening of the willingness of people to support each other through substances, dialogue, and physical labour. Similarly, they often insisted that bad-tempered or otherwise unpleasant people lost the good will of others. In such situations, they asked, whom can you ask for help if your child is sick, or if your tasks are too great? The speech of advice's counsels prescribed that people work with good will, evincing good humour and no irritation or bad thoughts. When possible, they were to volunteer to help others. In particular, they had to show great pleasure and willingness when they received tobacco as a summons to some large task or dance ritual. Mambeadores stated in different circumstances – informing me, counselling others, and in actual instances of receiving tobacco gifts – that neglecting to help, working grudgingly, or receiving tobacco apathetically stemmed from laziness and from a selfish lack of care for others. I heard several people individually use what must have been a standardized narrative frame, stating that another person who had been unwilling to help them or to share game, or who had done so unwillingly, would probably ask for help soon, and adding with a righteous tone that they would remind the miscreants of their unhelpfulness.

Perhaps the most emphatically commended attitude was *respeto*, 'respect.' The term in Muinane was 'not touching that which is another's', which revealed the wide scope of the value: people were not to steal from others, harm their children or other kin, or seduce their spouses. Some counsels appealed to empathy concerning this matter: in the mambeadores' idealized portrayals of the speech of advice, children were exhorted to think about what they would do if somebody stole something that belonged to them, or harmed a pet or a member of the kinship group. The proverbial father would explain to the paradigmatically male child: 'Little father, they too love their children, they too need their things, and care for them because they worked hard to produce them. If you touch these things, they will be angry and sad.'[1] They also used bodily idioms: harming one's kin was like harming one's body, and one should know that others' bodies hurt like one's own. Many other counsels, however, warned the addressee of danger rather than appealing to empathy. Elders and parents were supposed to warn of further consequences of touching the things of others: 'They may ensorcell you or harm you, and I will not be able to defend you because you touched, knowing that you should not have done so.'

People of the Centre's talk about the features of kinship relations was often couched in terms of memory, of people 'discerning' or 'remembering' who those around them were – whether they were kin, affines, visitors, or others – and how to address them. They also often made the case that the memories in question could, and indeed, should, be actively elicited. A very common narrative form – found in counsels of the speech of advice but also in other genres – described some individual suddenly saying, as if reminded, 'Oh! I *do* have a family!' upon being treated properly, as kin, by somebody else; such treatments included, for example, being addressed with a term such as 'grandfather,' or 'sister,' offered a refreshing drink by a solicitous woman, healed by an elder, or helped with the firewood by a young man. These and comparable gestures of support and care purportedly generated in those so treated attitudes and reactions corresponding to the relationships suggested by the treatment; in the examples in question, what was elicited was grandfatherly respect, love, and protectiveness, sisterly respect and care, or other kinspeople's recognition and thankfulness. To that extent, then, People of the Centre recognized a performative aspect to interpersonal relations, such that talk and other practices created the relationships they were supposed to be part of, rather than being merely products of such relationships.

## Gender Obligations, Virtues, and Complementarity

Men and women performed their gendered and moral subjectivity in talk and other practices that reproduced the footings of their relationships among themselves and with each other. The practices in question were reiterative and interpellated persons, letting them know what kinds of being they were and how to relate to others in their world, along the lines I described in the introduction and those drawn by Butler (1993). These acts established a gender binary; People of the Centre took for granted that most beings in the world – objects, cultigens, animals, meteorological phenomena, and certainly real people, came either in a male or a female version. In their understandings, the bodies of men and of women were endowed with different anatomical features and were constituted by overlapping but slightly different sets of substances that generated their gender-specific competencies and thoughts/emotions. The practices that established their division of labour expressed and reproduced these understandings and, thus, part of what it meant to be a woman or a man.

Ideally, couples were monogamous pairs constituted by a man and a woman who made and raised their children well and achieved a cool lifestyle, in a joint endeavour in which each partner depended on the other's contributions.[2] In my experience, each couple constituted a partially autonomous unit of production with two or three gardens of its own and occupied its own wooden house on stilts or, more rarely, its own corner of the patrilineal segment's maloca. Each was, for the most, part capable of producing its own sustenance with little or no help from others, although couples often helped each other out or provided food for each other.

Men's main productive activities were hunting, fishing, felling the forest to make gardens, making canoes and other work-intensive wooden artefacts,[3] collecting forest products, and helping their wives in the garden, as well as the work involved in making tobacco paste and mambe. The mambeadores portrayed many of these as endeavours that transformed some evil agent into a desirable substance – for instance, nasty forests into nourishing cultigens and diseases into meat – that would further empower men to produce stuffs and protect close ones, or that women could process in order to nourish kin or close ones. These transformative endeavours were central to People of the Centre's talk and practices that performatively reproduced their masculinity, and to their talk about what it was to be a true man (*imíyagaifi*). In my experience, these endeavours highlighted that true men possessed the knowledge, the thoughts/emotions, the discipline, the tough bodily constitution, and the substances that made them simultaneously competent producers and protectors. Men's roles as husbands, fathers, brothers, uncles, sons, grandsons, men of speech of tobacco and fathers-in-law centrally involved endeavours of protection of women, children, and youths from evil agents that threatened their bodily and intellectual/emotional well-being.[4]

On the other hand there was the true woman (*imíyagaigo*): hardworking, tough, conscientious, hospitable, nurturing, caring, and sexually faithful. In their talk, men and women treated women's responsibilities as centring on the alimentary nurturing of loved ones, mostly through the hands-on care for cultigens and children and the preparation and distribution of foodstuffs. Such nurturing was a vital contribution to a proper lifestyle, for only people fed proper foods in proper amounts had the bodies and thoughts/emotions that made them effectively sociable. Most people recognized that women's work was heavier than men's, in the sense that there were more tasks for them to carry out, and these occupied more of their time (see Griffiths 2001, 249–51). This view of women was coherent with rituals mambeadores described to me, in which they attempted to transform their womenfolk through different speeches – among others, the watering ritual invocations – into 'the true woman, the woman of satiety' and to keep them as such. A true woman's body was suffused with cool manioc juice, herbs, and water, making her resistant to fatigue, disease, and heat, and motivating her to care for others.[5]

Several men and women pointed out to me the mutual need of men and women when they spoke of abstractly conceived maloca owners as virtuous men and women living in an ideal good fashion. They described these proverbial couples as the 'parents' of their communities. Like any other couple and set of parents, a maloca owner and his wife depended on each other to fulfil their own obligations. They stressed that without a willing and hardworking wife, even a very diligent and knowledgeable man could not sustain a maloca and carry out dance rituals. But he too was obliged to enable her to do her part: he had to provide her constantly with meat, baskets, sieves, and healing concoctions.[6]

According to the prescriptions of the speech of advice, not being generally supportive of the spouse or thoughtful of their needs led to abandonment and the consequent suffering from lack of a necessary complement. Several counsels warned against behaviours that could lead to troubles with spouses: men were not to beat their wives, women were not to scold their husbands, and they were not to seek other lovers or be jealous of each other. The threat of losing a spouse was not an idle one: Lilith, for one, abandoned Jonás for his repeated beatings. As a result, Jonás had no garden, no true home, and little chance of producing food and substances for himself. He wandered between communities with his children, irking some, being pitied by others; by 2002 or 2003, he had moved to the city of Leticia.

The complementarity between the contributions of the genders to social life did not entail an understanding that they were equal, nor that men and women established thoroughly egalitarian footings in cross-gender relationships. Relationships between wives and husbands, brothers and sisters, and several others between men and women in certain categories, were in some ways hierarchical. For instance, their moral evaluations, presupposing causal links between moral personhood, cosmology, livelihood practices of substance production, and proper sociality, tended to assume implicitly or claim explicitly that men had greater moral acumen than women, and their competence was greater and more fundamental.

In their more egalitarian-sounding discourses, mambeadores stressed, with no hierarchical qualifications, that the contributions of both men and women were necessary for the achievement of a desirable lifestyle and for the propagation of kin. There was definitely a cycle involved in which mutuality and complementarity were fundamental: without women to process foodstuffs, men would quickly be bereft of the strength to produce ritual substances and carry out rituals; without men's contributions, women could not produce foodstuffs. On the other hand, however, the cycle of mutual dependency tended to appear lopsided and blown up on the male side. The mambeadores often expounded before me that it was men's substance-empowered thoughts/emotions and knowledge that ensured through ritual the continuous flow of human existence, encompassing men and women's non-ritual endeavours. Furthermore, different men and women explicitly stated that women did not have 'the capacity' – *la capacidad*, in Spanish – for speeches of the kinds required to ensure the production of foodstuffs and ritual substances and for the protection of close ones.

I should specify that People of the Centre did not found whatever hierarchical claims they did make concerning gender relations on the differential valuation of the different *foodstuffs* produced. Apparently, some Amazonian groups value differently the foodstuffs produced by men and those produced by women.[7] If there was a differential valuation in the production of each gender among People of the Centre, it lay, rather, in the opposition between foodstuffs, usually produced, but in any case prepared and distributed by women, and the ritual substances produced by men. All these substances were constitutive of real people, but in their discourses the mambeadores, and sometimes the women as well, clearly privileged the role of tobacco in the constitution of morally discerning persons and in the very relatedness of kin. Furthermore, they exalted tobacco's – and men's – effective predatory capabilities more than any other competence or virtue, male or female. In their discussions on patrilineal identity, healing rites, and dances, they often elided mentioning the theoretically indispensable use of manioc products, but they never failed to mention tobacco. And again, it was the men who produced, prepared, and distributed tobacco; it was their obligation and privilege, and one for which women 'had no capacity,' either. The 'knowledge of our own' and related practices could thus be treated as a 'soft, indirect form of violence, namely symbolic violence' (Lorrain 2001, 270) buttressing a distribution of labour and other aspects of gendered relations among People of the Centre.

People of the Centre expressed strong, if at times ambivalent, admiration for men's displays of aggression, or at least of potential for it; certainly men produced a great many moral self-portrayals that highlighted their own capacity for dealing angrily and effectively with others. Yet they also claimed that men were more competent than women at achieving coolness and peace. Women, Pedro told me, were thoroughly imbued with sweet manioc juice and were thus the mothers of coolness, but were actually less capable of subduing their anger and remembered their grievances for a long time; they, therefore, generated more interpersonal troubles than men did. Several men also noted that animals and other forest beings also made use of women's weakness to cause them to behave in ways that would generate troubles among men. Women rarely initiated diagnoses of troubles along these lines, but accepted them readily.

Even concerning childbearing, the recognized complementarity between men and women offered People of the Centre room for hierarchical claims, as well as for more egalitarian ones. On occasion, both claimed that men multiplied themselves in or through women, conveying an image of men as the more active parties interested in making new members of their patrilines and clan. They evaluated the moral features of women's biographies in terms of how their actions impinged upon unborn children and upon the actual process of giving birth, but they attributed to men's competence, more than to women's, the transformations involved in shaping the little body in a woman's womb.

Observations of People of the Centre's postulations of moral hierarchy between men and women elicit questions concerning whether there was a corresponding gender asymmetry and hierarchy in other matters. Is it appropriate to describe what happened there as a case of male control over women, exploitation of women's labour, or subordination of the interests of women to those of men?

As with moral acumen and the relative importance of the contributions of each gender to social life, there was room to push both for egalitarian practices and for more hierarchical ones. I found that there was considerable room in everyday life for personal autonomy, for concerted decision making, and for much mutual demand between spouses. People made many independent decisions about how to carry out their endeavours, but wives and husbands often decided together about issues such as whether to make a new garden or where to place it, what food to prepare or what animal to hunt on a certain occasion, and so on. They also made many mutual demands concerning gender-specific stuffs and services; often, these demands took the form of harsh critiques of the other's failure to provide something or other. However, side to side with both mutual demands and manifestations of autonomy, both men and women expressed the sense that it was men – as fathers, fathers-in-law, husbands, and to a lesser extent brothers and paternal uncles – who could exact obedience from their wives, and who constituted the ultimate authority in moments of conflicting opinions or of uncertainty. I particularly remember several women – even strong-willed, outspoken Elena – telling me that their husbands would not allow them to visit their families or to go to Araracuara; to some extent, thus, men were attributed with some restrictive control of their wives' bodies. This extended to their daughters, daughters-in-law, and, on occasion, to their sisters. Furthermore, if conflicts about miscreancy escalated, it was usually older men who were granted the authority to resolve them and to heal or punish the miscreants. By the same token, older women for the most part were not candidates for punishment, although until late in life they were subject to peremptory demands from their husbands.

Privileged symbolic forms – such as the highly objectified, ritualistic deployments of substances – tended to enable men to initiate certain kinds of complex interactions that women could not. A woman, for instance, could not have initiated the formalities that were involved in the struggle between David and Lilith, described earlier, where he conveyed a critical message along with the gift of a dead wild pig, and she responded by setting up a drinking bout. People of the Centre also generally assumed that it was men who sought out women to marry them, and not the other way around. There were counsels for a woman to follow if she wished to be a desirable choice for a good man seeking a spouse: she should be quiet, hard-working and well-behaved at all times, and solicitous concerning the hunger and thirst of guests. This was supposed to attract the favourable attention of a good man, who could ask her father to give her to him as a wife or as a daughter-in-law. Counsels to young men to work hard and willingly stated that they could impress a possible *father-in-law*, who would then offer them a daughter in marriage. In these formulaic prescriptions, men were the more active initiators, and women reactors; the latter could only agree or disagree to marriages, but not seek them out actively.

The practice of having decisions about community matters such as legal recognition of territorial boundaries and processes relating to government money transferences be taken in mambeaderos – where women were not supposed to sit – constituted an obstacle for women to assume the leadership position of community governor, which was purportedly non-traditional. Pablo, for one, claimed to find it undesirable for a woman in his community ever to assume such a position, given the need for all such decisions to be buttressed by distribution of tobacco paste and by mambeadero rituals. In a few Uitoto communities, however, rare women did assume such leadership roles, arranging for a transformation of the usual division of labour such that they would be in charge of moving monies and conversing to other governors and representatives of NGOs and governments, and the elders and mambeadores would provide esoteric guidance and ritual sanction to the processes these women engaged in.

Other aspects of social organization could be presented as examples of hierarchy, exploitation, or control. The normative preference for virilocal post-marital residence could be seen as systematically engendering iniquitous situations for women. An important proportion of the people men co-resided with tended to be kin they had lived with since childhood, while newly married women often found themselves surrounded by people they only sometimes were acquainted with, and with whom they had never lived. Upon arrival in their new post-marital homes, they could well be unloved strangers, at times even clearly unwelcome ones. Many girls had to wait months or years before they established the kinds of relationships with co-residents that would entail comfortable co-residence and, eventually, effective support in cases of conflict. Several women I met repeated a formula according to which it was women's lot to move away and live 'among other people'; an inmarried Tukanoan woman, reflecting on this, averred that she would take better care of her son than of her daughter, because the former would always remain with her.

Matters could be presented differently, however. For sure, counsels, talk about counsels, ritualistic deployments of substances, and explicit ideals concerning gender relations did not exhaust the symbolic resources available to People of the Centre. Some women could and did fly in the face of counsels and were coquettish, actively seeking to elicit a desired man's interest. They also had a strong say in accepting or refusing to marry or move in with a young man.[8] In some cases women left unhappy marriages to set up new ones, or returned to their parents' homes. And as for the possibility that the residence practices advanced the interests of men at the cost of those of women, the matter may also be framed differently, especially when focusing on the chronically tense relationships between the oldest male sibling in each family and his brothers, and often between a father and an eldest son. Men's life of nearly compulsory co-residence with resentful brothers was frequently unpleasant and constraining.[9]

In their sensibilities, hierarchical gestures between spouses and in many other cross-gender relationships were to be expected, and did not fly in the face of propriety. Even though enthusiastic about notions of political equality in certain contexts – for instance, when discussing the distribution of government monies and the rights of community members to benefit from these – both women and men rejected the image of the absence of gender hierarchy or gender labour specialization that some outsiders brought in for discussion. Nonetheless, there was also much room for voluntary choices for both men and women – choices that, like everywhere else, were bounded by the constraints of local meanings and practices – and it is clear to me that most men and women achieved ways of life they deemed dignified, respectable, and even admirable.

The historical nature of this state of affairs and values comes out clearly to me in view of my perception that Uitoto and Muinane people in the city of Leticia were citing less the discursive and non-discursive forms that reproduced ideals of moral personhood and efficacy that privileged membership in patrilines and compliance with corresponding values. In Leticia and its surrounding area, men of People of the Centre were more likely to move away from their kinsmen than their counterparts in the Medio Caquetá, making patrilineal corporativity less of a tangible reality. I did witness a few men producing discourses about belonging to this or that patriline, and, therefore, featuring this or that virtue, but these discourses simply did not have the kind of widespread hold they had in the Medio Caquetá. Furthermore, given men's greater itinerancy and the relative absence of residentially corporate patrilines, Uitoto women in Leticia had greater leeway to choose to co-reside with their mothers and sisters (Nieto 2006) after getting married, and often did so. This was less common in the Medio Caquetá, though all else being equal, women there would probably have *liked* to live with their mothers and sisters. One implication of this is that people understood what was most salient and important about themselves differently than their fellows in the Medio Caquetá, for whom imagery of patrilineal rootedness was much more compelling. Gender relations, livelihood, cosmology, and understandings of personhood were imbricated and spelled changes for each other.

## Affinity, Kinship, and the Proper Footings of Relationships

Viveiros de Castro (2004) claims that a general ontological premise underlying Amazonian worlds is that difference precedes and encompasses identity; the latter is a special case of the former, namely, its relative but never absolute absence. Alterity is the encompassing mode of sociality in these worlds, a background from which sociable, consanguineal relations must be extracted (see, for instance, 2004, 24, 25). Relations between beings are thus situated in continua of alterity, spanning from radical others such as gods, animals, and the dead to less radical others like enemies, to potential affines, to actualized affines, and then to co-residents and kin. Beings produce their kin by means of processes that consubstantialize or otherwise increase the commonalities between their bodies, reducing difference to its minimal expression but never absolutely.

In People of the Centre's cosmological rhetoric, the human world was indeed spatially and sociologically encompassed by a much more populated world of others; real people tapped into these domains of otherness, extracting from them, usually violently, places, substances, or capacities necessary to achieve the ultimate human purpose of multiplying real people and living well. This multiplication was not haphazard: it was the multiplication of persons as parts of patrilines and clans. People of the Centre's understandings of the moral features of persons tied these to the nature and processes of patrilines and clans. Men's features and capabilities, predatory or otherwise, stemmed from their embodiment of patrilineal and clanic substances through processes often carried out by kin; women's virtues and flaws corresponded to those of their constitutive substances and cohered with their tasks of nourishing their birth or adoption patrilines, and of multiplying the latter through their bodies. They placed much emphasis on the consubstantiality of the bodies of patrilineal kin, and on their consequent affective and intellectual similarities.

Clans and lineages were important institutions among People of the Centre, in terms of their entailments for the spatial distribution of the population as well as in their understandings of moral personhood. Along with the Tukanoans (see Hugh-Jones 1993), among whom descent and lineages were also of importance, they differed from the more emphatically cognatic arrangements described by Overing and Passes (2001) for much of the Amazon. Patrilineality had corporate implications; most settlements in the Medio Caquetá, for instance, were constituted by sets of brothers living with their parents, unmarried sister, wives, and children, and dance rituals were organized as encounters between different lineages and clans, each with different roles and ritual responsibilities.

Lineage leaders – usually the oldest brother in a set of siblings – but also the new governors, often spoke of themselves and were spoken of as fathers of their communities; the rhetoric on their wives as mothers of communities was not as common. Such leaders' central responsibility was to the ferocious defence of their people against the impingement of evil. The corresponding virtues were the capacity for esoteric violence, on one hand, but also generosity and gentle tact when dealing with others' troubles. Leaders, as true men, were supposed to be extremely knowledgeable and judicious. Bossiness, like anger, was a matter of ambivalence, both undesirable and yet admired; men loved to speak about scolding and ordering others about, and leaders did peremptorily order others about in certain contexts – mostly when planning rituals. However, there was also much rhetoric that made the case that authoritarian leaders were undesirable, for instance, because they treated people in the fashion of the terrible *mando militar* (the way of giving orders in the Colombian army).

Particular categories of kin relations within clans and lineages were subject to explicit typecasting. People produced and received counsels, critiques, and other interpellations that made explicit what the footings of such relationships should be, and demanded, on the ground that individuals so related think/feel and act accordingly. Part of their patrilineal emphasis took the form of marked solicitude concerning the relationships between fathers and sons and between brothers – sets of men who ideally co-resided throughout their lives. For instance, according to David and Pablo, sons were supposed to be told time and again that they should be reverentially obedient and solicitous towards their fathers, who in return should be protective, informative, and concerned. Brothers were supposed to support each other caringly, providing them with substances, partnership in ritual dialogues, and help in large tasks. Andrés, David's brother, told me that in the past Muinane adults would interrupt bickering siblings, making the children stand side by side with arms interlocked in the position of ritual dancers, and say with baby-like enunciation '*Abo, abo.*' This was to teach them not to fight with their '*naabo*' (brother or classificatory brother), but instead, to 'help/accompany each other well' (*iimino mágátavokasihi*) like adult siblings did at dance rituals.

On the ground, I found relationships between the oldest male in each set of siblings and his brothers often to be tense, and characterized by much criticism, resentment, and stress. Conflicts of interest were all the more poignant because of injunctions of docility to the younger members of families vis-à-vis the claims of their elders, and because of injunctions for men to remain with their siblings.[10] Every settlement I worked in featured examples of this. David's brothers found him to be bad-tempered and tyrannical, and to wish to control everything – from how government transference money was to be spent, to how gifts were distributed, to how to pursue rituals. Two of them had moved away, one of them, according to another brother, doing so particularly because he could not stand David's despotic ways. The speaker on that occasion told me that he too had wanted to leave, but he could not because a man away from his brothers and his territories was rootless and weak. In other words, it was in the context of a corporate patriline that a man could live a good and admirable life. In Emanuel's case, the generalized belief his numerous brothers had moved away from the settlement to escape his jealousy and pugnaciousness made him, and to a lesser extent them, the objects of much negative moral evaluation. The events people described in speaking about this clearly reflected the tensions between the brothers, but also the expectation that they should live together.

Father and mature son relationships were also often tense. There were abstract injunctions of filial obedience and respect and of paternal care. David, for instance, told me that in the past youths were counselled not to 'step ahead of the coca,' a metonymy that meant that just as a young man was not to step ahead of his father as the latter made his way home from the garden, carrying a basketful of coca, neither was the youth to speak in public before his father did, or use ritual knowledge without the father's blessing, if the latter were still alive. A man's father was his leader, healer, and caretaker, until he explicitly told his son that he could proceed to apply the knowledge which he had given him.

Pablo told me that like other elders of the past, his father used to warn him that if Pablo ever did speak before him in public, the old man would die of shame. 'I was always very fearful of this, and so I never spoke in public without my father's permission.' This issue was also touched upon in large meetings I attended, where elders decried the lack of humility and respect of young men, many of whom they said wished to be great leaders 'while their grandfathers and fathers were still alive.'

Other relationships were less subject to bossiness and tension. Among younger brothers, and between nephews and maternal uncles or paternal uncles other than the eldest in that generation, they were generally more relaxed and pleasant, and the object of less prescriptions and warnings. Relationships between men or boys and their grandmothers, mothers, aunts, sisters, classificatory sisters, and daughters were subject to counsels, most of these concerning gendered duties to provide nourishment, protection, and support. Relationships among co-resident and related women tended to be casual and pleasant, with the exception of those between mother-in-law and daughter-in-law, and more rarely, between sisters-in-law, which sometimes featured tensions.

Pablo once produced an account for me that retrospectively seemed to lend support to the view of Amazonian kinship as a process of reduction of affinity. He told me that he could not bear to sit next to white women and with women he did not know, because his tobacco would tremble and make him feel uneasy. He noted, however, that his body had become accustomed to two of his daughters-in-law, despite that, atypically for most in-marrying women in the region, they were Tukanoans from very far away. He explained that they had consumed his tobacco for a few years already, and therefore, his body did not reject them. To return to the notion of a continuum of alterity, their bodies, originally so different, had been transformed by consubstantialization, making them kin and, thus, comfortable company for Pablo. And men and women did explicitly state that people should be like caring parents towards their son's wives, who should become like daughters, and addressed as such. Daughters-in-law were in turn supposed to be counselled to address parents-in-law as parents – something I found people rarely to comply with, preferring to use the Spanish terms *suegro* or *suegra* (father-in-law or mother-in-law) and *nuera* or *yerno* (daughter-in-law or son-in-law).

As in much of the Amazon (see Overing 1993) relationships between affines were often intrinsically problematic, at least to start with and often later. Again, the image of a continuum of alterity is helpful here. Ideally, affines were people endowed with moral acumen and relationships with them were appropriate. Yet People of the Centre's speeches of apprising and other cosmological references featured more radically different and indeed inhuman kinds of affines, such as the immoral fathers-in-law of speeches of apprising. The latter were often dangerous sorcerers, eager to kill and cannibalize their sons-in-law and even their own grandchildren. Several men I knew well used these images explicitly when questioning the morality of men they addressed as 'father-in-law' of sorcery.[11] Lázaro told me he distrusted his wife's father because he belonged to a clan the members of which were perfectly willing to murderously ensorcell their own grandchildren. Emanuel claimed to have been the victim of his father-in-law's sorcery, and David broke off relations with Marco, who was both his wife's maternal uncle and his father's sister's husband, because he had learned from a *yagé* vision that Marco had killed his father with sorcery.

Counsels and evaluations prescribed that people get along with their spouses' parents and their children's spouses. I found that relationships between mothers-in-law and daughters-in-law varied; some were good, even if some respectful distance was always present, while others were problematic. Naomi showed much concern and a somewhat bossy educational interest in one of her daughters-in-law, respectful consideration for another, and great antipathy towards a third. Elena remembered her own mother-in-law's stinginess and manifest displeasure at her daughters-in-law's requests to borrow her manioc bread cooking plate. She noted that despite the poor treatment she received initially from the old woman, she still took care of the mother-in-law in her old age.

Men in particular were under the injunction to show special generosity towards their wives' parents, going to their home and helping them with their large tasks and giving generous amounts of tobacco paste and mambe to the fathers-in-law. Elena, with her frequent criticisms, provided me with a negative example of this: she spoke contemptuously of her daughter's city-born husband, describing him as a stingy young man who had not brought her or her husband any gifts from a recent trip to the city. Fathers-in-law could and occasionally did simply tell sons-in-law to come to their homes and help with some big job.

Sisters-in-law (the spouses of pairs of brothers, or the spouse and the sister of a man) differed in their relationships as well. Elena and Sara were related as aunt and niece (MZ and ZD, that is, mother's sister and sister's daughter), and though they married Lázaro and Pedro, a pair of brothers, they kept addressing each other as kin rather than as sisters-in-law. They got along relatively well, helping each other and sharing some food, despite some mutual criticism. Together, they waged a war of hate and gossip against Naomi, who was their husbands' brother's wife and was not otherwise related to them; they did not visit with her, and were particularly harsh in their talk about her. In another settlement, Emanuel's two daughters-in-law were classificatory sisters, and loved each other dearly and could be seen to help each other willingly and enjoy each other's company. At yet another community, the spouses of David's group of brothers got along well with each other despite being unrelated, but one of David's unmarried sisters resented Ariel's new wife's access to kitchen tools the sister had had exclusive access to before, and made life very difficult for her.

There were many counsels and much talk concerning the point that men were never to covet their brothers' and other kinsmen's wives. Some counsels even called for the avoidance of contact. Eneas stated this last point with the aphorism that for a man to gaze at a sister-in-law's face was like staring at the sun: embarrassing to the point of pain, so that one must look at the floor not to be dazzled. At the meetings on the speech of advice, the men described how in the past People of the

Centre would point out to all the men of the patriline that a new woman had arrived, that she was the woman of one of them and should be addressed as 'sister-in-law,' 'daughter-in-law,' or 'aunt,' and that she should definitely not be approached for sex. Misbehaviour was dangerous and destructive; in one of the patrilines, a young man cuckolded his own father's brother and, thereby, caused a very serious break in the patriline in question. In another patriline, a man's wife left him for his half-brother. The cuckolded husband left his settlement.

People of the Centre recognized that as with certain kinship relations, affinal relations could be induced or elicited by behaving as if the relationship were already established as such. They professed that if someone behaved as a good affine behaved, he (for this applied more to men than women) would eventually come to be treated as such. One counsel told young men that wherever they were, they should be on the lookout for opportunities to help others. The counsels went on to say that when visiting other malocas, a helpful youth could be observed and his diligence noted, and the owner of the maloca, wishful of acquiring a judicious and hardworking son-in-law, could offer him his daughter as a wife. Arad, a young man, tried to acquire Lázaro's and Elena's daughter Miriam for a wife in this fashion. I found out from Elena that Arad had helped Lázaro fell a section of forest on two occasions. Elena reported that Arad had said to Lázaro, 'This is to pay for Miriam,' meaning, perhaps half-jokingly, that he was working for Lázaro so that Lázaro would give him his daughter Miriam to be his wife.

Arad, perhaps, had the idea that if he behaved as a son-in-law should behave –working for the 'father-in – law,' addressing him in the proper fashion (as 'father-in-law,' though the somewhat joking tone I imagine he had at the time, if it was at all like other felling situations, involved running the risk that this might be deemed disrespectful by the addressee), providing him with tobacco and coca, and helping the 'mother-in-law' whenever possible – he could eventually effectively become a son-in-law. Arad's mother and sister tried to help him, respectively addressing Miriam on different occasion as 'daughter-in-law' and 'sister-in-law.' Unfortunately for Arad, however, his attempts faced a contesting use of performative utterances. Neither Miriam nor Elena wanted Miriam to go with Arad, and so the mother instructed the daughter to address Arad as 'cousin,' in Spanish. Elena told her that she was to say that though she knew they were not cousins, she perceived him as such, and that it would be strange and shameful for them to live as a couple. Arad tried to deny that they were cousins, to no avail.

## Categorization of People for Ritual Purposes

Perhaps the circumstances People of the Centre associated most saliently with the moral injunction to provide support were the great endeavours of building a maloca and holding the dance rituals that legitimated the maloca's existence. In their cosmological rhetoric, proper human life – perhaps life in general – simply could not continue without malocas and rituals. It was through these rituals that maloca owners ensured the procreation and well-being of their people, which included all the participants in the rituals. These people were categorized as 'insiders,' 'helpers,' 'men of the speech of tobacco,' and 'singers.' Maloca owners depended heavily on the support of these very people to carry out their rituals, and they explicitly stated this and talked about the footings of relationships that ensured others' support.

The 'insiders' or 'people of the maloca' (*jáhemɨna* or *hííjahooto*, in Muinane), and the 'helpers' (*jɨɨkávo*, in Muinane) were respectively the co-residents of the maloca owner and his out-marrying sisters and their nuclear families. When Pablo built his maloca, the insiders were himself and his two brothers, their spouses, their sons, their daughters-in-law and their unmarried daughters, and two young men who were the children of Pablo's classificatory brother (FBS). Pablo's helpers were his three sisters, one brother-in-law, and their numerous sons, daughters-in-law, and unmarried daughters. These people for the most part lived in the settlements of patriline segments located anywhere from half an hour to several hours' travel away. The affinal relations involved – in this case, just one – constituted a hierarchizing injunction to help, for a man was obliged to provide his father-in-law or his wife's brother (WB) with help when asked to.

These people all worked in various configurations to provide the maloca owner and his wife with tobacco, salt and coca, and manioc products for consumption and redistribution. The men also participated in the ritual dialogues necessary for the preparation of the dance ritual.

A third category of people linked to the maloca owner were his men of the speech of tobacco (*bááñojito),* who provided him with indispensable support as main ritual partners. Ideally, these men were neither kin nor actualized affines. A large ritual depended on the added esoteric 'strength' of several such men from different coca circles using various speeches with a common set of purposes: to ensure that there be enough food and drink for the ritual, that diseases and other tribulations dawn (become manifest) as game, that it not rain on the day of the arrival of the guests, that all involved be well counselled, and in general that the ritual be successful. For instance, Emanuel explained to me that a man holding a dialogue with his brother to keep rain at bay prior to a ritual would have limited 'strength' if the pair were alone. However, if the maloca owner's men of the speech of tobacco were to do the same with their own brothers, at the same time as he, their speeches would unite and gain great strength, to keep dry all the people travelling to the ritual. As he explained this to me, Emanuel made wide-sweeping gestures that mimed the speeches travelling across the sky overhead from the different directions of the malocas of his men of the speech of tobacco, and converging in the sky above his own. He stressed with gestures the strength and effectiveness of those converging speeches.

Most of the maloca owners I knew had two men of the speech of tobacco. These formal relationships were supposed to be inherited; thus, Pablo told me that Saúl had to be his man of the speech of tobacco because Saúl's father had been Pablo's father's man of the speech of tobacco. Pablo's other man of the speech of tobacco was Moisés, a young Uitoto man whose father had presumably also had a similar relationship with Pablo's father. However, new relationships of this kind could be established, though according to Pablo they had different names when untried or when few rituals had been carried out between the new ritual interlocutors. One important condition for two men to be able to establish such a relationship was that their lineages be entitled to hold the same kind of dance ritual: thus David and Emanuel were both entitled to hold Charapa Turtle dance rituals, which led David to ask Emanuel to be his man of the speech of tobacco.

Of importance in these relationships was the establishment of the 'path of speech' or 'path of tobacco.' These terms were sometimes used as a complex trope for the formal relationships established between maloca owners explicitly for ritual purposes. The 'path' referred to the geographical space – land or water – to be traversed by a traveller taking ritual tobacco from one clan's maloca to the other's in order to demand the other's help in some ritual endeavour, and by the guests who responded to those summons of tobacco and made their way to the ritual. The metonym involved not only the path itself, however, but also numerous other formalities: details of the form of the delivery of the tobacco package, who the actual purveyors could be, how many days prior to a dance ritual the tobacco would be sent out, and most importantly, some of the details of the footings of the relations between the men who sent and received tobacco along the path, and the behaviours of all involved when visiting another maloca. In the rhetoric, such paths ensured that each clan could request from each other much needed mutual support for great and vital endeavours, and that the other could respond accordingly. It was a moral path, traversed for moral purposes.

It was formal ritual protocol for the maloca owner to send or take – depending on how the formalities of the particular path of tobacco had been established – an *ímogaibɨ* to his men of the speech of tobacco, when he required their help to build a new maloca, to hold a dance ritual, or in other special circumstances. According to Pedro, men of the speech of tobacco would sometimes send for each other for help at moments other than dance rituals, when facing a particularly difficult problem or disease. When a man of the speech of tobacco received his counterpart's unswayable tobacco summons, he in turn had to distribute the tobacco among his kin and others whom he needed in order to live up to his responsibilities. Thus, when Pablo took tobacco to Saúl to demand his help in building his maloca, Saúl gave tobacco to his sons, his brothers, his nephews and their spouses, and then to Emanuel, his sons, and their spouses. Those to whom the man of speech of tobacco gave tobacco to summon them to a dance ritual were categorized as the dance ritual's guests or 'singers' (*másimɨnaha,*' in Muinane). Each of the men of the speech of tobacco was the leader of a group of singers and dancers who performed during much of the ritual.

Men of the speech of tobacco were supposed to receive each other with great respect, generous hospitality, and mutual concern. Though it seemed to me that these relationships on the ground were often those of fairly intimate acquaintances, the myths and stories people told about dance rituals in the distant past suggest that they understood these also to have been potentially dangerous relationships; men of the speech of tobacco were, after all, outsiders, and could well have sorcerous or otherwise malevolent intent. Dance rituals were thus dangerous: people could easily get ensorcelled if not on their best behaviour, and even then. Young men travelling to a dance ritual were warned against cuckolding the men of the host maloca or otherwise offending the maloca owner, lest they be ensorcelled too. Dances also involved esoteric dealings with dangerous beings in the cosmos, and a malevolent host or man of the speech of tobacco could well direct such beings to cause harm to their counterpart. In short, this relationship fit well with the more general Amazonian understanding that relationships with Others were necessary for the reproduction of kin and co-residential groups, but that they were always potentially dangerous.

People of the Centre's accounts of their collective lives pushed an image of patrilineal groupings whose individual workings required loving, caring, or at the very least mutually supportive relationships among co-residents. Patrilineal groupings also required complementary relationships with others and, hence, the importance of the virtuous skills of individuals to forge such relationships and keep them cool or better, lest the enormous task of achieving a desirable lifestyle and multiplying new generations fail from lack of support, or worse, from active and mutual ill will.

# 6 Shaped and Historical Moralities

In the previous chapters, I attempted to produce a textured interpretation of the talk and livelihood and other social organizational practices of a set of individuals of People of the Centre, involving their evaluative understandings of persons, subjectivities, and actions, and of the nature of human and inhuman purposes and capacities for action. I was particularly interested in grasping their own interpretive sense of and negotiations about what it was that they were doing when they did certain things, and what kinds of being they were, or could or should be, where this kind of being was defined by more or less articulated distinctions of worth. Their expressions of this sense seemed often to have been shaped by, and in turn to have reproduced, very coherent, phenomenologically persuasive accounts of self, in which they posited that human bodies were, indeed, constituted by cultivated substances, and their own and others' behaviours, whether human or inhuman, were caused by substances of outside origin. Individuals seemed to perceive intimately the moral worth of persons, events, subjectivities, and actions, in at least some of the terms of these accounts, and to be motivated by this perception.

My argument in this book thus converges with accounts that deem individuals' understandings of their world and of themselves in it to be structured or shaped to a great extent by their acquisition and citation of terms, concepts, narratives, and other symbolic forms in a lifelong process of social interaction with others, which they in turn reproduce transformatively. Claims about social life structuring individuals' experiences are often subject to objections on at least three related grounds:

1 They have difficulty addressing individuals' experiences of awareness and choice, reducing these to epiphenomena or side effects of a more fundamental underlying structure or process and denying human agency or creativity.
2 They reify 'culture' or some equivalent term, treating it as an integrated thing-in-itself rather than as a theoretical category used by scholars and other people to understand the diversity of human behaviour.
3 They posit too much homogeneity, too much similarity and sharedness of meanings, among the individuals that constitute social groups, communities, or societies.

I will address these objections in the next few paragraphs, specifically in terms of my interpretation of People of the Centre.[1]

Concerning the first objection, I believe I have shown how layered individuals can be, and that I had to consider their self-awareness if I was to understand what they said and did, but also decisions they made that impacted upon, or else maintained, the ways they organized themselves socially. I made a case, for instance, to the effect that they could be strategic in their moral self-portrayals. They also faced choices, concerning tacks they could follow in accounting for or otherwise portraying their own action, and so could and at times, indeed did, choose to use rhetoric and 'proper' ritual without 'meaning' it. They were manifestly aware that others evaluated their actions, and they could be portrayed in ways they did not like, and so sought to pre-empt the more disadvantageous portrayals and to encourage sweeter ones. But again, I emphasize that although they could be theatrical, strategic, and even insincere in their deployments of the accounts and related forms in question, this does not mean that underlying such performances there were basic, unconstructed selves, or essential, free, utilitarian subjects, or subjects endowed with universal cognitive capabilities that gave them access to some sort of unconstructed, pre-symbolic or pre-cultural reality that all human beings in their right mind would perceive in the same way. The claim is that the basic thinking, feeling self is always, already, a product or an achievement of social life.

The relationship between the dramatic expression and the sincere self I am referring to is comparable to people like me – middle-class, urban, male, white (-ish), English-speaking – expressing in various ways our sense of ourselves as classy, sophisticated, liberated, or tough individuals, or as featuring some other known virtue. We may matter-of-factly think of ourselves, or perceive certain others, as virtuous in these ways; we may also perceive others as phoney, or as posers, knowing their talk of wine or travel in Europe to be at best a delusion, at worst an imposture. We may even recognize impostures in ourselves, concerning, for instance, a conscious desire to be deemed examples of tough virility. But even as we question the substance of individuals' dramatic performances, wondering or doubting whether we or others are really classy or tough or competent, or whether it is an imposture, we tend not to question that the virtues of 'toughness,' 'classiness,' and 'sophistication' are truly virtues, and that some people actually feature them. We and people around us treat the categories in question as objective features of (some) subjects, and use them to understand ourselves and each other and to make choices that often reproduce certain kinds of groups and practices. In these processes, we end up making these categories available for ourselves and for others to cite, again and again, in our understandings, claims, and choices.

To summarize, the point is that our conscious self, the 'I' of my interlocutors among People of the Centre and of my imagined consociates, that could indeed fake, strategize, and so on, did not pre-exist individuals' social lives, but was shaped by these. Individuals' dramatic discourses concerning substances, virtues, animals, and so on, deployed many of the same symbolic forms constitutive of some of their intimate self-interpretations. They felt that they were people of this or that substance, that people could be admirably consistent and predatorial or else vulnerable to usurpation, and faced and made choices scaffolded by these symbolic forms. I must underscore that this was a dialogical process, such that the deployments, unselfconscious or strategic, then shaped further deployments.

Having said this, and concerning the second kind of objection, I very much wished to elide the picture of a monolithic culture that travels through the generations as a heavy, stable, clearly bounded mass programming entire populations – Amazonian or other – to perceive themselves and their world in a certain way, or to admire or despise certain qualities (an elision much like Urban 2000, 18; and Keane 2010, 68). This is a mirage produced when observing numbers of individuals citing more or less similar forms in a certain period of time. The image of social life that I espouse here incorporates temporality and individuality more centrally. It is individuals who generate social life, in an ongoing, processual fashion, by means of deployments of symbolic forms in exchanges with other individuals. Because each individual's life is unique, occurring in real space and time in unrepeatable circumstances, they renew and change the symbols they use, by associating them with other symbols that feature in their circumstances of use. Over time and through multiple citations, symbols acquire new historical associations and lose others. To reject an image of static culture is therefore also to reject that of a stable common essence, an 'authentic way of life' or unchanging kind of narrative characteristic of People of the Centre, or of any other people for the matter.

Rejecting an essentialized or reified 'authentic culture' implies, as well, rejecting the third grounds for the objections I listed: the expectation that individuals within a society will all 'share the same culture' and thus share, for instance, a fixed set of moral narratives and, thus, a common moral purview. Individuals in social groups often do cite many of the same symbols; some are cited so much that they become entrenched in the everyday lives of many people, for whom it is an immediate and necessary resource. The words and grammatical patterns of our thriving languages come to mind, as do our practices with clothing. Yet, as I underscored earlier, sharing some symbols and their associations does not entail that we share meanings radically; there are always some differences between the associations we make or cite for any symbolic deployment or circumstance, and those that our consociates make or cite.[2]

I have centred my descriptions here on People of the Centre's rhetoric and practices oriented towards the large moral project of making new generations of real people and achieving the good life. Many of the narratives and other forms in question were recognizable as reiterations, but clearly people interpreted and redeployed these forms from their own perspectives, with their own purposes, to make sense of their particular circumstances, to understand particular events in their lives. Any single event could be interpreted in different ways, even if very similar terms were used to interpret them. For instance, a man's violent outburst at a particular point in time could be perceived and portrayed as the product of tobacco's righteous indignation by some, as the product of animalistic impingement by others, or as mere 'vice' by yet others.

There *was* a great deal of coherence in People of the Centre's symbolic deployments – their talk and other practices – concerning their livelihood, their practices of consumption of substances, their kinship, their rituals, many of the actions of persons, and the terms of their moral evaluations concerning these matters. People often expressed their understandings of the nature and expression of moral and immoral subjectivity in similar ways in these milieus; these concepts thus appeared in casual gossip but also in rhythmic conjurations in the coca circles. It is beyond my methodology here, but I also noted interdiscursive relations between different genres such as their counsels, their gossip, their angry remonstrances, and their moral self-portrayals – for instance, in the way they portrayed certain matters as common sense by asking rhetorical questions that marked their sense that the answer was obvious, and in the ubiquitous voice People of the Centre deployed that situated the speaker in a position of purportedly unquestionable morality. I am persuaded that the reiterative, interdiscursive, coherent deployment of symbolic forms was part of what made these compelling, if necessarily imperfectly so.

## New Moralities, New Kinds of People

People of the Centre's moral subjectivities developed and reproduced in a way akin to gendered subjectivity in Judith Butler's account of performativity. According to Butler, we reproduce a gender binary by citing ideals – ideals that interpellate us and subjectivate us, and which exist only because we cite them. These ideals so shape our subjectivity that anything outside them seems unintelligible or monstrous. I recall how as an undersized teenager in Colombia I enacted typical manifestations of masculinity in a self-conscious, strategic or even fake way, but yet hardly questioned the purportedly essential reality of masculinity itself and its defining contrast with femininity.

In Colombia, UK, and Canada, places where I've lived, 'men' who do not perform their masculinity in compliance with gender norms puzzle or repulse those others who can neither see the virtue in engaging in such lives or imagine living them. Yet there have clearly been changes in the last few decades, and many people no longer react to gay and lesbian couples, or to the idea, with the repulsion I witnessed as a child. Some gender performances along other lines are no longer as widely deemed monstrous or unintelligible.

The kinds of lives that People of the Centre could engage in, and the kinds of persons they could be, have, by this account, always changed (see Taylor 1985, 238; Rorty 1989, 7). Colonists, merchants, missionaries, travelling scientists, and the like, with their own changing schools, guns, Spanish, Christian stories and worship, ways of getting spouses and raising children, and forms of exchange had been around for a long time, and changed the material context of People of the Centre's lives considerably. These must have generated new symbolic associations, and new interpellations.

In the 1990s, there were several important symbolic resources that offered clear discontinuities from those available twenty, fifty, or a hundred years back. I should note that by calling them 'resources' I am not treating them as stores from which people could choose freely to pick and choose; my sense is rather that changing material contexts were interpellating people in different ways, informing them – and thereby forming them as subjects – of the kinds of subjects they could be.

One important change concerned the new kinds of communities people could be members of. In the past, People of the Centre traditionally married and held rituals within their language groups. In the aftermath of the demographic devastation of the rubber holocaust, which annihilated entire lineages, clans, and even language groups, Uitoto, Muinane, Andoque and other survivors formed communities of a new kind that to some extent mixed people of different clans and language groups. People from different language groups intermarried more, and they started carrying out large dance rituals together. It was necessary to re-imagine the different groups now living together or in relative proximity as people of a kind, in what Echeverri (1997, 17), following Basso (1995, 21), calls a process of creating a new kind of 'moral community' that defined groups, and therefore their members, differently. Landaburu (1993, 150–1) provides a beautiful example of how an Andoque elder creatively reconfigured clanic myths of origin in such a way that they no longer accounted for the differences between certain Andoque clans, but rather enabled their co-residence and unity. Later, they developed the category of People of the Centre to its current use, as a response to engagement with the Colombian government.

These categories persuaded them, and they used them quite explicitly, for instance, in claims to the effect that People of the Centre were more knowledgeable, morally transparent, and trustworthy than other Amazonian Indians around them. They also understood themselves to be Indians as opposed to white or black people. Being 'Colombians' as opposed to 'Peruvians,' and later as opposed to 'gringos' (Americans or Europeans), was also a categorical possibility less than a century old; the former probably became important to them initially with the war against Peru in 1932 and then with the boarding schools, where they were taught to situate themselves in maps that coloured Peru and Colombia differently, and to take the part of Colombia in the national historical narratives.[3] This opened up the possibility for patriotism as a virtue and for the experience of nationalistic pride, expressed widely, for example, when they gathered in Araracuara to watch the World Cup.

Leadership categories, styles, and relations changed, as well. For instance, I witnessed young men making claims to virtue on the basis of their literacy and knowledge of government processes, gaining authority and people's ears in ways previously unavailable to them. I remember one young Uitoto man addressing an elder in a way that made this manifest. They had both been elected by vote to their positions of leadership in the CRIMA; the younger man was the president, and the elder purportedly the ultimate authority as the voice of wise tradition. At one large meeting, the young man retorted to a discourse of the elder's about their CRIMA work impatiently and sarcastically, asking the old man if he'd forgotten what the youth had taught him. This was a straightforward inversion of a typecast question that elders supposedly asked the young men they taught in their mambeaderos, and the public's reactions seemed to me to show that they recognized the subversion. The event cannot be oversimplified as a case in which a gerontocratic way of life was subverted by youths for whom a new path had opened. After all, all I witnessed ethnographically were some somewhat gerontocratic practices, and these were often assailed by younger people, but this may have been going on for a long time. What is a fact is that literacy was only one or two generations old for most families, and that relations between the Colombian government and NGOs on one hand, and indigenous peoples on the other, had changed recently. With NGO help, some created the CRIMA first to pursue their territorial rights vis-à-vis the government. This process reshaped local relations. It made new kinds of people: the young leaders, engaged in being new purveyors of outside resources, knowledgeable of the affordances of cities and bureaucracies, acknowledging publicly the foundational importance of elders' traditional knowledge and sometimes seeking it for themselves, but also ridiculing these same elders' relative ignorance of government and urban matters.[4]

Schools and their processes and accoutrements – whether the older boarding schools or the new community schools of the late 1980s and 1990s – were other forms of outside origin that had become important in people's moral understandings and portrayals of themselves, of others, and of their communities. For one thing, talk about communities with schools suggested these had greater standing or prestige than those without, and leaders clearly felt called to acquire the funds to build, equip, and maintain schools. The tangible presence of school houses and books in certain settlements and the presence of people identified as 'teachers' and 'students' had become part of social life in People of the Centre's communities. As for the effects of schools, one was the well-established distinction between judicious good students and *brutos* (stupid brutes, in Spanish) who could not read or write well. Some people also treated the manners learned at school – forms of washing the face and body, of greeting outsiders, of eating, of making a queue, and so on – as forms that could only be acquired in that milieu, and they expressed contempt for those bumpkins who had 'apparently never crossed a threshold into a school,' as one of Lázaro's sons scathingly commented about his father. Some people, like Pablo, protested that they had not gone to school, and so lacked important knowledge, yet a subset of these insisted that nonetheless they possessed other, powerful knowledge. Sara, to the contrary, felt that schools taught children to lose the necessary respect and fear for others that made them avoid thievery, cuckoldry, and other such miscreancies.

People of the Centre also changed the way they understood and drew personal entailments from malocas, perhaps the most heavily symbolically charged objects in their world besides human bodies. Some individuals pursued a moral contrast between people who actually inhabited their maloca and those who, while possessing one, did not reside in it. This contrast became strong in the late 1980s, in the context of much hortatory talk on the recovery of traditional ways and forms (Juan Echeverri, personal communication). Some of this talk cited the rhetoric of anthropologists and *indigenistas* (activists supporting indigenous people against the encroachments of the state and other outsiders) in the region: they spoke explicitly, for instance, about 'recovering' their tradition, their autonomy, and their 'uses and customs,' and wondered out loud and debated at length, even while I was there, about the meanings of these terms. The moral implications of the distinction between people's ways of using malocas was certainly important to at least some of the people in the households I visited, and an aspect of their lives that they highlighted in their self-portrayals. Emanuel, for instance, was quite proud that he was one of the few People of the Centre who slept in his maloca, and Pablo pointedly claimed in 1997 that when he built his maloca he would live in it, too. By the end of 1998, and when I visited him in 2007, he and at least one of his married sons resided in their maloca. For Pablo, this was living as one ought to live if one was People of the Centre. Again, these claims suggest that new articulations, new distinctions of worth, were appearing in the horizon of People of the Centre: by occupying a maloca, it was now possible to be, and to express the sense that one was, admirably and authentically indigenous, as opposed to living in a less than admirably 'modern' or 'invented' fashion.

I hasten to add that these very people insisted that they were not struggling for a 'return to the loincloth'; that is, that they sought to recover certain aspects of the knowledge and ways of life of their ancestors, but without giving up clothing and other accoutrements of white men.

Another contrast that was pertinent in the 1990s in the Medio Caquetá, and very prominent in 2008 in the Igaraparaná, concerned whether a maloca had been built properly, on the basis of the respect that people had for its owner, or whether it was a maloca built by workers who received money for their labour. Several men pointed out to me that six malocas had sprouted in recent periods near La Chorrera, because savvy individuals had managed to get the government – whose representatives I knew were interested in tangible manifestations of the recovery of traditional ways – to give them money to build them. Anybody can build a maloca like that, they said, but it would not work, because they did not have the ritual knowledge to 'keep it functioning' – that is, defending the community esoterically. Whether this turned out to be true or not I do not know; the important point for my purposes is the qualitative distinction of worth between the kinds of relations – based on money or based on respect – that came up at the time, and which became an issue at all because of the particular circumstances. Elsewhere in the Amazon, people also treat maloca-building as something akin to a vote of confidence in the individual who owned it; somebody disliked or distrusted simply would not have the help necessary to build a proper maloca.

The mutability of malocas as symbols was particularly clear in the case of the malocas of Muinane and Uitoto people in the diasporic setting of the city of Leticia. Malocas there depended more on communities of mixed groups than on the support of people organized in patrilines, and they were often deemed to be the property of communities rather than of a single, knowledgeable maloca owner who functioned as a ritual father for his patriline and for others attached to it in a community. Amy McLachlan (personal communication) found people to use malocas in Leticia to stress commensality in general, rather than specifically patrilineal, tobacco-centred consubstantiality.

More starkly than in the Medio Caquetá, malocas in Leticia had also become an image of indigenous authenticity and of age-old tradition that local people could deploy in interactions with each other and with the state, in the context of territorial and other legal claims concerning the distribution of state resources. Several communities and other collectives – in one case, a women's collective – built malocas in response to elicitation from the state, which required proofs of 'indigenousness' in order to grant groupings rights to land and deemed malocas to be such a proof (Amy McLachlan, personal communication).

This is not to say that malocas in Leticia, or their makers, were phoney. They were doubtless sometimes strategic in their considerations, but malocas still featured very much in their understandings of kinship, community, and moral personhood. I witnessed several dance rituals, and as in the Medio Caquetá, people rallied to these truly eager to get together, eat, and drink. Many wanted to make publicly manifest their knowledge and singing abilities, and said as much, proudly. In one case, it was a Uitoto woman, married to a man from some other indigenous group who did not have a maloca-building tradition, who decided, reportedly on the basis of a dream she had had, that she would have a maloca built in the way of her people, and that she would direct dance rituals and some other maloca events with her husband quite explicitly set up as a figurehead. At a dance ritual at that maloca, she was extremely attentive to performing the duties of a proper maloca owner's wife, receiving people, instructing them to drink, reciprocating gifts, and so forth. It seemed likely to me that she engaged in her performance with the sense that she was a certain kind of woman – an admirable, knowledgeable one and a real Uitota – and she desired to make this manifest to the public.

To summarize, over the previous century or so, the people I call People of the Centre were immersed in and engaged with a world into which new kinds of material objects were making their way quickly, and in which new ways of interrelating appeared as a consequence. There were new bodies – those of 'white' men, 'black' men, and 'Indians' from elsewhere in Colombia – new clothes, new foods, new tools, and new languages and vocabularies, including those about new gods. There were new kinds of communities, new kinds of hierarchy, new kinds of leaders, new kinds of differences between persons, new ways of talking to each other, new ways of getting married and of holding rituals, and new, monetized relationships. The imagined cosmos – and the stories that structured this imagination – changed as well. People who related in such changing ways with each other changed themselves.[5]

## The Amazonian Package and Continuity in Change

If the temporality of the symbolic deployments constitutive of social life entails that change is intrinsic to it, then that these deployments are citations or reiterations of past forms also entails that there will be some continuities, or at least family resemblances, among those whose symbolic forms derived from a common source.[6] This or some similar understanding of the potential of symbols to endure – or of symbolic deployments to resemble each other in time – underlies the growing chorus of scholarly voices that attempts to explain patterns in social change among Amazonian peoples, attributing causal pride of place in shaping these patterns to features of what I called 'the Amazonian package,' a widespread, lasting cluster of accounts or beliefs, or of what other scholars, on the basis of different understandings of symbolic processes, might refer to as 'structures' or 'narrative frames' or even 'unconscious dispositions.'

I have discussed elements of this package piecemeal in previous chapters. The claim is that it includes native understandings and practices to the effect that social life is centrally about dealing with bodies, that these dealings take place in a more or less perspectival cosmology, and that the processes involved require, at some point, relations with dangerous, outside Others.

My argument has been that just such a package shaped much of what mattered to People of the Centre about themselves, their relationships, and their ways of life. Citations of elements of this package, if not the only forms that people used to make evaluative sense of their lives, did feature very frequently in their intimate and compelling distinctions of worth. They averred, in many different ways, that the features of persons were a product of how their bodies were fabricated by kin, and of the features of the tobacco paste, manioc juice, and other substances that made up their bodies. They defined many of their virtues in terms of the humanity, as opposed to the animality, of subjectivities (perspectives) and actions. They also treated the process of making new kin and re-fashioning their co-residents, to a great extent, as a process of reducing the differences between the bodies of those involved, so that they would think/feel similarly and love each other. Their social organization, myths, rituals, tropes, terms, counsels, and gossip in this regard were densely interconnected and mutually buttressed each other, contributing to the effectiveness of performative symbolic deployments along its lines. They thus established and reproduced a certain image of what it was to be a human being, and what constituted an admirable, desirable, or common human way to be. They interpellated new generations of people, who therefore, to a great extent, came to understand the kinds of beings they were, to engage in certain ways of life, and to be sensitive to certain things and see that these mattered differently, in ways somewhat like those of their predecessors and peers. For sure, much of what they did was fairly unselfconscious (or habitus-like), but as I have shown, their understandings and concerns were a vital part of the reproduction of their way of life. This has been the gist of my contribution so far.

To go further, however, I will speculate about what the kind of light this might shed on the spread of the Amazonian package. If the reiterative interpellations that shape subjects and social existence are symbolic, the question remains why certain associations of symbolic forms seem to endure and be picked up sociologically more than others. The widespread presence of versions of the Amazonian package suggests that this was its case; that it had probably been around for a long time and become diffused. I'll extrapolate in time and space from what I interpret among People of the Centre, and claim that such a package may have been constitutive of people's understandings of themselves and of their relationships. Its conservatism was, perhaps, tied to its manifest forms that often explicitly pertained directly to people's experiences with bodies: with how these were conceived and borne, how they grew, sickened, and healed, how they developed competencies and suffered fatigue and pain, how they perceived smells, tastes, sounds, tactile impressions, and visual images, and how they were sometimes comfortable, and sometimes itchy and hot.

Bodies and their 'middle-size-dry-goods processes'[7] – among others, their birth, need for nourishment, initial limited competences, patterns of growth and aging, pregnancies, diseases, healing, and deaths – are themselves symbolic; they are sensible forms that feature widely in shared webs of associated symbols. The general shapes of human bodies, certain of their needs, and many of their temporal processes presumably remain quite similar over time and across human groupings. Perhaps – I do not wish to be more categorical – their continuities across time have the effect of keeping their associations with other symbolic forms more consistent than those that tied materially more mutable symbolic forms. This is in a limited sense a Saussurean account of the immutability of signs: they are complexly interrelated, and changes in one entail changes in others, but then this makes changes in general more difficult. Bodies and their processes could thus constitute a fairly constant public symbolic node, an attachment point for large and consistent symbolic webs, a centripetal force limiting if never eliminating *différance* and slippage.

Ethnographic accounts of other Amazonian peoples can be interpreted as revealing that elements of the Amazonian package feature centrally in people's morally evaluative understandings of themselves, and that they deployed the idioms of bodies. Vilaça's (2000) and Conklin's (2001a) descriptions of mortuary cannibalism, for example, suggest that Wari' people's highly valued compassion for grieving survivors was formulated in terms of body-making practices and perspectives; the survivors who had been consubstantial with the deceased could not cease to perceive it as a being of the same kind as they, and suffered for it. Affines, not under the thrall of this dangerous illusion, would eat the dead to show survivors that this was not a person any longer, but something edible, and therefore, a being of a different kind for which further, dangerous grief was no longer pertinent. Gow's (2001) account of Piro shamanism similarly shows that the kinds of beings people could be, their valued ways of relating to each other, and the admired and feared capacities of shamans, were all tied to the makings of like bodies and perspectives in a cosmos of alterity. Much work on shamanism and sorcery reveals that these are matters of considerable moral and aesthetic investment throughout the Amazon. The writings of many Amazonianists similarly seem to me to support the case that moral selfhood and sociality in the region are often shaped by, and reproduce, the Amazonian package.

I find that the widespread presence of the Amazonian package suggests a recursively branching historical process in which a group of people at one point in the distant past understood themselves and their relationships in its terms, and either they or their understandings, or both, spread out through the Americas.[8] The whereabouts and exact vicissitudes of this process are beyond me – my contribution is to claim that performative symbolic deployments that cited elements of the Amazonian package could have interpellated people effectively, telling them what kinds of beings they could and should be, and motivating them to act in ways that reproduced the conditions of their constitution, without such reproduction being under anybody's full ken or control. I thereby stress a key general message of this monograph: that morality, like its constitutive symbols, is both socially shared and a feature of individuals; it is also temporal, contingent, and slippery, and thoroughly pervades human existence.

# Appendix: Kinship Terminology

## Criteria for the Classification of Kin

An analysis of the classification of kin of a Muinane-speaking male ego suggests that he would 'box' each of his relatives on the basis of the following criteria:

1 Gender: whether the relative is male or female.
2 Generation: terms are distinct for relatives in each generation. This is not the case for a certain category of affine (or in-law), which will be discussed below.
3 Gender of the linking relatives: for kin in generation +1 (ego's parents' generation) and generation –1 (ego's children's generation) and, more specifically, whether the kinsperson is linked to ego via men only, or not. Note that MB ≠ FB, and there is a distinction between 'nephews' or 'nieces' (16 and 17 in table 3) linked to ego via a male sibling or male parallel cousin on the father's side, and 'nephews' or 'nieces' (18 and 19 in table 3) linked via a sister, an aunt (patrilateral or matrilateral), or female cousin. Thus, BD = FBSD ≠ ZD = FBDD = FZSD = FZDD = MBSD. Note that this coheres nicely with male members of a patriline tending to co-reside, and post-marital residence (where a couple lives after they become a couple) being virilocal; men would normally live in close proximity to men in table 3 categories 5, 8, 9, and 17, and unmarried women in categories 10, 11, and 18, but not with people in categories 19 and 20.
4 Relative age within the group of immediate siblings: whether the brother or sister is older or younger than ego.

## Some Notes on Marriage and Affinity

- People in table 3, categories 1–21 are ineligible for marriage to ego.
- The terms *gádoogo* and *gííyoobo* (in table 3, spouses of 5, 6, and 7) may be translated into English as stepmother and stepfather respectively. The reciprocal terms are *áikɨdoogo* (stepdaughter) when addressing a female and *áchiyoobo* (stepson) when addressing a male.
- Brothers, sisters, and some other kin of people categorized in table 3 as brother-in-law, sister-in-law, daughter-in-law, and son-in-law are known collectively as *nijɨɨto* (where individual men are referred to as *nijɨɨbo* and women as *nijɨɨg*o, independently of whether they are in generation 0 or generation +1.
- The term of reference for a male ego's wife is *taaba*, and for a female ego's husband is *tááje*. The parents and siblings (classificatory or not) of the parents of ego's spouse are all known individually as *baabo*, regardless of gender. The siblings and classificatory siblings of ego's spouse are known as brothers-in-law and sisters-in-law, the same terms used for the spouses of siblings and classificatory siblings.
- I heard two different terms for a male ego's WZH: *ikɨɨbo* and *dójɨhoobo* (or *dojɨɨbo)*. The first means 'he who takes,' and the second, one old man informed me, alluded to the situation of the ego and this man sharing the back of a maloca (since they had both married into it). A Muinane-speaking Nonuya elder told me the term *dojɨɨbo* applied as well to a man who had illicit sex with ego's wife.

## A Comparative Synthesis

Anthropologists often classify the kinship terminologies of people they work with according to their similarity to a number of 'basic' types of terminological systems (named Dravidian, Iroquois, Hawaiian, Eskimo, Crow, Omaha, and Sudanese types of kinship systems, after certain paradigmatic cases), each of which has its own criteria for classification. The terminology of the Muinane clans that I described features characteristics of Eskimo and Hawaiian types of kinship systems. In generations +2 and –2 all kin – in fact, everybody in those generations – are respectively either grandfathers or grandmothers, or grandsons or granddaughters. In generation 0, parallel cousins (the children of parents' same-sex siblings) and cross-cousins (the children of parents' cross sex siblings) are likened to siblings (for example,

Table 3
Kinship terminology for male ego among People of the Pineapple, People of the Grub, and People of the Wooden Drum (Chukikɨ)

| | | Muinane | | Equivalent terms in local Spanish and English approximation | | Of spouse: Muinane Equivalent terms in Spanish and English approximation | |
|---|---|---|---|---|---|---|---|
| Category number | | Term of reference | Vocative term† | Term of reference | Vocative term† | Term of reference | Vocative term† |
| | Generation +2 | | | | | | |
| 1. | FF, FFB, MF, MFB (and other men of this generation) | táádíyɨ | tyáádi | abuelo<br>grandfather | abuelito<br>grandpa | | |
| 2. | FM, FMZ, MM, MMZ (and other women of this generation) | táágóyɨ | tyáágo | abuela<br>grandmother | abuelita<br>grandma | | |
| | Generation +1 | | | | | | |
| 3. | F | kaani (a father)<br>giirubi (ego's father) | gííhi or gíí | papá<br>father | papito<br>daddy | If FW ≠ M:<br>sééjɨdoogo (a stepmother)<br>gáádoogo or gádahogo (ego's stepmother) | gáádoogo or gádahogo |

(*Continued*)

Table 3 (*Continued*)

| Category number | | Muinane: Term of reference | Muinane: Vocative term† | Equivalent terms in local Spanish and English approximation: Term of reference | Equivalent terms in local Spanish and English approximation: Vocative term† | Of spouse: Muinane Equivalent terms in Spanish and English approximation: Term of reference | Of spouse: Muinane Equivalent terms in Spanish and English approximation: Vocative term† |
|---|---|---|---|---|---|---|---|
| | | | | | | madrastra<br>stepmother | madrastra<br>stepmother |
| 4. | M | seejɨ (a mother)<br>gaarubi (ego's mother) | gáha or gáá | mamá<br>mother | mamita<br>mommy | If MH ≠ F:<br>kaaniyoobo (a stepfather)<br>gííyoobo (ego's stepfather)<br>padrastro<br>stepfather | gííyoobo<br><br>padrastro<br>stepfather |
| 5. | FB, FFBS (and in theory, any man in this generation linked to ego exclusively via men) | takoomoobo | takoomoobo | tío<br>(paternal) uncle | tío<br>uncle | sééjidoogo (a stepmother)<br>gáádoogo or gádahogo (ego's stepmother)<br>tía or madrastra<br>aunt or stepmother | gáádoogo or gádahogo<br><br>madrastra<br>stepmother |
| 6. | FZ, FFBD, MZ | takoomogo | takoomogo | tía<br>aunt | tía<br>aunt | kaaniyoobo (a stepfather or uncle)<br>gííyoobo (ego's stepfather or uncle)<br>padrastro or tío<br>uncle | gííyoobo<br><br>padrastro or tio<br>stepfather or uncle |

| | | | | | | | |
|---|---|---|---|---|---|---|---|
| 7. | MB | seejɨgaifiibo | gáágaifiibo | tío (maternal) uncle | tío uncle | sééjɨdoogo (a stepmother) gáádoogo or gádahogo (ego's step-mother) tía or madrastra aunt or stepmother | gáádoogo or gádahogo tia or madrastra aunt or stepmother |
| | Generation 0 | | | | | | |
| 8. | eB (brother, older than ego) | tahámiyaabo, and may also be called tañaabo (see 12) tagaifíibo (if female ego) | tahámiyaabo, and may also be called tañaabo (see 12) tagaifíibo (if female ego) | propio hermano mayor true older brother | hermano brother | atyaanɨɨgo cuñada sister-in-law | bɨ́ɨ́je cuñada sister-in-law |
| 9. | yB (brother younger than ego) | tagííhoobo, and may also be called tañaabo (see 12) tagaifíibo (if female ego) | bésha (if female ego) | propio hermano menor true younger brother | hermano brother darling (if female ego) | átyaanɨɨgo cuñada sister-in-law | bɨ́ɨ́je cuñada sister-in-law |

(*Continued*)

Table 3 (*Continued*)

| | | Muinane | | Equivalent terms in local Spanish and English approximation | | Of spouse: Muinane Equivalent terms in Spanish and English approximation | |
|---|---|---|---|---|---|---|---|
| Category number | | Term of reference | Vocative term† | Term of reference | Vocative term† | Term of reference | Vocative term† |
| 10. | eZ (sister older than ego) | tahámiyago, and may also be called tañaago (see 13) | tahámiyago or ñɨ́ɨba, | propia hermana mayor true older sister | hermana mayor sister or darling | átyaniibo cuñado brother-in-law | baadu cuñado brother-in-law |
| 11. | yZ (sister younger than ego) | tagííhogo, and may also be called tañaago (see 13) | tagííhogo or ñɨ́ɨba | propia hermana menor true younger sister | hermana sister or darling | átyanɨɨbo cuñado brother-in-law | baadu cuñado brother-in-law |
| 12. | B, FBS, FFBSS FZS, FFBDS, MBS, MZS FFBS (and in theory, any man in this generation who is not an affine) | tañaabo (see also 8 and 9) | fáñɨ bésha (as female ego may address younger men) | hermano brother | hermano brother darling (if female ego) | átyaanɨɨgo cuñada sister-in-law | bɨ́ɨje cuñada sister-in-law |
| 13. | Z, FBD, FZD, FFBSD, FFBDD(?), MBD, MZD | tañago (see also 10 and 11) | tañago or ñɨ́ɨba | hermana sister | hermana sister or darling | átyanɨɨbo cuñado brother-in-law | baadu cuñado brother-in-law |

| | | | | | | | |
|---|---|---|---|---|---|---|---|
| | Generation -1 | | | | | | |
| 14. | S | aachi | gíí or gííhi | hijo<br>son | papito<br>daddy | táhiyaja<br>nuera<br>daughter-in-law | gáá or gáha<br>mamita<br>mommy |
| 15. | D | áikigai | gáá or gáha | hija<br>daughter | mamita<br>mommy | aija<br>yerno<br>son-in-law | gíí or gíhi<br>papito<br>daddy |
| 16. | BS, FBSS, FFBSSS FFBS (and in theory, any man in this generation linked to ego exclusively via men, except for S) | tasííbakajeebe | tasííbakajeebe | sobrino<br>nephew | sobrino<br>nephew | táhiyaja<br>nuera<br>daughter-in-law | gáá or gáha<br>mamita<br>mommy |
| 17. | BD, FBSD, FFBS (and in theory, any woman in this generation linked to Ego exclusively via men, except for D) | tasííbakajege (rarely used) | tasííbakajege | sobrina<br>niece | sobrina<br>niece | áija<br>yerno<br>son-in-law | gíí or gíhi<br>papito<br>daddy |

(*Continued*)

Table 3 (*Continued*)

| | | Muinane | | Equivalent terms in local Spanish and English approximation | | Of spouse: Muinane Equivalent terms in Spanish and English approximation | |
|---|---|---|---|---|---|---|---|
| Category number | | Term of reference | Vocative term† | Term of reference | Vocative term† | Term of reference | Vocative term† |
| 18. | ZS, FBDS, FFBDS, FZSS, FZDS, MBSS, MBDS, MZSS, MZDS | taboobo | taboobo | sobrino nephew | sobrino nephew | táhiyaja nuera daughter-in-law | gáá or gáha mamita mommy |
| 19. | ZD, FBDD, FFBDD, FZSD, FZDD, MBSD, MBDD, MZSD, MZDD | taboogo | taboogo | sobrina niece | sobrina niece | áija yerno son-in-law | gíí or gíhi papito daddy |
| | Generation -2 | | | | | | |
| 20. | Sons of 15–20 (and all men in this generation) | iyachi | gíí or gííhi | nieto grandson | papito daddy | táhiyaja nuera daughter-in-law | gáá or gáha mamita mommy |
| 21. | Daughters of 15–20 (and all women in this generation) | aháikigai | gáá or gáha | nieta granddaughter | mamita mommy | áija yerno son-in-law | gíí or gíhi papito daddy |

Father = F; Mother = M; Brother = B; Sister = Z; Son = S; Daughter = D; Husband = H; Wife = W. The codes for other kin are read following the pattern of the following examples (from category 19): ZD = sister's daughter; FBDD = father's brother's daughter's daughter; MBSD: mother's brother's son's daughter.

† A vocative term is a term of address.

FZD = MBD). These are features of a Hawaiian kinship system. However, there is somewhat of a terminological distinction between immediate siblings and classificatory ones that is more like that of an Eskimo kinship system.

The terminology for generations +1 and –1 of the Muinane clans in question is also like that of the Eskimo system, but with an important patrilineal inflection, a difference created by the third criterion in the list above – gender of the linking relative(s). As with the Eskimo-type kinship system, the Muinane terminology distinguishes ego's parents from their siblings, and these siblings are furthermore distinguished by gender. However, parents' *male* siblings are distinguished by whether they are on the mother's side or the father's side (MB ≠ FB, yet MZ = FZ). In generation –1, children are distinguished by gender, one's children are terminologically distinct from sibling's children, and the latter, along with classificatory siblings' children, are mostly referred to with the same term: roughly, nephews and nieces. There is a non-Eskimo patrilineal bias in this generation too, however: nephews and nieces via exclusively male lines are distinguished terminologically from others in generation –1.

The kinship terminology in question features the same basic structure as that of Uitoto-speaking people in the Medio Caquetá and the Igaraparaná (Echeverri, personal communication); in other words, though the actual words differ, if each term in the Uitoto system were given a number, the diagram would look the same as the one I have provided here for the Muinane (figure A.1). The kinship terminology used by the Muinane-speaking Cumare Nut clan was more like that of the Miraña (and presumably Bora), which was quite similar but did not feature a patrilineal inflection. Thus, members of this clan did not distinguish terminologically between kin in categories 17 and 19, or between kin in categories 18 and 20. They tended to call the men in all these categories taboobo (19) and the women taboogo (20). I found women of all the clans to place little emphasis on the distinction between these kinds of nephews; some did not use terms 17 and 18 at all, and some found them to be exactly synonymous with terms 19 and 20. There is also great linguistic similarity between the Muinane and Miraña terms for each category of relative.

The differences in the terminologies between Muinane clans is probably causally related to the upriver clans (People of the Pineapple, Grub, and Wooden Drum) having lived in closer proximity with, and intermarried more, with Uitoto speakers. I imagine their terminology

Figure A.1 Diagram of Muinane kinship terminology for a male ego (Chukikɨ)

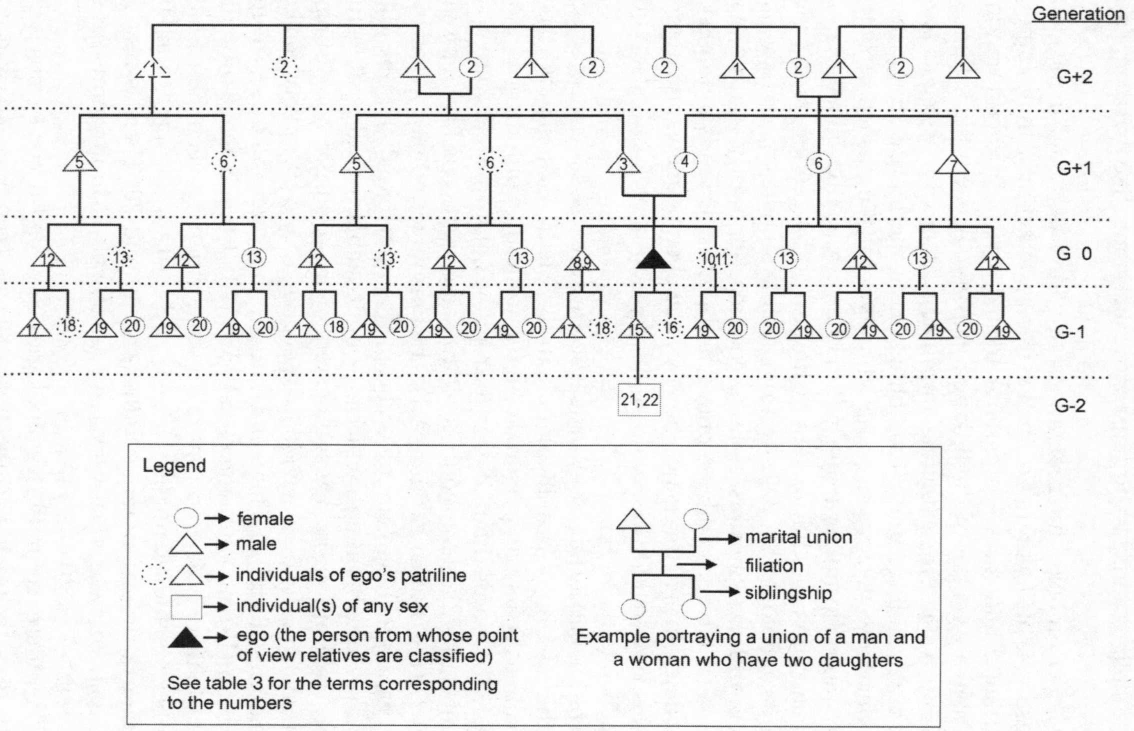

to have been the more widely shared Muinane terminology in the past. The Cumare Nut clan's terminology is closer to that of the Bora, probably for reasons relating to their closer proximity to the Bora while living in La Sabana del Cahuinarí, and having intermarried with them; the Bora influence was also discernible in this Muinane clan's songs and dance steps at dance rituals.

People of the Centre appeared to have followed a negative rule in seeking marriage partners, namely the specification of a large cognatic (bilateral) network of people within which ego could *not* marry. According to Karadimas (2000), terminologies such as that of the Miraña – and by extension, the Muinane and Uitoto – generated a growing number of kin with each marital alliance: the children of ego's parents' siblings were all ego's classificatory siblings, with whom marriage would be incestuous. This contrasts with the Dravidian-type terminologies of people to the north in the Vaupés, and to the south in the upper stretches of the Amazon, where there was what some anthropologists call 'a positive rule of exchange,' in the form of a preference for marriage with cross-cousins in a system of reciprocal alliances. In those neighbouring societies, some of the children of an ego's parents' siblings were actually preferred marriage partners for ego. Karadimas claims that among the Miraña, clans functioned not so much to establish groups of people tied by common lineal descent, but rather to delimit non-kin in a system that generated kin all the time. Karadimas articulates the 'canonical formula of Miraña alliance' as follows, with either of ego's parents as point of departure: 'the son's wife is the daughter of a classificatory brother or classificatory sister,' or 'the daughter's husband is the son of a classificatory brother or classificatory sister,' as long as ego's partner-to-be does not belong to any of the four clans of ego's grandparents (2000, 607; my translation). He notes that often it was parents who arranged their children's marriages.

Karadimas's account of Miraña kinship and marriage preferences resembles what I heard among Muinane people, and helps make sense of an apparent split in their injunctions concerning marriage: there were demands on one hand that they 'marry far,' and on the other, that they not marry too far. These rules and injunctions were pliable, however: people emphasized them at times, and at times found ways to reframe their decisions concerning partners in such a way that they could ignore the rules. In any case, with very few exceptions, marriages involving individuals of Muinane clans did take place with people outside of table 3, categories 1–21.

# Notes

**Introduction: People of the Centre**

1 Loosely, a narrative frame is a pattern within stories or narratives of a certain kind, and which makes these narratives recognizable and familiar to a group of people; they know what kinds of events or characters or qualities can be expected to appear in it, how the narrative is supposed to be told, and how it is closed.

2 These typologies do not correspond perfectly to each other, but there are some important convergences.

3 Juan Echeverri's PhD thesis features a lengthy discussion that describes the term 'People of the Center' as the reflection of a process of ideological construction of a new kind of 'moral community' (a concept developed by Ellen Basso), in the wake of the rubber boom holocaust that decimated the people in the region (1997, 16).

4 In Muinane there is a single term for thoughts and emotions: *ésámaje*. This volume attends to emotions at some length, taking its inspiration from Rosaldo (1984).

5 On this period in history in the region, see Domínguez and Gómez (1994, 123–7), Gómez et al. (1995, 47), Echeverri (1997, 94–9), Llanos and Pineda (1982, 59), Taussig (1987), and Londoño Sulkin (2001).

6 'Cumare' is the Spanish term for the *Astrocaryum sp.* palm from which husks or nuts (*nejéyi*, in Muinane) are harvested for traditional vessels for tobacco paste, and fibres extracted for various uses, including weaving.

7 The Matapí were a people historically related to the Yukuna, to such an extent the latter's Arawak language had become their own. The majority of the Matapí and Yukuna lived along the Mirití river and near La

Pedrera, but a few families had settled further upriver, in Araracuara and the communities slightly east of it.

8 For an excellent analysis of kinship terminology and marriage practices among the Miraña, see Karadimas (1997); much of what he states would apply to the Muinane as well, and the terms are morphologically and phonetically very similar.

9 Manioc (genus *Manihot*) is a staple food in much of Amazonia. It is a large tuber, very rich in carbohydrates. There are many varieties, some of which are poisonous and require special preparation to be made edible.

10 I use the term 'elders' as a translation of People of the Centre's references to mayores or ancianos in Spanish or *júúsito* in Muinane. The latter included adults who were among the oldest in their lineages and who were, therefore, recognized to be knowledgeable. Some could be as young as forty. Such elders did not constitute corporate age sets, that is, groups constituted by people of roughly the same age who went together through age-specific rituals, and who could act together as a group.

11 For a similar contrast between kinds of leaders among the Brazilian Kayabi, see Oakdale (2005, 62–5); for very clear discussions of the contradictions and other effects of the appearance of new kinds of leadership and new differentials in native people's access to resources, see Echeverri (1997) and Rubenstein (2002).

12 On this process and some of its unexpected effects on native communities, see Padilla (1994).

13 My attention to individuals' understandings resonates with that of interactionists (for example, Riches 1985) and transactionalists (for example, Barth 1966), but my approach differs fundamentally from these two in its more relational view of personhood – that is, in not presupposing that persons are logically prior to sociality; it also rejects the presupposition that individuals are maximizers (see Riches 1985).

14 I accept the Marxist rejection of Cartesian dualism that would treat ideas as part of an immaterial realm of existence, in contrast with a material one. Thoughts, emotions, and so forth, take place in material bodies, and are themselves sensible experiences. For a lovely old discussion of this, see Vološinov (1993 [1929]).

15 I rediscovered late in the process of writing this book a very similar understanding, formulated with a different vocabulary: 'because meaning is inherent in social relations, one has, in making meaning, to submit to the meanings that others have made. By the same token, others stand in a similar relation to oneself … Even while one makes meaning out of the meanings others have made, one cannot help but constitute those

meanings anew – and in the process introduce differences that are subtle or wide-ranging or even, sometimes, highly original. This perspective on meaning is inevitably historical for it allows our analyses to accommodate the material nature of social relations and thus to handle simultaneously both continuity and change' (Christina Toren, in Ingold 1996, 75) Geertz (1973) is of course a background figure in this discussion.

16 For an account convergent with mine on this point, see Lambek's (2010) discussion of the recognition and production of ethical criteria and judgment through ritual performance.

17 Along comparable lines, Taylor ranks what he calls different levels of expressive form, from projective body language, style, and rhetoric, to the symbolic (in works of art), to the descriptive. We may be unreflecting on what we project, but at some point it can be made an object of description and analysis (2006, 34, 35). Lambek (2010), in addressing the fact that criteria are intrinsic to ethical judgment, notes that they can be made objects of conscious discernment and deliberation. I would underscore that such discernment and deliberations are a *sine qua non* feature of human social life.

18 By *sensible experience* I mean associations established between perceptions and other symbolic forms. A personal memory of mine of such a sensible experience is of the feeling of pressure and fatigue in my jaw when biting into a fist-sized rubber ball of a kind popular in Medellín when I was a child; it featured in a recurrent dream I had back then, and I associate it with unpleasant frustration.

19 My vocabulary and concepts here are inspired by Judith Butler (1993).

20 Keane (2010), notes that Appiah, Derrida, Foucault, and Freud came to conclude, from different premises, that people are not fully aware of their motives for acting nor in full control of decisions they make. He disagrees with Derrida's Saussurean model of the sign, however: 'At this point, the analyst may find that the logic of deferral, posed as a critique of humanist notions of self-presence, situates the world of actions and interactions at the far reaches of an infinite regress' (2003, 412). For Keane, this impedes proper consideration of the entailments of the materiality of signs. For a good, brief discussion of the role of intentionality in the linguistic anthropological description and explanation of human social life, see Robbins and Rumsey (2008, 412–17). For a convergent discussion in literary theory, see Culler: 'If history is the name of the discrepancy between intention and occurrence, then literary theory has a pertinent model to hand in its debates about the problematical relation between meaning as intentional act (of a writer or reader) and meaning as textual fact (the

product of grammatical, rhetorical, textual, and contextual structures)' (1989, xiv).

21 Weber's 'value-spheres' (via Robbins 2007) could be deemed products of such patterns, too.

22 Rumsey's (2010) linguistic anthropological research makes a similar case to the effect that mundane communicative practices and interactional routines provide one of the bases on which more enduring sociocultural forms are reproduced and transformed.

23 An important limitation in my research is that I did not invest much time or focused methodological effort into researching socialization processes involving children. I did take note of who took care of them, of remarkable things that were said and done to them, and of goings-on at the incipient schools being set up in several settlements, but work like Kulick's (1992) and Ochs and Taylor's (1995) on child socialization underscores just how important this matter is, and the great deal of attention to detail it requires. A more detailed research specifically on language socialization would nicely complement my research to date.

24 Recent discussions of Amazonian understandings of embodiment and selfhood can be found in Belaunde (2000, 2001), Conklin (2001a, 2001b), Descola (2001), Fisher (2001). Gow (2000, 2001), Griffiths (1998), Hugh-Jones (2001), Lagrou (1998, 2000), Londoño Sulkin (2004), McCallum (2001), Overing and Passes (2000a), Rosengren (2006), Santos-Granero (2009), Seeger (2004), and Vilaça (2000, 2002, 2005), among many others. For important earlier work, see Seeger, da Matta, and Viveiros de Castro (1979); Turner (1980); and especially Seeger's (1980) concept of 'groups of substance.'

25 See Viveiros de Castro (2001), Descola (2001), or Erikson (1996), among a great many others, for pointed discussions of relations of alterity in the Amazon.

26 The literature discussing relations of alterity is extensive. A smattering of focused pieces is the following: Descola (2001), Erikson (1996), Fausto (1999), Overing (1993), Overing and Passes (2001b), Rivière (2001), and Viveiros de Castro (1996, 1998), recent, book-length expositions of the matter are Santos-Granero (2009) and, in the Andes, Peter Gose (2009).

27 Carneiro da Cunha and Viveiros de Castro (1985) make a similar claim for the Tupinamba, who created their societies on the basis of warring relations with enemy others.

28 This image of radial transformations is, of course, inspired by a Lévi-Straussian image of myths transforming in Amerindian time and space; my own reading of this is via Peter Gow's (2001) very important

monograph. Gow notes that it is becoming increasingly obvious that at some level, 'the socio-cosmological systems of all indigenous Amazonian peoples are topological transformations of each other in ways that are neither trivial nor over-generalized (300).

29 For instance, see Taylor's (1996) discussion of Achuar arutam searches.

**1 The Constitution of the Moral Self**

1 I take this concept from Harry Frankfurt, via Taylor (1985, 16–19).

2 I tend to treat the creator as a male figure linked to tobacco, following the preferences of the Cumare Nut and Pineapple Muinane-speaking clans. Their version of the creator had several names in Muinane that translated as 'Grandfather of Tobacco,' 'Grandfather of Our Creation,' and 'Our Father,' the latter perhaps a direct translation from the Christian Bible. The Grub and Wooden Drum clans were more akin to Uitoto-Nɨpóde clans in that they treated the tobacco deity as a female and the coca as male. Their prayers were thus often addressed to 'Our Mother.' Identification of all their deities with Christian ones was common.

3 The image of a single creator god above is most likely their adoption of Catholic and Evangelical missionaries' accounts; many – not all – amalgamated the Christian deity with the Grandfather of Tobacco.

4 For similar, morally imbued concepts of memory – or memory-centred concepts of morality – among Amazonians, see Gow (2000, 51) and Taylor (1996, 206).

5 See Seeger (1980), on a concept of 'corporeal groups' akin to People of the Centre's.

6 For two excellent ethnographic accounts of Amazonian people's understandings of the instability and fixity of bodies, see Vilaça (2005) and Lagrou (2000); see also Griffiths (2001) on how continual work among Uitoto people guarantees the retention of a human body and affirms human identity, in a world in which 'behaviour is a better guide than appearance' (Rivière, cited in Griffiths 2001, 257).

7 See Viveiros de Castro's (1998, 481) discussion on the performative character of the body among Amerindians in general; see also Vilaça (2005).

8 A mammalian species People of the Centre called 'zorro' in Spanish; it is not what is known in English as 'fox,' but I could not ascertain the species.

9 People of the Centre's version of *couvade* – practices based on the premise that there are links between a father, a mother, and their unborn or newborn child, such that what one of them does or experiences can cause the others to experience or do something similar – seemed to

extend, in tempered form, throughout life and to a broader range of people. See C. Hugh-Jones (1979, 132) on the seclusion of Barasana men and women during pregnancy, and Griffiths (1998, 212) and Gow (1991, 152–4, 197) for discussions concerning *couvade* in relation to notions of consubstantiality among Amazonian peoples.

10 For convergent descriptions of soft babies, baby-kneading, and aging as a process of hardening among Cashinahua, Uitoto, Barasana, Airo-Pai, and Kayabi people, see respectively Lagrou (2000), Griffiths (1998, 163), C. Hugh-Jones (1979, 149), Belaunde (1992, 110), and Oakdale (2005, 146).

11 People's names in Muinane and Uitoto were usually linked to the clan's *jávarata* although the kinds of connections varied. Thus, names of People of the Pineapple could be 'Beautiful Pineapple Plant,' or 'He of the Refuse Heap' (of pineapple peels), or 'Macaw Flower' (a variety of pineapple). Examples of names of People of the Grub were 'He Who Descends' (as a grub descends along a palm tree as it eats its core), 'Flier' (because the butterfly of the grub flies), and so on. On naming rituals and the recycling of names or souls among Uitoto, Barasana, and Yukuna people, see respectively Griffiths (1998, 173), S. Hugh-Jones (1979), and van der Hammen (1992, 329).

12 Belaunde (1992, 88–92, 106) states that for the Airo-Pai of the Peruvian Amazon, sexuality is not naturally given or independent of human agency. They symbolically manufacture children's sex organs, craft their (male and female) 'wombs,' pierce girl's hymens, and scratch the dark borders of their labia. 'In order to avoid an ever-present dangerous and infertile state of non-differentiation, the difference between men and women is constantly being recreated in a process which states their difference and also inverts their difference' (119). See as well Gow (1991, 120) and McCallum (2001, 41–64) on gender identity as constituted within social relations and not produced before them.

13 Nieto Moreno (2006, 187) provides a nice description of a Uitoto woman in Leticia describing how her own body had acquired its vigorous, itinerant, hard-working form because of her proper behaviour the first time she menstruated. See also Basso's description of self-cultivation among the Kalapalo (2003).

14 See Londoño Sulkin 2001, 2004, 2006, and 2010 for other examples of virtues becoming 'set' in bodies.

15 Vilaça finds that for the Wari', instability is the crucial feature of *jam* (souls), which can be realized in multiple forms of bodies and allows these to transform. However, transformations may be generated by other agents, and so must be controlled, the potential for metamorphosis annulled, if

specific humanity is to be achieved. Healthy, active human beings therefore have no *jam* (2005, 453).

16 The term for pain was also an augmentative adverbial or adjectival term; 'very strong,' in Muinane, would be 'painful strong.' For an interesting convergence, see Tambiah (1998, 76) on Sinhalese mantras which are said to 'hit with sound.'

## 2 Reflecting on Evil and Responsibility

Parts of this chapter appeared in Carlos David Londono Sulkin (2004), *Muinane: Un Proyecto Moral a Perpetuidad* (Medellín: Editorial Universidad de Antioquia).

1 Viveiros de Castro (1998, 481) has already noted that a deep existential problem for Amerindians lies in the danger of seeing the humanity of the Other, which then opens to question one's own. For other focused discussions of existential issues with deceit and impostorship among Amazonian peoples, see Griffiths (2001, 254, 255 and 261 n.19), Lima (2002, cited in Vilaça 2005, 458–9), Londoño Sulkin (2010), Opas (2008, 136–41), Taylor (1993), and Vilaça (2005, 451).

2 There are exceptions in the West, however: demonic possessions requiring exorcisms, and legal arguments of 'temporary insanity,' among others.

3 This contrasts with Santos-Granero's (1991, 41) description of Amuesha people's (Peruvian Amazon) implicit view of human nature, in which 'without the limitations imposed by social organisation actions tend towards evil.' Their reportedly Hobbesian image of humankind as naturally warlike would be opposed to People of the Centre's theories to the extent that the latter deemed true humanity to be intrinsically moral. Any antisocial behaviour was therefore not human, but bestial.

4 People remembered their experiences, because there was experiential continuity between the counterfeit self and the real one. This continuity did not puzzle People of the Centre, as it might a cognitivist theorist. The key to this lay in the body: selves could have false speeches, but I never heard of them having false bodies. It was the body that provided phenomenological continuity: all the speeches that went through it were remembered. The 'false' here as a qualifier articulated moral paucity; it did not deny the real existence of the immoral self.

5 Griffiths claimed that in some of the accounts of Uitoto people animals had malocas, food plants, and elders who provided counsel; in daily conversation and formal discourse, however, animals were defined by their anti-

social, non-human qualities rather than by parallels with humanity (1998, 71–3).

6 People of the Centre narrators animated the voices of characters in their stories and anecdotes. For a deep, persuasive examination of such animations among Kayabi people, see Oakdale (2005).

7 On the degradation of faunal races or the separation of immoral animality from humanity, and on animal threats, see Griffiths (1998, 55–8, 221), Overing (1990, 608, 613), Reichel-Dolmatoff (1997, 112), and Viveiros de Castro (1998, 472).

8 In Spanish, 'El tabaco de los animals no tiene sentido.' (Muinane people spoke of animal tobacco both in the plural and in the singular.)

9 Different beings' *jágába*, which my Muinane informants translated into Spanish as 'aliento' (breath) or 'atmósfera' (air, atmosphere, environment), were understood to generate subjectivities in the same way speeches did.

10 I refer to this anecdote in Londoño Sulkin (2003) and Londoño Sulkin (2004).

11 This supports Viveiros de Castro's (1998) point that it is the body that provides the point of view; bodies of others of the same species cannot but be perceived as humans. However, for People of the Centre the warped subjectivity of the jaguar motivated it to destroy others of its own kind – whatever body-kind that subjectivity happened to be 'speaking through.' Cf. Taylor (1996, 205, 206) and Conklin (2001a, 188).

12 Although other scholars engaged with the matter of cosmological perspectives – for example, Århem (1993) produced elegant work on point of view among the Makuna, and Tania Stolze Lima (1996) had underscored the importance of difference in perspective between peccaries and humans – the development of the full-fledged account of multinaturalist cosmological perspectivism and the ambitious argument to the effect that it is a thought system to be found among Amerindians in general is Viveiros de Castro's, and perhaps found in its most detailed form in his 1998 article. The discussion has since gone viral, with many Amazonians scrambling to address it. Examples from a young generation of Amazonianists doing so are Course (2010), High (2012), Kohn (2007), Opas (2008), Virtanen (2009), and Walker (2009). Prominent outsiders such as Sahlins (2008, 96) and Latour (2004, 2009) are joining in as well. For accounts of perspectival cosmologies outside the Amazon, see Howell (1996) on the Malaysian Chewong, Brightman (2002) on the Rock Cree in Canada and the US, and Pedersen (2001) on North Asia.

13 On the importance of avoiding the misattribution of metaphorical character to literal statements in ethnographic analysis, see Overing (1985c).

14 This wonderful man requested that I name him 'Rayo' – the Spanish word for lightning – because this was tied to his *jávarata*. I promised him I would follow the pattern of using Biblical or Hebrew names, and call him Barak, also 'Lightning.'

15 On evaluations of misbehaviour in terms of animality, see Kensinger (1995, 69) and Lagrou (1998, 28), on Cashinahua people, and on Achuar people, see Descola (1994, 91, 96, 97).

16 This possibility is not completely absent from Viveiros de Castro's discussion (1998, 483), and may be recognized in Lima (via Vilaça 2005).

17 Another Spanish term for these birds is 'oropéndola.'

18 The contributors to Overing and Passes (2000) provide converging accounts of the salience of anger as an emotion destructive of social life. See especially Overing and Passes's introduction, Belaunde (2000), Jamieson (2000), Kidd (2000), Londoño Sulkin (2000), and Rosengren (2000).

19 See Gonçalves (2000, 239) for an account of jealousy among the Brazilian Paresi, who understand it as a force that makes social relationships impossible.

20 Some scholars prefer the term 'entheogenic,' which defines the substance as one that 'puts one into contact with the gods,' to 'hallucinogenic,' which suggests that it makes one see something that is not really there.

21 Lynn (2005, 34) argues that Muinane people's attribution of human miscreancy to animals absolves persons of some responsibility and guilt; he sees this as a form of dissociation that fulfils a biological imperative. While recognizing people's capacity for strategizing, I distrust purportedly natural scientific accounts of agency or responsibility. My sense is that Western understandings of responsibility in relation to intentionality and the capacity for effective action are varied, parochial, and historically mutable, and are often imported casually into natural scientific arguments (see Laidlaw 2002 for a discussion of this). Anything we say about responsibility is already a performative claim that shapes the phenomenon, and already an interpretation of people's subjective understandings. It is, thus, not readily amenable to exploration modelled on the natural sciences and seeking to explain subjectivity radically in terms of causes other than subjective ones.

22 Zigon finds the analysis of narratives often to reveal competing and contested moral perspectives; it is common for the teller to frame his or her own moral position as somehow superior to another, in order to persuade others of the rightness of his or her moral position (2008, 147). Bakhtin – via Keane 2003 – argues that this multiplicity of perspectives, or rather of 'voices,' is constitutive of self-consciousness.

## 3 Agency and Transformation

1 For careful transcriptions, translations, and analyses of such speeches among Uitoto speakers, see Candre and Echeverri (1996). The contributions to Monod and Erikson (2000) describe a number of convergent features of ritual dialogues among different Amerindian peoples.
2 My Muinane hosts asked me not to record such speeches. I heard versions of this one many times, at times produced by a lone mambeador closing down a maloca for the night, at times by a man and a what-sayer. The cited version is my translation of speeches I reconstructed afterwards from memory, and is missing the answering 'hmms' and echoes.
3 See the contributions in Vidal and Whitehead (2009) and Wright (2004) for comparable accounts among different peoples in Amazonia and Papua New Guinea of malignant sorcery as an expression of the same powers used in benevolent shamanism.
4 It is not my intention to discuss here the 'scientifically objective' healing power of traditional medicines of People of the Centre, as if their knowledge were a shadow of Western science that prefigured it, as Lévi-Strauss claimed for magical thought (1964, 30).
5 This section also appears in Londoño Sulkin (2006).
6 There were several terms in Muinane that referred to the desirable visible manifestation of deployments of knowledge. *Seséévehi*, 'it whitens' or 'it dawns' was one; another was *állɨvɨ ɨ́fuvusuno*, literally 'above it makes itself be seen' which also described, for instance, a small plant sprouting and becoming visible above ground.
7 Cf. Echeverri (1997, 195) and Santos-Granero (1991, 12) on the moral use of knowledge among Uitoto and Yanesha people respectively.
8 Beauty can be a manifestation of morality, or else mere appearance, with no real substance behind it to guarantee its moral results. Cf. Overing (1985b, 274).
9 Cf. Overing (1985c, 167–9), on 'truth' and moral coherence and correctness.
10 See Overing (1993, 191–211) and Lagrou (2006), on the dangers of excess among the Piaroa and Cashinahua respectively.
11 Griffiths (2001) addresses at length the importance of work among Uitoto people, and their long work days.
12 See Griffiths (1998, 252–4) for an excellent discussion of gardening as 'proper work' among the Uitoto, and involving the participation of garden divinities that eat the felled forest.
13 See Belaunde (1992, 167, 168), Descola (1994, 270), Echeverri (1997, 151, 152), Griffiths (1998, 114–18), Nieto Moreno (2006, 174), and Taylor (2001,

51, 52) for discussions on Amazonian groups' images of plants as children and of children as plants.

14 See Echeverri (1997, 8–102) for a lengthy discussion of this.

15 See Goldman's (1963, 155) commentary to the effect that Cubeo house building was the equivalent of an election; see also Rivière (2000).

16 Following the descriptions of Emmons and Feer (1990, 11), the animal People of the Centre know as *tintín* (Spanish) or *jíkimo* (Muinane) is known to zoologists as the 'green acouchy,' or *Myoprocta pratti*.

17 According to Pineda, quoted in Espinosa (1995, 101), the pillars of Andoke malocas were understood to be four anacondas that cared for the community.

18 See van der Hammen (1992, 140), on the purpose of the maloca among the Yukuna.

19 In my experience, Muinane and Uitoto malocas were all understood to be female entities. However, according to Horacio Calle as discussed by Griffiths (1998, 162), Uitoto people also had male malocas. For a discussion of female, male, and androgynous houses in Amazonia, see S. Hugh-Jones (1993, 100; 1995) and Guyot (1972).

20 There was a verb in Muinane that referred specifically to the act of gaping at dead game brought home by a hunter. I believe this related to the reported past custom of hunters to place their game where people could see it, presumably, so that they would know that the hunters' or healers' knowledge had dawned, and so that others could claim their part.

21 Emanuel often insisted that sleep deprivation could make someone 'see' things in a manner similar to how *yagé* could provide the consumer with a privileged, all-seeing perspective.

22 These were claims to strength, destructive power, invulnerability, and immortality.

23 Again, that which was moral was manifest, transparent, clear, and available to sight. That which was immoral was often obscure, dark, and concealed from sight.

24 Plowing the ground for peanuts was a stereotypical agricultural endeavour of women.

25 See Lorrain (2001, 207) for a discussion of debates concerning gender hierarchy and equality in the Amazon; she finds that gender hierarchy in the division of labour among the Kulina is enforced by a 'soft, indirect form of violence, namely the symbolic violence expressed in rituals, myths, implicit mythology, shamanic practices, and the discourses of everyday life.'

**4 The Substances of Humanity**

1 See van der Hammen (1992) for a lengthy discussion of the distribution of manioc strains among Yukuna women in the Lower Caquetá.
2 On Uitoto healers' ability to see that which is invisible to others, see Echeverri (1997, 171).
3 Some of these forms of exchange and gifting of tobacco appear in descriptions of the customs of people along the Caquetá river from a century back; see Whiffen (1915) and Casement (1985).
4 'To dazzle painfully' and 'to cause to feel shame' were the same term in Muinane. Shame was supposed to make a person drop their head, unable to bear looking at others' faces, much as they were unable to look at the midday sun.
5 The term in Muinane was *Ájevabañoho*, constituted by the stems *bañoho*, meaning tobacco, and *ájeva*, which I translate as 'itchiness.' Walton et al. (1997, 12) translated the term as 'madness' and 'sexual desire.' People of the Centre spoke of fixating, uncontrollable sexual desire as a form of extreme itchiness or as akin to the latter in its capacity to occupy people's attention and distract them from their endeavours.
6 Clear sight, light, and disclosure were opposed to undesirable sightlessness, darkness, and opacity in People of the Centre's rhetoric on knowledge. On the other hand, darkness and opacity could be used as protection. Calling the Tobacco of Opacity an evil tobacco was a matter of perspective: if what it did was make animals opaque and inconspicuous, it was evil.
7 Cf. van der Hammen (1992, 292, 344) on references to different species' tobaccos, among Yukuna, Makuna, and Desana people.
8 For similar views in Amazonia, see Belaunde (1992, 2000), Gow (1991), and Lagrou (2000). On becoming people of a kind in Hawaii through common consumption of substances, see Sahlins (1985, 28, 29).
9 Echeverri's (1998, 99) discussion of 'public' versus 'private' discourses in Muinane and Uitoto settlements concerned their contestations of leadership and unity, expressed in cosmogonic accounts. See as well Hugh-Jones (1993, 108), on Tukanoan's 'vegetable lines' – cuttings of coca and manioc plants transmitted over generations as part of the group patrimony.
10 The species of the genus Cecropia tree in question is known as 'yarumo,' in Spanish, or *távi* in Muinane. People of the Centre used the ashes of this or of one or two other species in the coca powder mix.
11 See Griffiths (1998, 163) on the concept of 'sitting firmly' among Uitoto people, Belaunde (1992, 103) on the Peruvian Airo-Pai's valuation of

'erectness of posture' as a manifestation of moral personal disposition, Alès (2000) on both 'sitting' and 'standing' as matters of attention among Yanomami people, and Chernela (1993, 125, 136) on 'seated ones' among the Wanano. See also Griffiths (1998, 123) and Santos-Granero (1991, 103–5) on the links between coca and knowledge among Uitoto and Amuesha people respectively.

12 'Maloca people' in such references were paradigms of morality, very hard-working, orthodox in form, and obedient of the counsels of the speech of advice.

13 Manioc and other cultigens were real people's food. Meat was a much cherished addition to manioc products, and people often claimed to miss it and want it, but they did not deem it to be superior stuff to what women cultivated and prepared. Perhaps this was because at a 'shamanic' level, game was also cultigens that matured and were harvested by men. On differential as opposed to egalitarian valuations of men and women's products in different Amazonian groups, see C. Hugh-Jones (1979, 173), Belaunde (1992, 155), and Nieto Moreno (2006, 165).

14 See Hugh-Jones (2001, 254) for a very similar understanding of manioc starch juice in the Vaupés region.

15 On starch as a paradigmatic process of purification, see Echeverri (1997, 254). For an interesting convergence between the People of the Centre and the Tukanoan Barasana, concerning the link between the processing of manioc and human reproduction, see C. Hugh Jones (1979, 180).

16 I never identified their species, though one of them tasted very much like basil.

17 Uitoto people spoke about a herb they planted in their gardens and which they called 'Lying-in-Wait Mother,' who stamped her foot and scared black agoutis (*Dasyprocta fuliginosa*) away from the garden (Griffiths 1998, 116).

## 5 Virtuous Relationships and Social Organization

1 Perhaps the fact that these accounts, for the most part, feature male children is tied to a local sense that males are the more likely initiators of many salient, reiterated kinds of action and interaction.

2 In the past, some men had two or more wives; in the 1990s I knew of only one living example of polygyny: a Miraña man who had two homes and a wife in each one.

3 Among other artefacts, men made drums, cylinders for pulverizing coca leaves, and heavy, flat wooden pestles for crushing fermented manioc.

4 To some extent, People of the Centre converged with the Achuar as described by Descola (2001), among whom men are in charge of predatory relations with figures of alterity such as animals and affines, and women in charge of parental care of plants and much of the hands-on consanguinealization or consubstantiation with children. However, among People of the Centre men's tobacco was perhaps the most prominent substance in talk about the engendering and consubstantialization of new generations of kin. These people then provide support both for a Western sociological paradigm that assumes that men are universally in charge of the domain of the public and women of the domestic, and for Overing and Passes' (2001) critique of such paradigms.

5 See Griffiths (1998, 198) and Nieto Moreno (2006) on the Uitoto ideal of the nourishing, mythical 'woman of abundance.'

6 For an account of gender interdependency in rituals among the Barasana, see S. Hugh-Jones (1979, 42). See also Belaunde (1992, 16, 139), Gow (1991), McCallum (2001), Overing (1986), and Santos-Granero (1991, 232) on the complementarity of and interdependency between the 'sexes' in native Amazonian groups; these last four scholars reject the notion that there is male domination among the people they studied. See also Whiffen (1915, 91).

7 According to C. Hugh-Jones (1979, 72, 173), for instance, Barasana esteemed fish and meat acquired by men through unreliable interactions with the forest and river, more than the more dependable, cultivated food women produced, and men had greater prestige because of this. The Piaroa, on the contrary, 'insisted on the equal value of products of the hunt and products of the garden' (Overing 1986, 153).

8 Nieto Moreno (2006, 90) offers a perspicacious if incipient discussion of women's autonomy among Uitoto migrants to the urban centre of Leticia, Colombia. She describes these women as valuing their autonomy and independence, and tending to construct their narratives in such a way that the vicissitudes of their relationships with men, kin, and others appeared as a conscious process in which the speakers were judiciously selective and in control.

9 Gender inequality or domination – or, for the matter, equality – cannot be assumed to exist or to take the same form in all societies. Belaunde (1992), Gow (1991), Lorrain (2001), and McCallum (2003), among others, have addressed this issue in Amazonian societies. Overing (1986) rightly warns against assuming a catch-22 position in the analysis of gender that *a priori* treats anything women do as a reflection of their subordinate place in society, any message relating to women as one that debases them, and constraints as pertaining to women and not to men (142). See Cohen

(1985, 34–6) for a general critique of the use of the term 'equality' in social anthropology.

10 On tense relations between brothers in Amazonian groups, see Gonçalves (2000) and Griffiths (1998, 273).

11 In local kinship terminologies, WF, WFB, WMB are fathers-in-law for a male ego, as are HF, HFB, and others, for a female ego.

## 6 Shaped and Historical Moralities

1 For examples of the first objection, see Rapport (1997) and Cohen (1985, 1994); for discussions that formulate versions of the second and third objections, see Urban (2000, 1–28) and Strathern, Toren, and Ingold in Ingold (1996, 57–98). There is a great deal of literature critical of the emphasis on codes over performance that would make similar objections (such as Dell Hymes's body of work, or Vološinov 1993); I hope it is clear that my attention to dialogism, materiality, and temporality pre-empts these objections, with which I agree.

2 Cohen (1985) makes this point insistently. Toren (in Ingold 1996), Urban (2000, 9), and Rorty (1989, 14–16) make similar cases against the concept of shared meanings. Taylor's (1985, chapter 1) concept of a background of distinctions of worth does suggest a level of intimate sharedness that I find problematic, but profitably re-interpretable in terms of a differentiation between our more widely shared symbolic forms deployed 'out there' and the (also symbolically constituted) meanings we make of them.

3 On the role of maps and schools in shaping nationalist awareness, see Benedict Anderson (1983).

4 See Jackson (1995) and Oakdale (2005) on indigenous Amazonian organizations and styles of leadership.

5 Peter Gow's (2001) account of the Piro lived world suggests that the Piro lived world had similarly been changing for many centuries as new figures of alterity swam into view – from Inca conquerors and traders to Spanish conquistadores to a variety of missionaries, hacienda owners, and anthropologists. The Piro, he argues, sought to transform their bodies in order to reshape their relationships with others; in good perspectival logic, they donned the clothing of white people to appear to be like them and thus to relate more peacefully and profitably with them. The paradox is that for many current outsiders – including some anthropologists – Piro people's donning of white people's clothing signalled acculturation, rather than a very Amazonian practice of transforming the body to engage better with others. Though myths hide this fact from them

somewhat, Gow's argument is that this is what the Piro have been doing for centuries.

6 This is clear with language: our grandparents, and the books our predecessors wrote, used terms and grammars many of which we still use, reiterating them for our own purposes. In the case of what we call religion, stories about a single god becoming incarnated and dying on a cross seem to have reproduced very effectively. Fables and children's stories also exemplify this: there are innumerable versions of Beauty and the Beast, Little Red Riding Hood, and so on, in books, movies, and video games, including versions for toddlers and versions for porn surfers. Despite the diversity, most remain recognizable as 'versions' of each other.

7 Taylor speaks of a domain of 'middle-sized dry goods,' the ordinary material objects that surround us and that are likely to be salient to most people 'in virtue of their similarity as human beings' (1985:275). I use the term to refer to processes most human beings would recognize, even if their terms and explanations for them would differ. I did not wish to use the term 'biological processes' because I very much want to bear in mind that biological accounts, though extremely useful and persuasive, are also historical, mutable, and contingent.

8 This argument complements Lévi-Strauss and Peter Gow's (2001) account of the distribution of myths across the Americas, and Viveiros de Castro's and his students' analyses of perspectivism.

# References

Alés, Catherine. 2000. Anger as a Marker of Love: The Ethic of Conviviality among the Yanomami. In *The Anthropology of Love and Anger: The Aesthetics of Conviviality in Native Amazonia,* ed. Joanna Overing and Alan Passes, 133–51. London: Routledge.

Anderson, Benedict. 1983. Imagined Communities: Reflections on the Origin and Spread of Nationalism. London: Verso.

Århem, Kaj. 1993. Ecosofía Makuna. In *La selva humanizada: Ecologia alternativa en el trópico húmedo colombiano*, ed. Francois Correa, 105–22. Bogotá: Instituto Colombiano de Antropología.

– 1996. The Cosmic Food Web: Human-Nature Relatedness in the Northwest Amazon. In *Nature and Society: Anthropological Perspectives,* ed. Philippe Descola and Gísli Pálsson, 185–204. London: Routledge.

Balée, William. 1994. Footprints of the Forest: Ka'apor Ethnobotany: The Historical Ecology of Plant Utilization by an Amazonian People. New York: Columbia University Press.

Barth, Fredrik. 1966. *Models of Social Organization*. London: The Royal Anthropological Institute of Great Britain and Ireland.

Basso, Ellen B. 1995. *The Last Cannibals: A South American Oral History*. Austin: University of Texas Press.

– 2003. Translating 'Self-Cultivation.' In *Translation and Ethnography: The Anthropological Challenge of Intercultural Understanding*, ed. Tullio Maranhão and Bernard Streck, 85–101. Tucson: University of Arizona Press.

Belaunde, Luisa E. 1992. Gender, Commensality and Community among the Airo-Pai of West Amazonia (Secoya, Western-Tukanoan Speaking). PhD thesis, London School of Economics.

– 2000. The Convivial Self and the Fear of Anger amongst the Airo-Pai of Amazonian Peru. In *The Anthropology of Love and Anger: the Aesthetics of*

*Conviviality in Native Amazonia*, ed. Joanna Overing and Alan Passes, 209–20. London: Routledge.
– 2001. *Viviendo Bien: Género y Fertilidad entre los Airo-Pai de la Amazonía Peruana*. Lima, Perú: Centro Amazónico de Antropología y Aplicación Práctica (CAAAP); Banco Central de Reserva del Perú (BCRP) – Fondo Editorial.
Bloch, Maurice. 1977. The Past and the Present in the Present. *Man* (N.S) 12 (2): 278–92.
Brightman, Robert. 2002. *Grateful Prey: Rock Cree Human-Animal Relationships*. Regina: Canadian Plains Research Centre.
Butler, Judith. 1990. Gender Trouble: Feminism and the Subversion of Identity. New York: Routledge.
– 1993. Bodies that Matter: On the Discursive Limits of 'Sex.' New York: Routledge.
– 1997. Excitable Speech: A Politics of the Performative. New York: Routledge.
Candre, Hipólito, and Juan Alvaro Echeverri. 1996. Cool Tobacco, Sweet Coca: Teachings of an Indian Sage from the Colombian Amazon. Devon: Themis.
– 1993. *Tabaco Frío, Coca Dulce*. Bogotá: Colcultura
Carneiro da Cunha, Manuela, and Eduardo Viveiros de Castro. 1985. Vingança e temporalidade. *Journal de la Sociéte des Américanistes* 71: 191–208.
Casement, Roger. 1985. Putumayo, Caucho y Sangre. Relación al Parlamento Inglés (1911). Quito: Ediciones ABYA-YALA.
Chernela, Janet M. 1993. *The Wanano Indians of the Brazilian Amazon: A Sense of Space*. Austin: University of Texas Press.
Cohen, Anthony P. 1985. *The Symbolic Construction of Community*. London: Routledge.
– 1994. Self Consciousness: An Alternative Anthropology of Identity. London: Routledge.
Conklin, B.A. 2001a. Consuming Grief: Compassionate Cannibalism in an Amazonian Society. Austin: University of Texas Press.
– 2001b. Women's Blood, Warrior's Blood, and the Conquest of Vitality in Amazonia. In *Gender in Amazonia and Melanesia: An Exploration of the Comparative Method*, ed. Thomas A. Gregor and Donald Tuzin, 141–74. Berkeley: University of California Press.
Culler, Jonathan. 1989. *Framing the Sign: Criticism and Its Institutions*. Norman: University of Oklahoma Press
Derrida, Jacques. 1988. *Limited Inc*. Evanston: Northwestern University Press.
Descola, Philippe. 1994. *In the Society of Nature: A Native Ecology in Amazonia*. Cambridge: Cambridge University Press.
– 2001. The Genres of Gender: Local Models and Global Paradigms in the Comparison of Amazonia and Melanesia. In *Gender in Amazonia and*

*Melanesia: An Exploration of the Comparative Method*, ed. Thomas A. Gregor and Donald Tuzin, 91–114. Berkeley: University of California Press.

Echeverri, Juan Álvaro. 1997. The People of the Centre of the World: A Study in Culture, History, and Orality in the Colombian Amazon. PhD thesis, New School for Social Research.

– 2000. The First Love of a Young Man: Salt and Sexual Education among the Uitoto Indians of Lowland Colombia. In *The Anthropology of Love and Anger: The Aesthetics of Conviviality in Native Amazonia*, ed. Joanna Overing and Alan Passes, 33–45. London: Routledge.

Domínguez, Camilo, and Augusto Gómez. 1994. Nación y etnias: Los conflictos territoriales en la Amazonia 1750–1933. Bogotá: Disloque.

Emmons, Louise H., and François Feer. 1990. *Neotropical Rainforest Mammals: A Field Guide.* Chicago: University of Chicago Press.

Erikson, Philippe. 1996. La Griffe des Aïeux: Marquage du Corps et démarquages Ethniques chez les Matis d'Amazonie. Louvain: Peeters/ SELAF [PE].

Espinosa Arango, Mónica L. 1995. *Convivencia y Poder Político entre los Andokes.* Bogotá: Universidad Nacional de Colombia.

Fausto, Carlos. 1999. Of Enemies and Pets: Warfare and Shamanism in Amazonia. *American Ethnologist* 26 (4): 933–56.

Fausto, Carlos, and Michael Heckenberger. 2007. *Time and Memory in Indigenous Amazonia: Anthropological Perspectives.* Gainesville: University Press of Florida.

Fisher, William H. 2000. *Rain Forest Exchanges: Industry and Community on an Amazonian Frontier.* Washington and London: Smithsonian Institution Press.

– 2001. Age-based genders among the Kayapo. In *Gender in Amazonia and Melanesia: An Exploration of the Comparative Method*, ed. Thomas A. Gregor and Donald Tuzin, 115–40. Berkeley: University of California Press.

Geertz, Clifford. 1973. *The Interpretation of Cultures*. London: Fontana Press.

Goffman, Erving. 1959. *The Presentation of Self in Everyday Life.* New York: Doubleday.

Goldman, Irving. 1963. *The Cubeo Indians of the Northwest Amazon.* Urbana: University of Illinois Press.

Gómez, Augusto, Ana Cristina Lesmes, and Claudia Rocha. 1995. *Caucherías y Conflicto Colombo-Peruano – Testimonios 1904–1934*. Bogota: Disloque.

Gonçalves, Marco. 2000. Jealousy and the Predation of Sociality. In *The Anthropology of Love and Anger: The Aesthetics of Conviviality in Native Amazonia*, ed. Joanna Overing and Alan Passes, 235–51. London: Routledge.

Gose, Peter. 2009. Invaders as Ancestors: On the Intercultural Making and Unmaking of Spanish Colonialism in the Andes. Toronto: University of Toronto Press.

Gow, Peter. 1991. Of Mixed Blood: Kinship and History in Peruvian Amazonia. Oxford: Oxford University Press.

– 2000. Helpless – The Affective Preconditions of Piro Social Life. In *The Anthropology of Love and Anger: The Aesthetics of Conviviality in Native Amazonia*, ed. Joanna Overing and Alan Passes, 46–63. London: Routledge.

– 2001. *An Amazonian Myth and Its History*. Oxford: Oxford University Press.

Griffiths, Thomas F.W. 1998. Ethnoeconomics and Native Amazonian Livelihood: Culture and Economy among the Nipóde-Uitoto of the Middle Caquetá Basin in Colombia. PhD Thesis, University of Oxford.

High, Casey. 2012. Shamans, Animals, and Enemies: Locating the Human and Non-Human in an Amazonian Cosmos of Alterity. In *Personhood in the Shamanic Ecologies of Contemporary Amazonia and Siberia*, ed. M. Brightman, V. Grotti, and O. Ulturgasheva. Oxford: Berghahn.

Hill, Jonathan D. 1988. Introduction: Myth and History. In *Rethinking History and Myth: Indigenous South American Perspectives on the Past*, ed. Jonathan D. Hill, 1–17. Urbana: University of Illinois Press.

Howell, Signe. 1996. Nature in Culture or Culture in Nature? Chewong Ideas of 'Humans' and Other Species. In *Nature and Society: Anthropological Perspectives*, ed. Philippe Descola and Gísli Pálsson, 127–44. London: Routledge.

Hugh-Jones, Christine. 1979. From the Milk River: Spatial and Temporal Processes in Northwest Amazonia. Cambridge: Cambridge University Press.

Hugh-Jones, Stephen. 1979. The Palm and the Pleiades: Initiation and Cosmology in Northwest Amazonia. Cambridge: Cambridge University Press.

– 1993. Clear Descent or Ambiguous Houses? A Re-Examination of Tukanoan Social Organisation. *L'Homme* 126–8 (1): 95–120.

– 2001. The Gender of Some Amazonian Gifts: An Experiment with an Experiment. In *Gender in Amazonia and Melanesia: an Exploration of the Comparative Method*, ed.Thomas A. Gregor and Donald Tuzin, 245–78. Berkeley: University of California Press.

Ingold, Tim, ed. 1996. *Key Debates in Anthropology*. London: Routledge.

Jackson, Jean E. 1995. Culture, Genuine and Spurious: The Politics of Indianness in the Vaupés, Colombia. In *American Ethnologist* 22 (1): 3–27.

Jamieson, Mark. 2000. Compassion, Anger, and Broken Hearts: Ontology and the Role of Language in the Miskitu Lament. In *The Anthropology of Love and*

*Anger: The Aesthetics of Conviviality in Native Amazonia*, ed. Joanna Overing and Alan Passes, 82–96. London: Routledge.

Karadimas, Dimitri. 1997. Le Corps Sauvage: Ideologie du Corps et Representations de l'Environment chez les Miraña d'Amazonie Colombienne. PhD thesis, Université de Paris X.

– 2000. Parenté et alliance miraña. *L'Homme* 154–5: 599–612.

Keane, Webb. 2010. Minds, Surfaces, and Reasons in the Anthropology of Ethics. In *Ordinary Ethics: Anthropology, Language and Action*, ed. Michael Lambek. 64–83. New York: Fordham University Press.

– 2003. Semiotics and the Social Analysis of Material Things. *Language and Communication* 23: 409–25.

Kensinger, Kenneth M. 1995. *How Real People Ought to Live: The Cashinahua of Eastern Peru.* Prospect Heights, Illinois: Waveland Press.

Kidd, Stephen W. 2000. Knowledge and the Practice of Love and Hate among the Enxet of Paraguay. In *The Anthropology of Love and Anger: The Aesthetics of Conviviality in Native Amazonia*, ed. Joanna Overing and Alan Passes, 114–32. London: Routledge.

Kohn, Eduardo. 2007. How Dogs Dream: Amazonian Natures and the Politics of Transspecies Engagements. *American Ethnologist* 34 (1): 3–24.

Kulick, Don. 1992. Language Shift and Cultural Reproduction: Socialization, Self and Syncretism in a Papua New Guinean Village. Cambridge: Cambridge University Press.

Lagrou, Elsje M. 1998. Cashinahua Cosmovision: A Perspectival Approach to Identity and Alterity. PhD thesis, University of St. Andrews.

– 2000. Homesickness and the Cashinahua self: A Reflection on the Embodied Condition of Relatedness. In *The Anthropology of Love and Anger: The Aesthetics of Conviviality in Native Amazonia*, ed. Joanna Overing and Alan Passes, 152–69. London: Routledge.

– 2006. Laughing at Power and the Power of Laughing in Cashinahua Narrative and Performance. *Tipití* 4 (1/2): 33–56.

Laidlaw, James. 2002. For an Anthropology of Ethics and Freedom. *Journal of the Royal Anthropological Institute* (N.S.) 8: 311–32.

Lambek, Michael. 2010. Introduction. In *Ordinary Ethics: Anthropology, Language and Action*, 1–36. New York: Fordham University Press.

Landaburu, Jon. 1993. Du Changement de Nom de Certains Dieux ou Péripéties de la Reconstruction d'un Univers Religieux Amazonien. In *Mémoire de la Tradition*, ed. Aurore Becquelin and Antoinette Molinié, 145–59. Nanterre: Société d'Ethnologie.

Latour, Bruno. 2004. Whose Cosmos, Which Cosmopolitics? Comments on the Peace Terms of Ulrich Beck. *Common Knowledge* 10 (3): 450–62.

– 2009. Perspectivism: 'Type' or 'Bomb'? *Anthropology Today* 25 (2): 1–2.

Lévi-Strauss, Claude. 1964. *El Pensamiento Salvaje*. México: Fondo de Cultura Económica.

Lima, Tânia Stolze. 1996. O Dois e Seu Múltiplo: Reflexões sobre o Perspectivismo em uma Cosmologia tupi'. *Mana* 2 (2): 21–47.

Llanos Vargas, Hector, and Roberto Pineda C. 1982. *Etnohistoria del Gran Caquetá (siglos XVI–XIX)*. Bogotá: Banco de la República (FIAN).

Londoño Sulkin, Carlos David. 2000. 'Though it Comes as Evil, I Embrace it as Good': Social Sensibilities and the Transformation of Malignant Agency among the Muinane. In *The Anthropology of Love and Anger: the Aesthetics of Conviviality in Native Amazonia*, ed. Joanna Overing and Alan Passes, 170–86. London: Routledge.

– 2001. The Making of Real People: An Interpretation of a Morality-Centred Theory of Sociality, Livelihood and Selfhood among the Muinane (Colombian Amazon). PhD thesis, University of St. Andrews.

– 2002. The Narrative Framing of the Self among the Muinane. In *Travelling Concepts II: Meaning, Frame and Metaphor*, ed. Joyce Goggin and Michael Burke, 12–18. Amsterdam: ASCA Press.

– 2003. Paths of Speech: Symbols, Sociality and Subjectivity among the Muinane of the Colombian Amazon. *Ethnologies* 25: 173–95.

– 2004. *Muinane: un Proyecto Moral a Perpetuidad*. Medellín: Editorial Universidad de Antioquia.

– 2005. Inhuman Beings: Morality and Perspectivism among Muinane People (Colombian Amazon). *Ethnos* 70: 7–30.

– 2009. Response to Fernando Santos-Graneros 'Hybrid Bodyscapes: A Visual History of Yanesha Patterns of Cultural Change.' Cultural Anthropology 50 (4): 499, 500.

– 2010. People of No Substance: Imposture and the Contingency of Morality in the Colombian Amazon. In *Ordinary Ethics: Anthropology, Language and Action*, ed. Michael Lambek, 273–91. New York: Fordham University Press.

Lorrain, Claire. 2001. 'The Hierarchy Bias and the Equality Bias: Epistemological Considerations on the Analysis of Gender.' In *Beyond the Visible and the Material: The Amerindianization of Society in the Work of Peter Rivière*, ed. Laura Rival and Neil L. Whitehead, 263–72. Oxford: Oxford University Press.

Lynn, Christopher Dana. 2005. Adaptive and Mal-Adaptive Dissociation: An Epidemiological and Anthropological Comparison and Proposition for an Expanded Dissociation Model. *Anthropology of Consciousness* 16 (2): 16–50.

McLachlan, Amy L. 2010. Bittersweet: Hazard and Intimacy in a Moral Sensorium. Paper presented at 'Explorations in Sensory Anthropology Symposium,' CASCA, Montreal, June.

Manning, Paul, and Anne Meneley. 2008. Material Objects in Cosmological Worlds: An Introduction. *Ethnos* 73 (3): 285–302.

Mauss, Marcel. 1979 [1950]. *Sociology and Psychology: Essays*. London: Routledge & Kegan Paul.

McCallum, Cecilia. 2001. Gender and Sociality in Amazonia: How Real People are Made. Oxford; New York: Berg.

Monod Becquelin, Aurore, and Philippe Erikson, eds. 2000. *Les Rituels du Dialogue: Promenades Ethnoglinguistiques en Terres Amerindiens*. Nanterre: Société d'ethnologie.

Nieto Moreno, Juana Valentina. 2006. *Mujeres de la Abundancia*. Tesis de Magíster en Estudios Amazónicos. Leticia: Universidad Nacional de Colombia, Sede Leticia.

Oakdale, Suzanne. 2005. I Foresee my Life: the Ritual Performance of Autobiography in an Amazonian Community. Lincoln: University of Nebraska Press.

Ochs, Elinor, and Carolyn Taylor. 1995. The 'Father Knows Best' Dynamic in Dinnertime Narratives. In *Gender Articulated: Language in the Socially Constructed Self*, ed. K. Hall and M. Bucholtz, 97–120. New York: Routledge.

Opas, Minna, 2008. *Different but the Same: Negotiation of Personhoods and Christianities in Western Amazonia*. PhD thesis, Department of Comparative Religions, University of Turku, Finland.

Overing, Joanna. 1985. Introduction. In *Reason and Morality*, ed. Joanna Overing, 1–28. London: Tavistock Publications.

– 1985b. There Is No End of Evil: The Guilty Innocents and Their Fallible God. In *The Anthropology of Evil*, ed. David J. Parkin, 244–78. Oxford: Basil Blackwell.

– 1985c. Today I Shall Call him 'Mummy': Multiple Worlds and Classificatory Confusion. In *Reason and Morality,* ed. Joana Overing, 152–79. London: Tavistock Publications.

– 1986. *Men* Control Women? The 'Catch 22' in the Analysis of Gender. *International Journal of Moral and Social Studies* 1 (2): 135–56.

– 1987. Translation as a Creative Process: The Power of the Name. In *Comparative Anthropology,* ed. Ladislav Holy, 70–87. Oxford: Blackwell.

– 1993. Death and the Loss of Civilized Predation among the Piaroa of Orinoco Basin. *L'Homme* 26–8: 191–211.

– 2000. The Efficacy of Laughter: The Ludic Side of Magic within Amazonian Sociality. In *The Anthropology of Love and Anger: The Aesthetics of Conviviality in Native Amazonia*, ed. Joanna Overing and Alan Passes, 64–81. London: Routledge.

Overing, Joanna, and Alan Passes, eds. 2000a. The Anthropology of Love and Anger: The Aesthetics of Conviviality in Native Amazonia. London: Routledge.

– 2000b. Introduction: Conviviality and the Opening up of Amazonian Anthropology. In *The Anthropology of Love and Anger: The Aesthetics of Conviviality in Native Amazonia*, ed. Joanna Overing and Alan Passes, 1–30. London: Routledge.

Padilla, Guillermo. 1994. Los indígenas en la nueva Constitución. *Revista Coama*, no. 001, Diciembre de 1994–Febrero de 1995. COAMA. Bogotá.

Passes, Alan. 2001. The Value of Working and Speaking Together: A Faced of Pa'ikwené (Palikur) Conviviality. In *The Anthropology of Love and Anger: The Aesthetics of Conviviality in Native Amazonia*, ed. Joanna Overing and Alan Passes, 97–113. London: Routledge.

Patiño Roselli, Carlos. 1987. Aspectos Lingüísticos de la Amazonía Colombiana. *Boletín de Antropología, Universidad de Antioquia* 6 (21): 125–40.

Pedersen, Morten A. 2001. Totemism, Animism and North Asian indigenous Ontologies. *The Journal of the Royal Anthropological Institute*
(N.S.) 7: 411–27.

Pineda Camacho, Roberto. 1982. Chagras y Cacerías de la Garza Siringuera: El Sistema Hortícola Andoke (Amazonía Colombiana). Bogotá: Universidad Nacional de Colombia.

Rapport, Nigel. 1997. Transcendent Individual: Towards a Literary and Liberal Anthropology. London: Routledge.

Reichel-Dolmatoff, Gerardo. 1997. *Rainforest Shamans: Essays on the Tukano Indians of the Northwest Amazon*. Dartington: Themis Books/COAMA Programme Colombia/The Gaia Foundation London.

Riches, David. 1985. Power as a Representational Model. In *Power and Knowledge: Anthropological and Sociological Approaches*, ed. Richard Fardon, 83–101. Edinburgh: Scottish Academic Press.

Rivière, Peter. 2001. 'The More We Are Together …' In *The Anthropology of Love and Anger: The Aesthetics of Conviviality in Native Amazonia*, ed. Joanna Overing and Alan Passes, 252–67. London: Routledge.

Robbins, Joel. 2007. Between Reproduction and Freedom: Morality, Value, and Radical Cultural Change. *Ethnos* 72 (3): 293–314.

Robbins, Joel, and Alan Rumsey. 2008. Introduction: Cultural and Linguistic Anthropology and the Opacity of Other Minds. *Anthropological Quarterly*

81 (2): 407–20.
Rorty, Richard. 1989. *Contingency, Irony, and Solidarity*. Cambridge: Cambridge University Press.
Rosaldo, Michelle Z. 1984. Toward an Anthropology of Self and Feeling. In *Culture Theory: Essays on Mind, Self, and Emotion*, ed. Richard A. Shweder and Robert E. LeVine, 137–57. Cambridge: Cambridge University Press.
Rosengren, Dan. 2000. The Delicacy of Community: On Kisagantsi in Matsigenka Narrative Discourse. In *The Anthropology of Love and Anger: The Aesthetics of Conviviality in Native Amazonia*, ed. Joanna Overing and Alan Passes, 221–34. London: Routledge.
– 2006. Matsigenka Corporeality: A Non-biological Reality. On Notions of Consciousness and the Constitution of Identity. *Tipiti* 4 (1–2): 81–102.
Rubenstein, Steven. 2002. *Alejandro Tsakimp: A Shuar Healer in the Margins of History*. Lincoln: University of Nebraska Press.
Rumsey, Alan. 2010. Ethics, Language, and Human Sociality. In *Ordinary Ethics: Anthropology, Language and Action*, ed. Michael Lambek, 105–22. New York: Fordham University Press.
Sahlins, Marshall D. 1985. *Islands of History*. Chicago: University of Chicago Press.
– 2008. *The Western Illusion of Human Nature*. Chicago: Prickly Paradigm Press.
Santos-Granero, Fernando. 1991. The Power of Love: the Moral Use of Knowledge amongst the Amuesha of Central Peru. London: Athlone Press.
– 2000. The Sisyphus Syndrome, or the Struggle for Conviviality in Native Amazonia. In *The Anthropology of Love and Anger: The Aesthetics of Conviviality in Native Amazonia*, ed. Joanna Overing and Alan Passes, 268–87. London: Routledge.
– 2009a. Vital Enemies: Slavery, Predation, and the Amerindian Political Economy of Life. Austin: University of Texas Press.
– 2009b. Hybrid Bodyscapes: A Visual History of Yanesha Patterns of Cultural Change. *Current Anthropology* 50 (4): 477–512.
Seeger, Anthony. 1980. Corporaçao e corporalidade: ideologia de concepç o e descendencia. In his *Os índios e nós*. Rio de Janeiro: Campus.
2004. Why Suyá Sing: A Musical Anthropology of an Amazonian People. Urbana: University of Illinois Press.
Seeger, Anthony, Roberto da Matta, and Eduardo Viveiros de Castro. 1979. A construçao da pessoa nas sociedades indígenas brasileiras. *Boletim do Museu Nacional* 32: 2–19.
Storrie, Robert. 2006. The Politics of Shamanism and the Limits of Fear. *Tipití* 4 (1/2): 223–6.
Tambiah, Stanley J. 1968. The Magical Power of Words. *Man* (n.s.) 3: 175–209.

Taussig, Michael T. 1987. *Shamanism, Colonialism, and the Wild Man: A Study in Terror and Healing*. Chicago: University of Chicago Press.

Taylor, Anne-Christine. 1993. Des fantômes stupéfiants: Langage et croyance dans la pensée achuar. *L' Homme* 126–8: 429–47.

– 1996. The Soul's Body and Its States: An Amazonian Perspective on the Nature of Being Human. *The Journal of the Royal Anthropological Institute* (N.S.) 2 (2): 201–15.

– 2001. Wives, Pets, and Affines: Marriage among the Jivaro. In *Beyond the Visible and the Material: The Amerindianization of Society in the Work of Peter Rivière*, ed. Laura Rival and Neil L. Whitehead, 45–56. Oxford: Oxford University Press.

Taylor, Charles. 1985. *Human Agency and Language*. Cambridge: Cambridge University Press.

– 2006. An Issue About Language. In *Language, Culture, and Society*, ed. Christine Jourdan and Kevin Tuite, 16–46. Cambridge: Cambridge University Press.

Tobón, Marco Alejandro. 2008. 'La mejor arma es la palabra.' *La Gente de centro* –kigipe urúki *y el vivir y narrar el conflicto político armado. Medio río Caquetá – Araracuara 1998 – 2004*. Tesis de Magíster en Estudios Amazónicos. Leticia: Universidad Nacional de Colombia, Sede Leticia.

Turner, Terence. 1980. The Social Skin. In *Not Work Alone*, ed. J. Cherfas and R. Lewin, 112–40. Beverly Hills: Sage.

Urban, Greg. 2000 [1991]. A Discourse-Centered Approach to Culture. Tucson: Hats Off Books.

Useche Losada, Mariano. 1994. *La Colonia Penal de Araracuara*. Bogotá: Tropenbos Colombia.

van der Hammen, Maria Clara. 1992. El Manejo del Mundo: Naturaleza y Sociedad entre los Yukuna de la Amazonia Colombiana. Bogotá: Tropenbos Colombia.

Vengoechea, Consuelo. 1995. El Verbo y la Dimensión Aspecto-Temporal en Muinane. Monografía de grado, Magister en Etnolinguística. Bogotá: Uniandes (CCELA).

– 1996. Comentarios sobre los Datos de la Lengua Muinane Recogidos por Tastevin en 1920 y Datos Actuales. In *Documentos sobre Lenguas Aborígenes de Colombia del Archivo de Paul Rivet: Vol. I, Lenguas de la Amazonía Colombiana*, ed. Jon Landaburu, 553–62. Bogotá: Ediciones Uniandes

Vidal, Silvia, and Neil L. Whitehead. 2004. Dark Shamans and the Shamanic State: Sorcery and Witchcraft as Political Process in Guyana and the Venezuelan Amazon. In *In Darkness and Secrecy: The Anthropology of Assault Sorcery and Witchcraft in Amazonia*, ed. Neil Whitehead and Robin Wright, 51–81. Durham: Duke University Press.

Vilaça, Aparecida. 1992. Comendo como Gente: Formas do Canabalismo Wari' (Pakaa Nova). Rio de Janeiro: Editora UFRJ.

– 2000. Relations between Funerary Cannibalism and Warfare Cannibalism: The Question of Predation. *Ethnos* 65: 83–106.

– 2002. Making Kin out of Others in Amazonia. *The Journal of the Royal Anthropological Institute* (N.S.) 8: 347–65.

– 2005. Chronically Unstable Bodies: Reflections on Amazonian Corporalities. *Journal of the Royal Anthropological Institute* (N.S.) 11: 445–64.

Virtanen, Pirjo Kristiina. 2009. New Interethnic Relations and Native Perceptions of Human-to-Human Relations in Brazilian Amazonia. *Journal of Latin American and Caribbean Anthropology* 14 (2): 332–54.

Viveiros de Castro, Eduardo B. 1992. From the Enemy's Point of View: Humanity and Divinity in an Amazonian Society. Chicago: University of Chicago Press.

– 1996a. Images of Nature and Society in Amazonian Ethnology. *Annual Review of Anthropology* 25: 179–200.

– 1996b. Os Pronomes Cosmológicos e o Perspectivismo Ameríndio. *Mana* 2 (2): 115–44.

– 1998. Cosmological Deixis and Amerindian Perspectivism. *The Journal of the Royal Anthropological Institute* (N.S.) 4: 469–88.

– 2001. GUT Feelings about Amazonia: Potential Affinity and the Construction of Sociality. In *Beyond the Visible and the Material: The Amerindianization of Society in the Work of Peter Rivière*, ed. Laura M. Rival and Neil L. Whitehead, 19–44. Oxford: Oxford University Press.

Vološinov, Valentin Nikolaevic. 1993 [1929]. *Marxism and the Philosophy of Language*. Cambridge: Harvard University Press.

Walker, Harry. 2009. Baby Hammocks and Stone Bowls: Urarina Technologies of Companionship and Subjection. In *The Occult Life of Things: Native Amazonian Theories of Materiality and Personhood*, ed. Fernando Santos-Granero, 81–104. Tucson: University of Arizona Press.

Walton, James W., Janice P. Walton, and Clementina Pakky de Buenaventura. 1997. *Diccionario Bilingüe Muinane-Español Español-Muinane*. Bogotá: Editorial Alberto Lleras Camargo.

Whiffen, Thomas. 1915. *The North-West Amazons. Notes of Some Monthes Spent among Cannibal Tribes*. London: Constable and Company.

Whitehead, Neil L. 2003. Introduction. In *Histories and Historicities in Amazonia*, ed. Neil L. Whitehead, vii-xx. Lincoln: University of Nebraska Press.

Wright, Robin. 2004. The Wicked and the Wise Men: Witches and Prophets in the History of the Northwest Amazon. In *In Darkness and Secrecy: The Anthropology of Assault Sorcery and Witchcraft in Amazonia*, ed. Neil Whitehead and Robin Wright, 82–108. Durham: Duke University Press.

Zigon, Jarrett. 2008. *Morality: An Anthropological Perspective*. Oxford: Berg.

– 2009. Within a Range of Possibilities: Morality and Ethics in Social Life. *Ethnos* 74 (2): 251–76.

# Index

ANTHROPOLOGICAL HORIZONS

Editor: Michael Lambek, University of Toronto

Published to date:

1 *The Varieties of Sensory Experience: A Sourcebook in the Anthropology of the Senses* / Edited by David Howes
2 *Arctic Homeland: Kinship, Community, and Development in Northwest Greenland* / Mark Nuttall
3 *Knowledge and Practice in Mayotte: Local Discourses of Islam, Sorcery, and Spirit Possession* / Michael Lambek
4 *Deathly Waters and Hungry Mountains: Agrarian Ritual and Class Formation in an Andean Town* / Peter Gose
5 *Paradise: Class, Commuters, and Ethnicity in Rural Ontario* / Stanley R. Barrett
6 *The Cultural World in Beowulf* / John M. Hill
7 *Making It Their Own: Severn Ojibwe Communicative Practices* / Lisa Philips Valentine
8 *Merchants and Shopkeepers: A Historical Anthropology of an Irish Market Town, 1200–1991* / Philip Gulliver and Marilyn Silverman
9 *Tournaments of Value: Sociability and Hierarchy in a Yemeni Town* / Ann Meneley
10 *Mal'uocchiu: Ambiguity, Evil Eye, and the Language of Distress* / Sam Migliore
11 *Between History and Histories: The Production of Silences and Commemorations* / Edited by Gerald Sider and Gavin Smith
12 *Eh, Paesan! Being Italian in Toronto* / Nicholas DeMaria Harney
13 *Theorizing the Americanist Tradition* / Edited by Lisa Philips Valentine and Regan Darnell
14 *Colonial 'Reformation' in the Highlands of Central Sulawesi, Indonesia, 1892–1995* / Albert Schrauwers
15 *The Rock Where We Stand: An Ethnography of Women's Activism in Newfoundland* / Glynis George
16 *Being Alive Well: Health and the Politics of Cree Well-Being* / Naomi Adelson
17 *Irish Travellers: Racism and the Politics of Culture* / Jane Helleiner
18 *Writing and Colonialism in Northern Ghana:* The Encounter between the LoDagaa and the 'World on Paper,' 1892–1991 / Sean Hawkins
19 *An Irish Working Class: Explorations in Political Economy and Hegemony, 1800–1950* / Marilyn Silverman
20 *The Double Twist: From Ethnography to Morphodynamics* / Edited by Pierre Maranda

21 *Of Property and Propriety: The Role of Gender and Class in Imperialism and Nationalism* / Edited by Himani Bannerji, Shahrzad Mojab, and Judith Whitehead

22 *Guardians of the Transcendent: An Ethnography of a Jain Ascetic Community* / Anne Vallely

23 *The House of Difference: Cultural Politics and National Identity in Canada* / Eva Mackey

24 *The Hot and the Cold: Ills of Humans and Maize in Native Mexico* / Jacques M. Chevalier and Andrés Sánchez Bain

25 *Figured Worlds: Ontological Obstacles in Intercultural Relations* / Edited by John Clammer, Sylvie Poirier, and Eric Schwimmer

26 *Revenge of the Windigo: The Construction of the Mind and Mental Health of North American Aboriginal Peoples* / James B. Waldram

27 *The Cultural Politics of Markets: Economic Liberalization and Social Change in Nepal* / Katherine Neilson Rankin

28 *A World of Relationships: Itineraries, Dreams, and Events in the Australian Western Desert* / Sylvie Poirier

29 *The Politics of the Past in an Argentine Working-Class Neighbourhood* / Lindsay DuBois

30 *Youth and Identity Politics in South Africa, 1990–1994* / Sibusisiwe Nombuso Dlamini

31 *Maps of Experience: The Anchoring of Land to Story in Secwepemc Discourse* / Andie Diane Palmer

32 *Beyond Bodies: Rain-Making and Sense-Making in Tanzania* / Todd Sanders

33 *We Are Now a Nation: Croats between 'Home' and 'Homeland'* / Daphne N. Winland

34 *Rural Nostalgias and Transnational Dreams: Identity and Modernity among Jat Sikhs* / Nicola Mooney

35 *Kaleidoscopic Odessa: History and Place in Post-Soviet Ukraine* / Tanya Richardson

36 *Invaders as Ancestors: On the Intercultural Making and Unmaking of Spanish Colonialism in the Andes* / Peter Gose

37 *From Equality to Inequality: Social Change among Newly Sedentary Lanoh Hunter-Gatherer Traders of Peninsular Malaysia* / Csilla Dallos

38 *Dimensions of Development: History, Community, and Change in Allpachico, Peru* / Susan Vincent

39 *'We Are Still Didene': Stories of Hunting and History from Northern British Columbia* / Thomas McIlwraith

40 *People of Substance: An Ethnography of Morality in the Colombian Amazon* / Carlos David Londoño Sulkin